WHAT DO JEWS BELIEVE?

WHAT DO JEWS BELIEVE?

The Spiritual Foundations of Judaism

DAVID S. ARIEL

SCHOCKEN BOOKS / NEW YORK

Library of Congress Cataloging-in-Publication Data

Ariel, David S.
    What do Jews believe?: the spiritual foundations of Judaism
  David S. Ariel.
      p.   cm.
    Includes bibliographical references and index.
    ISBN 0-8052-1059-8
    1. Judiasm—Essence, genius, nature.   I. Title.
BM565.A77   1995
296.3—dc20

                                   94-3550
                                     CIP

Book design by JoAnne Metsch
Manufactured in the United States of America
First Paperback Edition
9 8 7 6 5 4 3 2

To Judah, Micah, and Aviva
The future is in your hands

Contents

Preface		ix
Introduction		3
1.	God	11
2.	Human Destiny	50
3.	Good and Evil	84
4.	The Chosen People	108
5.	The Meaning of Torah	134
6.	The *Mitzvot*	159
7.	Prayer	186
8.	The Messiah	211
9.	Why Be Jewish? A Letter to My Children	247
Notes		253
Glossary		267
Bibliography		271
Index		279

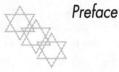 *Preface*

Writing a book such as this involves both solitary pursuit and the generous support of many people. The Cleveland College of Jewish Studies has provided me with a stimulating community of degree students, professional educators, and adult learners who engage in Jewish learning because it is important in their lives. I have written this book in response to their questions over the years. Some students in my courses on Jewish thought have read early drafts. They have been excellent critics, reviewers, and questioners and have provided me with valuable suggestions about the book. I owe them a great deal for having insisted on clarity, relevance, and pluralism in explaining Jewish beliefs.

I have found great professional satisfaction in working within the Cleveland Jewish community. Thanks to many people, lifelong Jewish learning is now part of the fabric of Jewish life for individuals, for families, in congregations, at the Jewish Community Federation, and in the Cleveland College of Jewish Studies. The college has also brought together a community of faculty members devoted to the academic and personal implications of Jewish learning. My academic colleagues—Nili Adler, Moshe Berger, Roger Klein, Alan Levenson, Lifsa Schachter, and

Jeffrey Schein—make the teaching of Judaism a noble profession and continue to inspire me with their knowledge and understanding.

My colleagues in the Cleveland College of Jewish Studies' administration have made it possible for me to pursue my writing and teaching with confidence that our institution will continue to advance. Together, we have built an organization that is dedicated to the professional advancement of people who work in the Jewish community and to the lifelong learning of Judaism in a committed, pluralistic, and open-minded environment. Lance Colie, Pat Evans, Patty Kaplan, Leah Kaplan-Samuels, Jean Lettofsky, and Michael Nutkiewicz are an excellent team of leaders and managers who share a vision of a learning community. My assistants, Jennifer Isabella and Susan Brown, have provided me with outstanding support.

The Cleveland College of Jewish Studies' Board of Governors has facilitated the renewal of Jewish communal life through their support of Jewish learning. I have served as president of the college under the chairmanship of outstanding leaders and colleagues who include Dan Aaron Polster, Eli Reshotko, Alvin Siegal, and Donna Yanowitz. The officers and trustees are individuals with unique talents and a commitment to the sacred task of strengthening higher Jewish learning. In particular, Bob Apple, Ilana Horowitz Ratner, Earl Linden, Allen Miller, David Shifrin, Michael Siegal, Marc Silverstein, and Jim Spira have taught me a great deal about leadership and planning.

I have found in the Jewish community of Cleveland a rare combination of pioneering willingness to improve Jewish education and a philanthropic commitment to implement the goals of educational improvement. The story of how Jewish communities in North America are tackling the challenges of Jewish education is still unfolding. The professional contributions of Stephen Hoffman and Mark Gurvis of the Jewish Community Federation and the leadership of Morton Mandel, Dr. Art Naparstek, and Charles Ratner have been an inspiration to me.

Close friends have provided me with more support and care than I can express. As I have grown and faced the unanticipated challenges of life, which are supposed make us wiser, I realize how blessed I am with good friends. They have played a role in this book with their constant inspiration to reach higher. They include Dr. Arthur and Diane Lavin,

Joshua Rubenstein and Jill Janows, Peter Geffen and Sue Kessler, Professor Lawrence and Debbie Fine, Dr. William Greenberg and Elissa Fenster, Margerie Hecht and Stanley Kugelmass, Professor Susannah Heschel, and Professor Daniel Pekarsky.

I have been fortunate to have Bonny Fetterman, senior editor of Schocken Books, as my mentor and guide on this project. The idea for the book was conceived over dinner several years ago. Bonny's skill, insight, patience, and persistence through the writing and editing process have helped me draw on ideas and beliefs that I might not otherwise have written about. Her focus on the concerns of the reader and insistence on clarity of expression have challenged me in new ways. Her confidence in the writer and in the finished book have made the project enjoyable.

More than from anyone else, I have learned from my wife, Kay, and our three children, Judah, Micah, and Aviva, that intimacy and openness go hand in hand. Kay has taught me that true spirituality finds its home in relationships. My children have taught me that intentions and actions are inseparable. To my children, whose patience during the writing of this book was often tested, I dedicate this book.

WHAT DO JEWS BELIEVE?

Introduction

I recall a conversation with a college classmate and her parents during my undergraduate years. As an exuberant sophomore immersed in studying Western civilization, I was fascinated by the connections I saw between religion and philosophy. My friend's father, an art connoisseur and financier, was equally intrigued by art, literature, and culture. We talked late into the night about the relationship between religious beliefs and life.

I do not recall exactly what we said in that stimulating discussion, but I remember becoming conscious for the first time of how deeply I was immersed in a search to understand my own Judaism. That evening, I decided to devote myself to the study of Jewish civilization with the same degree of intensity I had brought to my work in Western civilization. That conversation launched me on a return to my Jewish roots and to a spiritual quest within Judaism. Instead of seeking answers outside my religion, I began to search within my own heritage. I started by immersing myself fully in the literature, philosophies, and spiritual teachings of Judaism. Whatever I had sought in Western civilization, I began to find in Judaism.

I came to realize that I was seeking to understand why the Jewish way of life still held such appeal for me. I chose to study Judaism instead of other philosophies because I sensed a durability in Judaism that other belief systems lacked. I was not disappointed in my search and soon found myself digging deeper and deeper into Jewish literature. I came to appreciate the endurance and adaptability of Judaism as an evolving, continuous tradition. I saw new significance in Jewish beliefs, the shared values of the community, the culture with which I identify, the literature that moves and inspires me, and the rituals that mark the celebrations and tragedies of life.

In the years that followed, I discovered a diversity and depth in Judaism I had not anticipated at the outset. I found myself returning time and again to basic questions about the relationship between Jewish ideas and personal beliefs. I continued my search for the explanation of why Judaism has endured for so long.

Judaism is not a religion of fixed doctrines or dogmas but a complex system of evolving beliefs. Despite its diversity, there is an overarching rubric that unites Jews of every persuasion, from the most Orthodox to the most liberal or secular. This rubric, at once so dynamic and so compelling in its possibilities, I call "sacred myths," a term borrowed from the field of religious studies. No matter how literally or metaphorically we choose to interpret them, these sacred myths form the framework for the Jew's ongoing search for personal meaning in his or her own life, the life of the Jewish community, and society at large.

Contrary to a narrow definition, religion is not concerned just with the formal actions and rituals prescribed by the priests, rabbis, or holy texts of a tradition. Religion offers explanations, values, and beliefs, as well as the categories of meaning into which these beliefs and values can be ordered.[1] Religion utilizes an array of strategies to convey meaning, including myth and ritual. Sacred myths are articulations of our most deeply held beliefs that are not subject to verification for truth or falsehood. While the truth of these myths is valid and sacred for those who hold them, it does not necessarily follow that other people's myths are false or wrong. All people hold to sacred myths in one way or another— whether the sacred myth of the American nation, the individual's life-story in psychotherapy, or Australian aboriginal dream-time. The sacred myths can be about the creation of the world, the ancestors and sacred history, virtuoso figures in history, human purpose, or the future. The stated belief system of a religion is the framework that delivers meaning to those who are part of its religious community.

To call the most cherished beliefs of a culture "myths" does not mean that they are fairy tales. Every culture presents its understanding of the world in the language of its own sacred myths which might not make sense to outsiders. For example, the Christian beliefs in Jesus' resurrection and salvation through faith are important elements of the sacred myth of Jesus Christ. The Founding Fathers' beliefs in individual rights and freedoms are indispensable to the sacred myth of American liberty. The sacred myths of Judaism present different and unique categories of meaning and values. As Jews came upon other sources of knowledge through their encounters with other cultures, the sacred myths of Judaism also changed.

This book will explore the sacred myths of Judaism and how they have developed over time. My goal, however, is to provide more than a guided tour through the lively terrain of Jewish intellectual history from ancient to modern times. The sacred myths of Judaism are the key to understanding the special nature of Jewish spirituality.

What is the relationship between religion and spirituality? We often view religion as the formal set of beliefs and behaviors one follows as part of one's attachment to a particular tradition. Religion is also a system of meaning that provides a comprehensive frame of reference for its adherents. Spirituality need not imply an otherworldly approach but rather a highly personal outlook on the transcendent dimensions of life, emphasizing the connection between what is sacred to us and our innermost selves. Spirituality relates to the deeper meaning of things, heightened awareness, and a sense of higher purpose. It is "heart-knowledge"[2]— a highly individual outlook based on personal experience and certainty of the validity of that experience which does not always fit into an institutional framework.

Sacred myths are the expression of the deepest beliefs of Judaism, but they also express Jewish spirituality. Judaism is often described as a

worldly religion because of its emphasis on ethics, justice, and community. Nevertheless, the sacred myths of Judaism are the expression of a
spirituality that is tested in the real lives of ordinary people on a daily
basis. They provide the explanation of why Jews believe it is so important to express their spirituality in how they see themselves, how they
live their lives, how they relate to other people, and how they create
their communities.

Many Jews search for spiritual answers from a variety of religious traditions and sources because they believe that their own tradition is not
sufficiently spiritual. This is a particular problem for those who feel some
attachment to the Jewish traditions but are dissatisfied with what they
see as the lack of spirituality in Jewish life. While Jewish spirituality is
evident in the beliefs of Judaism, it has not always been apparent in the
formal organizations and institutions of Jewish life.

The failure of Jewish education in recent decades to engage children
and adults in serious discussion of challenging ideas and philosophies is
another factor that has led many to conclude that Judaism is spiritually
empty. Too many people have had negative experiences with their own
Jewish education or have had no such education at all. Many learned
about Judaism only during their childhood and, so, have only a child's
understanding of its sacred myths. To them, sacred myths are fairy tales.
Many Jews enter adulthood with a childish conception of Jewish ideas
that becomes all too easy to discard. What they reject, however, is not Judaism but the childish version of it that was presented to them. The person who wants to develop an adult Jewish identity or find a spiritual
home in Judaism often does not know where to begin. I believe that en-
countering the sacred myths of Judaism is the right place for adults to
begin the search. Adults approach the world through ideas, and compelling ideas can often touch our hearts and become beliefs. One of my
goals in writing this book is to restore Jewish spirituality to its proper
place by providing a truer understanding of Jewish beliefs to those who
have not yet had an opportunity to encounter them.

What Jews believe today is often different from what was believed in
generations past. What Jews believe has changed as Jewish values have
changed. For example, until recently something new in religion was regarded as undesirable. Today, change and innovation are considered as

necessary and beneficial. Self-denial was once regarded as worthwhile, but self-fulfillment is now esteemed. Loyalty to one's group used to involve not accepting outsiders. Today, tolerance of differences and acceptance of people from different backgrounds are seen as healthy. The belief in a supreme being was once the cardinal belief. Belief in ourselves—empowerment—is now thought to be an important key to self-fulfillment. Religion was once centered on institutions that commanded loyalty. Today's seekers are skeptical of institutions, authority, dogmas, and claims to possess exclusive truths. Religion was once the provenance of men. Gender equality makes women full partners in many religions. Religion was once understood as an inherited tradition. It is understood today as a matter of personal choice and an experience to be explored and examined. What Jews believe has, therefore, changed as the world has changed. This has always been the case.

Each generation retells the sacred myths of the Jewish people. In each telling of the story, we relate to the narratives told by previous generations while modifying and changing them. For example, the sacred myth of the Exodus from Egypt became the basis of the Passover Seder and the Haggadah, the written account of the Exodus. Each Passover, the story of how God freed the ancient Israelites from Egypt in order to give them the Torah is retold. In each retelling, however, we find new significance or read new meanings into the narrative. The same account might lead one person to believe that the sacred myth of the Exodus is about universal human freedom and equality, while another might conclude that it is about the special mission of the Jewish people to be the vanguard for human and political liberation. Another may view the narrative as stressing the centrality of Torah and the Land of Israel in Jewish destiny. Still another might conclude that Jews must always defend themselves against the pharaohs and Hitlers in every generation. The narrative is each generation's way of saying what is significant to it.

Judaism is a spiritual process based on continuous attempts throughout history to find answers to the perennial questions of human life. It is not a religion of dogmatic formulations approved by powers with the authority to define belief. Rather, every literate and knowledgeable Jew has the right to define Jewish belief as he or she sees fit within the framework of Judaism. Judaism is a continual debate about what Jews believe. This does not mean that "anything goes" in the arena of Jewish belief. There are certain sacred myths that establish central themes and fundamental beliefs. Judaism is sufficiently fluid and dynamic to encourage the continuous redefinition of its own sacred myths. These myths inspire a continuing dialogue among committed Jews. Change is ongoing in light of individual interpretation and the understanding of each age. The compelling and enduring beliefs survive and keep Judaism alive. The diversity and vitality of Jewish belief are part of what makes it worthwhile to be a Jew.

It is only fair to admit that I, as any author, bring a particular outlook to this task. I am not a theologian, a rabbi, or a spokesperson for a particular denomination. I write as an engaged historian of Jewish thought whose professional and academic training has exposed him to the range of Jewish thought and literature from the biblical, rabbinic, medieval, and modern periods and to the contemporary critical and analytical literature of the field of Judaic studies. I also write as a teacher who is deeply committed to understanding and communicating the spiritual dimensions of Judaism. I do not write as an apologist for any particular point of view but regard myself as "just Jewish." Yet every author writing about Judaism has a perspective and a particular orientation. As Gershom Scholem said, "Everyone cuts the slice suiting him from the big cake."[3] I hope to cut a slice that offers the flavor of the whole cake.

This is not a work of original scholarship but a synthesis of Jewish knowledge drawn from my own work over twenty years. Modern scholarship has contributed greatly to understanding Jewish thought. I believe that it is important to provide access to knowledge and, in particular, to communicate the research findings of contemporary Jewish scholarship to those who are interested in learning more about Judaism. The growing inaccessibility of Judaic scholarship to the members of the Jewish community is a problem I labor to overcome. In writing this book, I have drawn on the work of many outstanding Judaic scholars of the last fifty years. They are acknowledged in the notes for each chapter and in the bibliography.

I have set out to write a book that will help the reader find an answer to his or her questions about Judaism. The questions I address can be identified as: What are the enduring Jewish beliefs that have survived from antiquity to the present? How have these beliefs developed over time? What are the distinctive beliefs of Judaism today? This book is based on a broad array of Jewish sources and an equally broad presentation of Jewish beliefs. It does not provide simple answers or dogmas, although I hope it will be responsive to the questions that the reader brings to the subject. It will not tell the reader what to believe, although it will explain what others have believed throughout the history of Judaism. My goal is to assist the person who is searching for his or her own answers within the context of authentic Jewish belief.

I also hope to provide my own answer to the essential Jewish question of our age: Why be Jewish? I believe that Judaism is the longest continuous tradition in Western civilization to ask fundamental questions about life, its purpose, and human destiny. It is the only tradition that has drawn on all the other Western traditions and philosophies in its search for answers, and it embraces perspectives beyond its own teachings. Judaism is a continuing struggle with old and new ideas about the human experience. It is the arena in which the most significant ideas of human civilization have been addressed.

In one area, however, this book will leave the author and the reader disappointed. Although there is a growing body of knowledge about women and Judaism, the perspective of women has been generally missing from Jewish thought. The sources from which I have reconstructed the great Jewish ideas were written mostly by men for men. They represent a male perspective on Jewish experience. For this, I can neither defend Judaism nor apologize for it. It simply reflects the reality that, until recently, women were not regarded as equals in Jewish or many other cultures. I have attempted to portray Jewish ideas as they are, even when they fail to take into account female sensibilities. I have tried to avoid sexist language when possible, but not at the cost of making the sources mean something other than what they say.

1

God

It is difficult to imagine Jewish identity without a belief in God. Yet, for many Jews today, belief in God is a major stumbling block in relating to Judaism. For some, Jewishness has nothing at all to do with God. The reasons why Judaism and monotheistic faith are no longer inseparable arise out of the great challenges to and attacks on traditional belief. Unlike our ancestors, we often seek material, scientific, political, economic, and psychological explanations for events and experiences in our lives. As children of the modern Enlightenment, we no longer look for explanations in heaven. We are also heir to the great challenges that intellectuals of the last two centuries directed against traditional religious faith. Social scientists, following Karl Marx, attacked belief in God as an antiquated idea whose purpose was to maintain the social order by persuading the members of society that their suffering in this world served a higher purpose and would be requited by rewards in the afterlife. Psychoanalytic thinking, following Sigmund Freud, derided belief in God as a neurosis arising from the Oedipus complex: simultaneous fear of and longing for a father figure projected onto an imaginary heavenly father. Some European Jews also abandoned Jewish belief on account of anti-Semitism and disillusionment with the conditions of Jewish life. They turned to political activism, Zionism, and revolutionary movements as secular alternatives to traditional Judaism. The catastrophic events of the Holocaust further alienated many Jews from the notion of God. How could God, if He is good, permit the Holocaust to happen? Finally, the materialist outlook of the twentieth century persuaded other Jews that God was a fictional character from the premodern era who might deserve occasional mention but no real honor.

Many people who believe in God have in mind a concrete image of a benign heavenly figure who can be called upon in time of distress. Others have discarded belief in this particular idea of God because it is too primitive and unrealistic. Having rejected this belief in God, it sometimes follows that one should reject everything else associated with religion. The Jewish conception of God, however, was never as simplistic and concrete as those who reject it claim. Moreover, the rejection of this conception is merely a rejection of a certain notion of God without having thought through the idea in a more sophisticated manner. The God whom they reject is, in some respects, a "straw man" who was never the God of Jewish belief. Many Jews, including Marx and Freud, were indeed at the forefront of the attack upon what they viewed as the traditional belief in God. Their criticism of belief, however, was based on a simplistic and incorrect understanding of the conception of God. Jewish thinkers themselves criticized simplistic conceptions of God. Within the tradition, Jewish philosophers argued that infantile caricatures of God were worthy of rejection. No less an authority than Abraham Isaac Kook, the chief rabbi of Palestine until 1935, believed that atheism was valuable in that cut it through the thickets and cobwebs of specious ideas about God.

Most of us carry in mind an image of God shaped by our religious traditions, our education, our experience, and our personal belief. Beginning at an early age, we hear about God, ask questions about God, experience religious moments, and think about our own beliefs. For some, the private belief in God plays an important role in life and provides a foundation of faith and certainty. Many people believe that God is the higher, supernatural being who has created life and presides over the universe and humanity as a benign, moral, and watchful ruler, one who is accessible to us at special moments, like a caring parent who provides reassurance and comfort when we are in distress.

This common faith is what theologian David R. Griffin calls the generic idea of God.[1] While the generic idea of God may represent the common denominator of religious belief, many people find it bland and uninspiring. It is not spiritually compelling for those looking for a way to feel God's presence in the daily lives of ordinary human beings. It does not explain the gap between the belief in our being created "in the image of God" and the reality of living in a world of continued suffering and conflict. The generic idea often presents God in masculine terms, as a father, rather than in ways that might have more meaning to women seekers. It is difficult to develop brand loyalty to the generic idea of God.

Many people associate the generic belief in God with the teachings of traditional religions such as Judaism and conclude that organized religion is not sufficiently spiritual. The Jewish belief in God, however, is far more spiritually compelling than the generic belief. It asserts that God's presence can be felt in the daily lives of ordinary human beings through specific beliefs and actions that translate the belief in being created "in the image of God" into reality. The Jewish belief in God is not a static dogma but the result of active spiritual seeking over the course of four thousand years. In fact, there are many Jewish ideas of God that have developed over the course of time as old ideas lose credibility and new ideas emerge. Each of these offers a different approach to the questions people ask about God: How is it possible to believe in one, unknowable, invisible God? How can a supernatural being have a presence in the daily lives of ordinary people? How can a moral, good, and purposeful being permit suffering and injustice? What are God's characteristics and why is God often portrayed by sacred tradition only in masculine, fatherly terms? As our knowledge and understanding have grown, our beliefs about God have likewise evolved, and in a variety of ways. All these beliefs are equally legitimate as Jewish beliefs. Therefore, we can speak about "the magnificent gods of Jewish belief" but each one is a different perspective on the one, true God.

There is no one authoritative Jewish conception of God, although all Jewish thinkers agree that God is one and invisible. Among the range of views, some emphasize God's otherness (transcendence), while others emphasize God's accessibility (immanence). Some emphasize the personal aspects of God, some the impersonal; some stress God's supernaturalism, while others stress God as process. Some see God as a masculine figure, others as a neutral or androgynous being with elements of a masculine and feminine goddess. Each of these views is an authentic Jewish view. They are authentic because they are honest attempts by committed Jewish thinkers to explore ideas about God within the context of Jewish tradition.

Does this mean that all Jewish formulations of theism, pantheism, and other views of God are equally valid? Perhaps the diversity of Jewish points of view on God demonstrates that genuine certainty and knowledge of God are impossible. God may be unknowable despite human efforts to find God in heaven, nature, and human relationships. A legitimate point of view, given the range of Jewish conceptions of God, is agnosticism. This is not the agnosticism of doubt but the principled and reasoned admission of the impossibility of knowing about God that is coupled with the impulse to search for knowledge of Him. This search takes place through study of religious texts, intuitive understanding, and personal experience.

Judaism is a spiritual force whose sacred myths and rituals are based on successive attempts throughout the course of human history to find answers to the fundamental questions of human life and its meaning. Each generation understands God in its own terms and based on what it has received from earlier generations. The sacred myths generated by Jews throughout history are the ways in which our people have struggled to make sense of God and how God relates to us. The sacred myths, the bedrock of our deeply held beliefs and convictions, will continue to be refined, modified, revisited, and reformulated.

What, then, do Jews believe about God? We must start with the premise that God is the transcendent reality which exists beyond the limits of our knowledge. We cannot fashion any image of God or worship anything else in God's stead. The Jewish belief in God is rooted in the paradox that the most powerful force in the universe is the one least visible and knowable in the world. The second of the Ten Commandments states: "You shall not make for yourself a sculptured image, any likeness of what is in the heavens above, or on the earth below, or in the waters under the earth" (Exodus 20:4). There is no representation of any kind of God. This idea requires a level of abstraction that is difficult to understand. It also requires that we subordinate our sense perception—which tells us that God cannot be known—to an unprovable or not-yet-proven idea: that the unknowable God exists. Although belief in God may appear to be counter to what our senses tell us, accepting belief in invisible forces is part of our daily experience of the world.

The God we worship is the invisible creator of all life. To worship anything other than God is idolatry and leads to evil. Jews believe that God is invisible and yet has a presence that draws us constantly. Even though God is unattainable, we seek Him and strive for a relationship with Him. Although we can never truly know God, we cannot resist the urge to try to understand Him. God may be abstract and unknowable, yet we believe that human beings are created in the divine image. We imagine God as transcendent and impersonal, yet the God we worship is also a deeply personal God whose true presence is found in ourselves, in others, and in the world around us. We can only relate to God through the world.

Judaism presents two interconnected sacred myths about God. The first presents God as transcendent and above the world. God created the world but He Himself stands above and beyond all living things. Everything stands in awe of Him and praises Him for His majesty and power. He is the Lord of all, who at any moment could return the world to nothingness. He is a fearsome God who judges the world and has the power to bring down His judgment upon the world.

This sacred myth views existence as a series of polarities: God creates and sustains nature but cannot be identified with it. He is different from nature and stands above and outside it. God created man but He cannot be compared to humanity. The world is divided into polarities of the holy and the profane, Israel and other nations, the Sabbath and weekdays, good and evil. Everything is either one or the other but not both. This sacred myth invites us to be drawn to God's transcendence, which lifts us out of the mundane into the sacred. We can overcome the polarities by choosing God over nature, the holy over the profane, Israel over the other nations, the Sabbath over the other days of the week, and good over evil. We can choose transcendence over immanence.

The other sacred myth in Judaism views God as an accessible, personal being. God is a nurturing and comforting parent who is near to us and all humanity. God has created us in His image and endowed us with His own characteristics. God expects us to be like Him. God hears our prayers and answers us. We can choose immanence over transcendence. We can draw the transcendent to us and infuse the sacred into the everyday. We can see the transcendent in nature and in other human beings, the profane can be made sacred, Israel can live as a sacred people among other nations, the holiness of the Sabbath can be applied to life throughout the week, and we can overcome evil through our deeds.

These two sacred myths coexist within Jewish belief. Sometimes they are intertwined into a seamless system of belief that affirms both transcendence and immanence. At other times Jews believe more strongly in one myth than the other. All Jewish belief begins with these sacred myths, and each age develops its own categories of meaning in which its beliefs and values are ordered. All of Jewish belief is commentary on the two, interrelated sacred myths of God.

The rabbis of the talmudic era softened the polarities of biblical Judaism by emphasizing the sacred myth that holds that God is both transcendent and immanent. The medieval philosophers and Kabbalists added new categories of meaning that reemphasized the polarities of divine transcendence and immanence. The philosophers held that God is more transcendent, hidden, and remote than earlier generations had believed. The Kabbalists agreed with the philosophers that God is wholly transcendent but offered their own explanation of how God can be made accessible through mystical rituals. Modern Jewish belief builds on this historical quest and offers new spiritual alternatives. In a simple sense, each age creates God in its own image and expresses this image through sacred myth.

THE ONE, INVISIBLE GOD

The sacred myth of the Bible is that God is the author of all life who brought the world into being and, when He completed His work, He rested. He created human life as the pinnacle of creation and fashioned the first human being in His own image. He established a covenant with Abraham and promised him that if he and his descendants obeyed Him, he would guide them and make his descendants a great people. Later, God established an eternal covenant with the descendants of Abraham, the people Israel whom He led out of slavery in Egypt, and gave them the Torah. God's Torah taught that human life has purpose and dignity because God is a moral being who alone created the entire universe. God expects that just as He is holy, so too we will be holy. God's moral nature is a guarantee that He will sustain and protect the world. In order to do so, He gave a moral law and judges humans by its strict standards, meting out reward and punishment accordingly.

The most highly valued knowledge in modern society is psychological and scientific. Psychoanalysis has shown that the forces that truly shape our personalities are unconscious drives, hidden impulses, defenses, memories, and fears that reside deep within us. These forces have greater influence over us than we often care to acknowledge. Physics has shown that the universe is an intricate organization which follows a systematic and mathematical regularity and whose deepest structures and forces are invisible and in many cases not yet provable. Most of us accept that psychology and science are true because psychologists state "facts" we seem to recognize in our own experience and scientists produce explanations of phenomena we could never otherwise comprehend. Yet even these ways of knowledge are paradoxical because they credit the greatest sway over our lives to the least perceptible forces within us and within the universe. They also require reliance on the authority of others rather than the evidence of our senses and experience.

The same is true for the Jewish belief in God. Even today, belief in God requires a suspension of our usual means of knowing in favor of inner certainty. When this belief was first introduced by the Israelites four thousand years ago, it required a daring suspension of belief in idols and myths about the many gods of the Babylonian pantheon. Belief in *one* God, however, was the defining issue of Judaism, the feature that made the religion of Israel different from all other religions in the ancient Near East, and the unique Jewish contribution to civilization.

The God in whom we believe is ultimately unknowable. The Torah recounts how, after God revealed the Ten Commandments, Moses goes back up the mount and asks God to reveal Himself directly. Moses is not satisfied with having heard God's commanding voice or having seen the consuming fire on top of the mountain—he wants to know who is this

God who has guided him and his people. God rejects Moses' request by saying, "You cannot see My face, for man may not see Me and live" (Exodus 33:20). God then tells Moses to station himself on the mountain and God will shield him as His Presence passes by. God passes by Moses, and Moses sees the shadow of God's Presence, but his longing is not satisfied.

This Torah passage states that we can know nothing about God's true nature, only God's actions. God remains always inscrutable, unimaginable, and invisible. Still, despite these strictures against portraying God's image, the very first chapters of the Torah tell us that we are created in the image of God. This challenges us to understand the way in which we are created in the image of God. Even though God is invisible and inconceivable, we are compelled to imagine Him.

The sacred myths about God in Judaism reflect this paradox. Jews believe in a very abstract God. Every time we talk about God or what we believe about God, we are creating Him in our own image. It is impossible to avoid committing an act of idolatry if we are to say anything about God. Jewish belief must always be critical of itself and constantly attempt to challenge itself. Every time we have an image of God, we must destroy that image and create the image anew. There has been a progression in what Jews believe about God because of the constant self-criticism of Jewish belief from antiquity until today. Certain overarching assumptions, however, have not changed, such as the belief in God's oneness, invisibility, and goodness.

THE MORAL GOD OF THE UNIVERSE

The Hebrew Bible begins with the self-evident proposition that God exists, that there is no other God, and that He created the world and all that is in it. The opening passage presupposes the existence of God: "When God began to create the heaven and the earth . . ." There is no hint at God's biography before He created the world. Only at the moment of creation is there any story to tell. The biblical God acts intentionally to create a good universe where moral behavior is expected and order prevails. The biblical creation account establishes an ironclad connection between ethical human behavior and divine action. If individuals act morally, they will be rewarded with prosperity, longevity, and happiness. If they act contrary to God's law, which is the moral law, they, their families, their crops, and their property will suffer.

This assumption was not taken for granted by the other peoples in the Near East among whom the early monotheists lived. Around 1900 B.C.E., the age of biblical Abraham, the Babylonians believed that heaven was populated by many gods whose contentious, jealous tendencies brought conflict in heaven and suffering on earth. The gods were capricious beings whose immoral actions caused chaos for humanity. In contrast, the biblical view introduced the idea that bounty, good harvests, and longevity were divine rewards for moral human behavior just as floods, disasters, crop failures, and death were God's punishment of errant human behavior. Biblical monotheism was a significant departure from the Babylonian assumption that love, wars, strife, and treachery among the gods determined arbitrarily the course of human destiny. The Babylonian creation epic, *Enuma Elish,* dating from this period, illustrates the difference between the prevailing religion and the Israelite religion, which takes the existence of God as a given. *Enuma Elish* begins with the creation and early biography of the gods. The mother and father gods of Babylonian religion, Tiamat and Apsu, gave birth to other gods:

> When, on high, the heaven had not been named,
> firm ground below had not been called by name,
> naught but primordial Apsu, their begetter,
> and Mummu-Tiamat, she who bore them all,
> their waters commingling as a single body;
> No reed hut had been matted, no marsh land had appeared,
> when no gods whatever had been brought into being, uncalled by name,
> their destinies undetermined—
> Then it was that the gods were formed within them.[2]

Tiamat and Apsu gave birth to gods who challenge them and provoke them into jealous fits of rage. From these heavenly battles the world was formed, a place of chaos, suffering, and disaster.

For biblical Judaism, however, the world was a place of goodness and fullness if humans lived according to the moral law. The Hebrew God who created a universe from nothing presides over a world that is inherently good and perfectible. In this purposeful universe, "God saw all that

He created and it was very good." The biblical view introduced the idea that a moral cord binds the world and human destiny together.

The belief in the one, invisible God was the result of a belief in the possibility of the moral goodness of humanity. In a world governed by disregard for human life and by pessimism and defeatism, the biblical God was an assertion that humans are created in a divine image and, therefore, human life is worthwhile. The supernatural God has a presence in the daily lives of people when they act in a moral manner consistent with the image of God. The biblical belief in God is belief in an ideal of strict justice and morality which makes uncompromising demands upon human behavior. No human action escapes the scrutinizing eye of God and no immoral action can be hidden from Him. The introduction of morality into belief was the unique contribution of ancient Israel and has been the decisive feature of Judaism ever since.

The cause-and-effect relationship between moral action and human destiny does not seem as persuasive today as it did to our biblical ancestors because we understand that natural, social, political, and economic forces affect our lives. Still, the biblical idea must be seen within the context of introducing moral responsibility into human understanding of the universe. The earliest Jewish monotheism emphasized moral responsibility and should be viewed as a counterforce to Babylonian polytheism, which suggested that fate is not in human hands. Biblical Judaism asserted that God is loving and caring with the morally upright and just but avenging with the wicked. Although God is the ultimate author of all things, human behavior determines whether God rewards or punishes the world and its inhabitants.

The belief in a moral God shaped the character of the Jewish religion from its beginning. Because people are created in the image of God, any offense against another person is an offense against God. The call to imitate the moral character of God is the challenge placed before every human being. According to the Torah, murder is not only a criminal act but an attack upon the very image of God inherent in each person. Later authorities claimed that one who saves one life saves, as it were, the entire world and one who destroys one life, destroys the entire world.

Just as God created the world and rested on the seventh day, humans are commanded to cease from their productive labors on the Sabbath in order to be refreshed. An employer must let his employees—Jewish and non-Jewish—and his slaves and animals rest on the seventh day. The reason given is: "Remember that you were a slave in the land of Egypt and the Lord your God freed you from there with a mighty hand and an outstretched arm; therefore the Lord your God has commanded you to observe the Sabbath day" (Deuteronomy 5:15).

The moral law extends throughout the universe to people, animals, and the environment. Animals and the environment have the right to rest on the seventh day. Animals should be spared the pain of having their young slaughtered and cooked in the mother's own milk. Since the land belongs to God, not to people, it can be cultivated for six years but in the seventh year must lie fallow. For the same reason, the benefits of the land must be shared with all people. A landowner must leave unharvested a portion of every field and may not return to pick up bits of the harvest he dropped along the way. These must be left for the poor and non-Israelites, who are guaranteed by God a portion of every harvest. Every fifty years, debts are annulled, and land sold to pay a debt must revert to its original ownership. The reason given is: "For the land is Mine; you are but strangers resident with Me" (Leviticus 25:23). The moral God of the universe is the fundamental axiom of Jewish belief.

THE HIDDEN GOD AND THE PRESENCE OF GOD

How can the hidden God have a presence in the daily lives of ordinary people? The rabbis of the talmudic era believed that God is both transcendent and immanent. As we noted earlier, transcendence is the idea that God is remote, distant, and inaccessible—reachable only by overcoming the limitations of earthly existence. Immanence is the concept that emphasizes God's presence in the world and His nearness or accessibility to humans. The rabbis believed that God is the powerful, invisible, transcendent ruler of the world. Following the biblical legacy, the less visible God is, the more powerful He is. The rabbis, however, emphasized that there are many ways to make this invisible God a living presence in one's own life. They taught that God is immanent—present—in the world and that it is not necessary to look outside our own experience to find God.

The rabbis emphasized the immediacy of the connection with divine transcendence whenever a Jew prays, offers a blessing, or learns Torah: "If two sit together and occupy themselves with words of Torah, the divine Presence abides in their midst."[3] This is what the rabbis had in mind when they spoke of *kedushah* (holiness). They understood *kedushah* as the experience of becoming momentarily aware of the impact of divine transcendence on the world. *Kedushah* is the experience of creature-consciousness, that is, of the relationship of the created being to the creator, of the transient and mortal to the eternal, of the partial to the whole, of the moment to eternity, of the good to the ideal, and of the perfectible to the perfect.

The rabbis believed that God is present at every moment that human beings become conscious of their createdness by, dependence on, and indebtedness and gratitude to God. They introduced a series of metonyms or substitution terms to express the idea that the transcendent God is accessible to human experience. They implied that God becomes accessible to the consciousness of an individual when he reaches out to God. This does not mean that God becomes localized physically in the world. The metonym rabbinic Judaism employed to suggest consciousness of God is the *Shekhinah* (divine Presence), a euphemism for the immanence of God.

The range of rabbinic views of God preserves the belief in God as creator, lawgiver, sustainer, judge, and protector of the world. The rabbinic God is a personal God whose transcendence is tempered by His immanence and His abiding concern with the world. God's connection with the world was sometimes expressed in anthropomorphism—statements that described God in physical terms—which the rabbis understood as metaphors. At other times, the rabbis expressed God's personality in anthropopathism—expressions that described God's emotions—which they took literally. The rabbinic conception of God is based on the paradoxical formulation that God is accessible to man even as He remains remote and hidden across the unbridgeable abyss. While the Torah contains many accounts of the ancestors who maintained a close relationship with God, the rabbinic tradition emphasized the abyss between man and God, and found means of bridging the abyss within the tradition itself through prayer and study rituals.

The rabbis asked how it is possible to relate to a transcendent being. They addressed this issue by way of an explanation of the biblical verse "After the Lord your God you shall walk" (Deuteronomy 13:5). "And is it possible for a man to walk after the *Shekhinah?* Rather, this means that one should emulate the virtues of the Holy One, blessed be He."[4] Here, as in many instances, the word *Shekhinah* is substituted for God to avoid suggesting an anthropomorphic description of God, that is, a depiction of the transcendent God in human terms. At the same time, the rabbis suggested that consciousness of God is possible at every moment a Jew emulates the moral virtues of God. The universal moral God is the role model for human activity.

The rabbis believed that nature itself provides proof of God's otherness. God's very invisibility is corroboration of His transcendence. One rabbinic passage draws an analogy between God and the sun. If the sun is too powerful to be viewed directly, then how much more difficult it is to view God, who is more powerful than the sun by orders of magnitude. Still, God is an even more influential presence in human life than the sun. Therefore, the less evident God is, the more powerful He is. In the following rabbinic passage (which illustrates the considerable interaction between the Jews in Palestine and their Roman rulers during the period of the Roman Empire), Caesar, who expected that the Jewish God could be shown in statuary like Zeus, asked one rabbi to show him his God. The rabbi answered that his God was invisible and went on to explain that his invisible God was more powerful than any force in the universe:

> A Caesar said to R. Joshua ben Hananiah, "I want to see your God." R. Joshua: "You cannot see Him." Caesar: "Nevertheless, I want to see Him." So R. Joshua had Caesar stand facing the sun during the summer solstice of Tammuz and said to him, "Look directly at the sun." Caesar: "I cannot." R. Joshua: "If you say of the sun, which is only one of the servitors standing before the Holy One, Blessed be He, 'I cannot look directly at it,' how much less could you look at the Presence [*Shekhinah*] itself?"[5]

God is generally regarded in rabbinic Judaism as different from and above the world, on one hand, and closely involved and concerned with the world and its inhabitants, on the other. This paradoxical formulation of God's simultaneous transcendence and immanence is central to understanding the rabbinic conception of God. Sometimes God appears in more earthly manifestations, but this is only in the eye of the beholder. People perceive God in different ways and imagine God in various forms. It is not God but our perception of God that changes. According to the rabbis, even though God made Himself visible in different forms to the biblical patriarchs and prophets, He is still fundamentally one, transcendent, and invisible:

> Because the Holy One appeared to Israel at the Red Sea as a mighty man waging war, and appeared to them at Sinai as a teacher teaching Torah, and appeared to them in the days of Daniel as an elder teaching Torah, and appeared to them as a young man in the days of Solomon— the Holy One said to Israel: "Even though you see Me in many different images, I am the same. I am He who was with you at Sinai: 'I am the Lord your God.'"(Exodus 20:2)[6]

Rabbinic Judaism maintained that studying the holy texts and learning from the great sages of Judaism were the proper substitutes for attempting to relate directly to the transcendent God. Although the rabbis believed that God is by nature transcendent and unattainable, His intentions can be deciphered and known by studying and interpreting Torah, His sacred word. It is impossible for a mere mortal to relate directly to the transcendent God, but the rabbis maintained that they themselves could serve as mediators and interpreters of God's transcendent message. One midrash (a rabbinical homily) interprets the verse "And cleave to Him" (Deuteronomy 11:22) by asking: "How is it possible for man to ascend to heaven and cleave to fire, seeing that it has been said, 'The Lord your God is a consuming fire' (Deuteronomy 4:24)? Rather, cling to the sages and to their disciples. I will consider it as if you had ascended to heaven and had received the Torah there."[7] The rabbis imply that it is possible to relate directly not to the transcendent God but only to his designated disciples. This does not suggest that the rabbis saw themselves as divine; rather, they were interpreters of the divine.

THE CARING GOD

The rabbinic conception of God stressed the notion of God as a protecting and nurturing parent. This idea was expressed in a popular midrash on the verse "The angel of God who went before the camp of Israel moved and went behind them" (Exodus 14:19). In explaining the notion that God, or an angel, can walk before or after the tribes of Israel marching through the desert, the midrash states that such an anthropomorphism is meant to suggest God's parental protectiveness: "It is like a man who was walking on the way and letting his son go before him; came robbers in front to take the boy captive, the father put him behind him; came a wolf from behind, he put him in front; came robbers in front and wolves behind, he took him up in his arms; did he begin to be troubled by the heat of the sun, his father stretched his own garment over him; was he hungry, he gave him food; thirsty, he gave him to drink."[8]

The concept of God as parent or father is expressed in another rabbinic passage that portrays God taking pleasure in seeing His children outsmart Him. Here, Rabbi Eliezer is arguing an unpopular position on a relatively obscure matter of Jewish law with his colleague Rabbi Joshua. Rabbi Joshua, along with the rest of the sages in the rabbinic court, reaches a conclusion from which Eliezer vigorously dissents. Unwilling to concede, Eliezer resorts to some extraordinary measures to persuade Joshua and the majority of his rightness. After he performs three sets of miracles and Joshua is still not persuaded, Rabbi Eliezer appeals to God directly, who quite forcefully states that Eliezer's legal rulings are to be followed in this and every other case. Despite the authoritative statement by God that Eliezer has carte-blanche legal authority, Joshua is still not persuaded. He even chastises God by quoting God's own words, albeit out of context, against Him. He first admonishes God that He has no standing in courts of Jewish law after the Torah was given once and for all at Mount Sinai. Joshua quotes the Torah against God, the lawgiver, by reminding God that He has transferred all legal authority to the rabbis and established the principle of majority rule as their guide. The controversy ends with Joshua victorious over Eliezer and even over God, who accepts that He can no longer intervene in disagreements among His children:

One day, Rabbi Eliezer was in dispute with the other sages on a matter of law. He brought all the proofs of the world in support of his opinion but the other sages would not accept them. He said to them: "If the law is according to me, let this locust tree prove it." And the locust tree moved one hundred cubits. (Some say four hundred cubits.) The sages said to him: "The locust tree cannot prove anything." Then he said to them: "If the law is according to me, let this stream of water prove it." And the stream of water turned and flowed backward. They said to him: "The stream cannot prove anything." Then he said to them: "If the law is according to me, let the walls of the house of study prove it." The walls of the house of study began to topple. Rabbi Joshua reprimanded the walls: "If scholars are disputing with one another about the law, what business is it of yours?" The walls did not fall down out of respect for Rabbi Joshua and did not straighten up out of respect for Rabbi Eliezer. They are still so inclined! Then Rabbi Eliezer said to them: "If the law is according to me, let the heavens prove it." A voice then came forth from heaven and said: "Why do you dispute with Rabbi Eliezer? The law is according to him in every case." Thereupon, Rabbi Joshua rose to his feet and said: " 'It is not in heaven' (Deuteronomy 30:12). The Torah has been given once and for all at Mount Sinai. For You have already written in the Torah at Mount Sinai: 'After the majority one must incline' (Exodus 23:2)." Later on, Rabbi Nathan came upon Elijah the Prophet. He said to him: "What was the Holy One, Blessed be He, doing at that moment?" Elijah said to him: "He was smiling and saying: 'My children have defeated Me! My children have defeated Me!' "[9]

The passage attributes to God the natural parental inclination to intervene in disputes among His children. At the same time, God as a wise parent admits that His children are mature enough to resolve matters without His involvement. The passage admonishes God for not exercising greater self-restraint in remaining apart from human affairs. He is asked to abide by His own self-imposed restrictions, which include respect for the autonomy of human activity and judgment, nonintervention in the world, and avoidance of miracles.

Miracles represent a violation of the normal relationship between God and the world. Usually, God acts indirectly and predictably by allowing events to occur in response to human behavior and in such a way that the effect is proportionate to the cause. Good actions are rewarded and bad actions are punished. Miracles, on the other hand, are unpredictable, direct, and disproportionate results of the incursion of the transcendent God into the world. Both Rabbi Eliezer and Rabbi Joshua accept the occurrence of miracles but they differ on their relevance to Jewish legal debates. Rabbi Eliezer thinks that miracles and the power of the transcendent God can prove his case. Rabbi Joshua is unmoved by the miracles because he believes that they are irrelevant to the legal process of deciding matters of Jewish law; only the majority rule of a court of law has standing. Along the way, however, Rabbi Joshua decides to show that he too can perform miracles, if only to show that they are legally worthless.

The relationship between God and the Jewish people is analogous to that of a father and a child. God's treatment of the Jewish people in history is even portrayed as a process similar to the way in which a parent contributes to the maturity of a child. Jewish history is seen as a progression from thorough dependence upon God to greater self-reliance. God the parent guides the child along until the child can stand on its own. One passage characterizes this relationship as so powerful that God must voluntarily withdraw from the child in order for the child to achieve his or her own dignity and self-respect.

One midrash describes the construction of the Tabernacle, the ark containing the commandments which the Israelites transported from Sinai to the Land of Israel, as a result of the voluntary withdrawal or contraction of God into a specific location. Instead of appearing to Israel in many locales, after Sinai God viewed the people Israel as worthy of a more mature relationship with Him. He withdrew from His previous, rather intimate relationship with the Israelites to show them and others that they deserved to be respected as adults. The midrash equates greater parental intimacy with infancy and parental recognition of the child's maturity with withdrawal from casual contact and the establishment of more formal relations. The greatest expression of parental love is seen here as holding back from too much intimacy, which would smother rather than nurture the child into adulthood. The child may want to continue the dependency, but the parent distances himself for the sake of the child. This passage even offers a slightly suggestive nuance by implying that the father does not want anyone to suspect an illicit sexual rela-

tionship between himself and his daughter. Out of respect, he with-
draws. The Jewish people are described in the midrash as a daughter,
even though the biblical passage refers to Israel as "he":

> The case of a king who had a daughter who was a minor: Until she
> grew up and came of age, he used to speak with her when he saw her in
> the street; he spoke to her in the alleyways. But when she grew up and
> came of age, he said, "It is not in keeping with my daughter's dignity that
> I should talk to her in public. Make, therefore, a pavilion and I shall speak
> with her inside the pavilion." Thus, at first, it is written, "When Israel was
> a child, then I loved him." Said God, "They saw Me in Egypt; they saw
> Me at the Red Sea; they saw Me at Sinai." But, once they had accepted
> the Torah and became a complete nation unto Him, He said, "It is not in
> keeping with the dignity of My children that I should speak with them
> publicly, but let them make Me a tabernacle and I shall speak with them
> from the midst of the tabernacle."[10]

From the rabbis' perspective, the transcendence of God is a consequence
not of God's nature but of His voluntary withdrawal or self-contraction
to allow the Jewish people to reach maturity. The implication of this notion is that God is a caring parent who intervenes on behalf of His children minimally and, then, only as necessary. Otherwise, He allows His
children to direct their own affairs and fulfill the father's wishes and expectations as best they can, thereby vesting the Jewish people with responsibility for their own actions and placing their destiny in their own
hands. This is a humane theology that emphasizes the freedom, autonomy, responsibility, and accountability of the Jewish people. It also defines Judaism as the arena in which human freedom and responsibility
are worked out.

Another passage suggests that God's withdrawal can be caused invol-
untarily through human sin, which repels God from His people. In referring to the destruction of the Jerusalem Temple, the rabbis placed the
burden for its destruction not on the Babylonians or Romans, who destroyed the First and Second Temples, respectively, but on the sinfulness
of the Jewish people, which alienated God and forced Him to retreat
from intimacy. God's presence in the Temple provided protection from
outside attacks, but Jewish sinfulness caused God to withdraw and leave

the Temple vulnerable to destruction. God is pained by the sins of the Jewish people, which compel Him into withdrawal. This is the anguish of a parent who sees His children in distress but who cannot set things right for them. The rabbinic conception of God as caring parent is a metaphor that is both powerful and troubling. Its power resides in its providing comfort and consolation as well as reassurance that God has not abandoned His children. It is troubling because it humanizes God as a suffering victim of His own high expectations of His children:

> When the Holy One, Blessed be He, wished to destroy the Temple, He said, "So long as I am in it, the gentile nations will not harm it. I shall, therefore, cease to regard it and shall swear not to give it heed until the time of the End." At that moment, the enemy entered the Temple and burned it. When it was burnt, the Holy One, blessed be He, said, "I no longer have a seat upon the earth. I shall remove My Presence therefrom and ascend to My first habitation." At that moment, the Holy One, blessed be He, wept and said, "Woe unto Me! What have I done? I caused My Presence [*Shekhinah*] to dwell for Israel's sake, and now that they have sinned, I have returned to My original place."[11]

God as parent is not a gender-specific motif. God is neither male nor female but exhibits what the rabbis must have seen as ideal characteristics of any parent: love, nurturance, empathy, placing the child's needs first, self-sacrifice, and self-restraint. The rabbis attributed to God the best of human characteristics—only more so. They promoted the analogy between God and parents in order to stress that God, like a parent, gives life, nourishes and protects the child, promotes the child's growth, and remains ready to goad, encourage, or punish the child as necessary. The parent is both restrained and nurturing, just as God is transcendent and immanent. The belief that God's parental and protective aura can preserve us from pain and suffering has provided consolation and comfort to many. God's transcendence has offered certainty that the world will continue to function through all its changes. God's presence has offered stability and reassurance to many who feel lonely and afraid. God offers hope that the continuity of life itself is assured.

THE MASCULINE GOD

Why is God often portrayed in masculine, fatherly images? The rabbinic concept of God as parent is only one of several rabbinic metaphors. God is also king and judge. The familiar rabbinic prayer recited on the High Holy Days, "Our Father, Our King" (*Avinu Malkeinu*), combines the themes of compassionate parent with majestic king and righteous judge. It expresses a popular idea of God as a strict judge of human behavior who is still compassionate and responsive to His subjects. The archetype of father is invoked to stress that God is responsive to our pleas for mercy and compassion, although we are guilty by His standards as king. We ask God not to punish us, although we might deserve punishment, because our resulting pain will cause Him pain. We ask Him to remember that a punishment will hurt Him more than it will hurt us: "Help us for Your own sake." The king archetype stresses the objective and stern judgment of God about human worthiness. It implies that when human activity is weighed in the scales of judgment, it is measured by the standards of God's law and found wanting. Thus, humans are deserving of punishment.

The king also has the power to relieve us from the unwarranted oppression of our enemies and to grant us our wishes. We remind the king of our loyalty to Him as the only true king:

> Our Father, our King, we have no King but You.
> Our Father, our King, help us for Your own sake.
> Our Father, our King, grant us a blessed New Year.
> Our Father, our King, annul all evil decrees against us.
> Our Father, our King, annul the plots of our enemies.
> Our Father, our King, frustrate the designs of our foes.
> Our Father, our King, rid us of tyrants.
> Our Father, our King, rid us of pestilence, sword, famine, captivity, sin
> and destruction.
> Our Father, our King, forgive and pardon all our sins.[12]

This long prayer concludes with a plea for a response to our prayers and divine mercy for our sins. The king-and-father motif reinforces the idea that we are subjects and children who ask for mercy not on the basis of our own merits but from the compassion of the divine judge: "Our Father, our King, answer us though we have no deeds to plead our cause; save us with mercy and lovingkindness."

The masculine portrait of God as father and king has received considerable emphasis, particularly in the High Holy Day liturgy. It has led many people to a distorted image of God as a stern, unforgiving male figure which carries with it all the negative associations of some male stereotypes. However, it represents only one among several metaphors the rabbis employed to convey their beliefs. It should not obscure metaphors that are more nurturing and spiritual.

THE GOD OF ARISTOTLE
AND THE GOD OF ISRAEL

The biblical and rabbinic beliefs about God are quite distinct from other philosophies of God that developed in neighboring cultures and that later had a powerful impact on how Western civilization viewed God. Jews have always sought to learn from other peoples and have been receptive to the best efforts of foreign cultures to address the questions that interest Jews. Even though biblical Judaism began in opposition to Babylonian religious beliefs, later Judaism looked to other cultures for new ideas. The teachings of Plato and Aristotle held a great attraction for Jewish thinkers, who saw in them new and original approaches to what one can believe about God.

Greek civilization, beginning around the sixth century B.C.E., developed a new philosophy about God and the universe. Although they grew in close geographical and temporal proximity, neither Israelite nor Greek civilization was aware of the ideas of the other until centuries later. By way of comparison with biblical ideas, the Greek philosopher Plato, in the fifth century B.C.E., believed that one of the gods—the good demiurge—created the universe in order to replicate his own ideal perfection. The perfect existence of the gods could not be duplicated, so the world was created by a lesser god in poor imitation of that of the gods. This led Plato to the idea that God represents the ideal and that the universe of human experience is a pale reflection of God's perfection. Such a belief differed from the biblical view, which saw God as an all-

powerful creator who fashioned a perfect universe. Plato's negative estimation of the physical world is in contrast to the Jewish view of the
world as perfect or perfectible and ruled by a moral God. Plato stated:
"Before beginning the story of the genesis of the world, let us state
the cause wherefore he who constructed it did construct the universe. . . . He desired that everything should be so far as possible like
himself. God desired that all things should be good and nothing bad, so
far as this was attainable."[13]

The early Jewish beliefs differed also from another ancient Greek philosophy. Aristotle, in the fourth century B.C.E., introduced a new conception of God that influenced not only Jewish thought but all of
Western civilization until the late Middle Ages: God is an impersonal,
incorporeal principle of being, the Unmoved Mover of all existence
who does not act to create. The universe is not created but is made up of
matter that has existed as long as God, that is, eternally. This god does
not act at all, although its perfection is so complete that it influences and
attracts the eternal matter of the world. Matter aspires to perfection and
is drawn to the Unmoved Mover. Thus, the Mover does not really move
anything but is called "Mover" because it attracts everything. It is almost
meaningless to call this god and the God of the Bible by the same name.
The connotation of the term is fundamentally different in each case. The
God of the Bible is a "Moved Mover," a moral and personal being of
pathos, creation, and action. Aristotle's god is a static, impersonal, inac-
tive, abstract principle of being, so far removed from the world that it
does not even know, let alone care about, individuals.

The god of Aristotle is a perfect being which has no moral influence
upon the world. The world functions according to its own nature, and
human moral activity has no influence on nature. The biblical God directs nature in response to human activity, and the means of achieving
perfection in the world reside in the arena of human activity. God directs the course of the world morally and acts in history in a manner responsive and proportionate to human action. In the account of Noah
and the Flood, God declares that an impending natural disaster could
have been avoided. God says to Noah: "I have decided to put an end to
all flesh, for the earth is filled with lawlessness because of them. I am
about to destroy them with the earth" (Genesis 6:13). In the account of

Sodom and Gomorrah, Abraham challenges God not to destroy the innocent with the guilty by reminding God of His moral law: "Shall not
the judge of all the earth deal justly?" (Genesis 18:25). God, however,
can be a harsh and unforgiving judge: as the prophet Isaiah warned his
contemporaries, "In that day, the Lord will punish with His great, cruel,
mighty sword" (Isaiah 27:1).

The biblical God governs nature and is not governed by it. God is
above and beyond nature, which He created: "You spread the heavens
like a tent cloth. . . . He [God] sets the rafters of His lofts in the waters,
makes the clouds His chariot. . . . He makes the winds His messengers,
fiery flames His servants" (Psalms 104:2–4). Centuries later, the rabbis
explained: "Every entity regards itself as exalted over another entity.
Darkness regards itself as exalted over the deep, because it is above it. Air,
as exalted over water, because it is above it. Fire, as exalted over air, because it is above it. The heavens, as exalted over fire, because they are above
it. But the Holy One, blessed be He, is truly exalted over them all."[14]

The biblical God is the universal, transcendent, omnipotent moral
being who creates, governs, and sustains the world. God transcends the
world in every respect. The Bible reiterates the superiority and transcendence of God over all human endeavors: "For My plans are not your
plans, nor are My ways your ways, declares the Lord. But as the heavens
are high above the earth, so are My ways high above your ways and My
plans above your plans" (Isaiah 55:8–9). Divine omniscience or providential knowledge is a corollary of His transcendence. One midrash explains that God is like an architect who built and then governs a city
with passages, alleys, and tunnels. While thieves might think it is possible
for them to hide from the governor within the city, they are mistaken.
The architect knows the hidden places and can reach the thieves anywhere. So, too, with God, who created and rules the universe and knows
the actions and whereabouts of all humanity.

The biblical and rabbinic notions that God personally causes the rains
to come in their seasons, crops to grow, flocks to increase, and the world
to prosper reflect a view of human cause and divine reaction that might
appear simplistic today. It should be considered, however, in relation to
the values of its time. The Jewish belief in God was a forceful departure
from the amoral, arbitrary, and capricious universe of the ancient Baby-

lonians and the indifferent, mechanistic God of Aristotle. It introduced a novel view of a benign universe governed by a moral God. As human consciousness matured, new understandings of God supplanted the biblical and rabbinic perception.

THE GOD OF MOSES MAIMONIDES

In the Middle Ages, the encounter between Jewish theology and the legacy of Plato and Aristotle would reshape Jewish theology. Many medieval Jewish thinkers were influenced by the ideas of Plato and Aristotle. Jewish philosophers attempted to reconcile the impersonal God of Plato and Aristotle with the biblical and rabbinic belief in a moral and personal God. The medieval Jewish conceptions sought to preserve the purity of divine transcendence while removing some of the more egregious expressions used to describe God's immanence. In particular, the medieval Jewish thinkers challenged the view that God could be described in human terms, especially through anthropomorphism and anthropopathism. At the same time, they sought to preserve God's accessibility. In preferring the king archetype, they were in danger of losing the father archetype.

The attempt to purge the Jewish conception of God of anthropomorphism produced the reaffirmation of belief in God's incorporeality. For those who believed that God was truly unique, the rejection of anthropomorphism still left them with a vulnerability to anthropopathism, the belief that God experiences emotion and feeling, characteristics of humans. Jewish thinkers in the Middle Ages concluded that a pure notion of God must be free of all human physical and emotional characteristics. This was the contribution to Jewish theology of Moses Maimonides.

Moses Maimonides (Rambam) (1135–1204), the greatest Sephardic rabbinic scholar and philosopher, introduced a sweeping new codification of Jewish law called *Mishneh Torah* (Repetition of the Law). The title boldly suggests a recapitulation of the law code and a book second in importance only to the Torah. This fourteen-volume work was strongly attacked by his critics for many reasons, including the fact that it did not cite earlier rabbinic authorities. His critics suspected that Maimonides went too far beyond his predecessors and thereby set himself up as a greater authority than they. *Mishneh Torah,* however, soon gained acceptance and assumed great importance as the basic codification of Jewish law.

Maimonides' *Guide of the Perplexed* is the most influential of the medieval efforts to convey the belief in God's absolute transcendence. Maimonides did not find the rabbinic explanation of divine transcendence wholly satisfactory. He thought that the scientific knowledge and philosophic belief of his day contradicted rabbinic beliefs about God. The teachings of the ancient Greek philosophers such as Plato and Aristotle had been translated into Arabic and interpreted by the medieval Islamic philosophers Alfarabi, Avicenna, and Averroes. Maimonides' intellectual development was rooted in equal measure in traditional Jewish studies and in contemporary Arabic philosophy. As a rabbi, he was troubled by the fact that he personally found the teachings of Arabic philosophy about God more persuasive than the familiar rabbinic teachings. To avoid claiming that Aristotelian and Arabic thought was closer to the truth than Judaism, he tried to prove that Jewish belief is compatible with the teachings of those philosophies. His critics attacked this claim as a distortion and an attack on the integrity of authentic Jewish traditions.

Maimonides accepts the rabbinic notion of the abyss between God and man, and refines the idea in many novel ways. As did the rabbinic sages, he teaches that God is absolutely unique and transcendent. He goes further than they did, however, in claiming that God is therefore unknowable. Maimonides' philosophic challenge to the rabbinic conception of God produced a revolution in Jewish thought.

All we can know, Maimonides asserts, is that God exists; we cannot know anything about His essence. If that is the case, he asks, how is it possible to explain all the biblical and rabbinic descriptions that portray God as having physical characteristics such as a face, hand, and arm or emotional attributes such as compassion and anger? How is it possible to pray to God in language that describes Him in concrete terms?

The Bible speaks of God's hand, face, front, back, and eyes, as well as His hearing, seeing, and anger. The rabbinic literature even portrays God as crying and wearing a prayer shawl. Were these images to be taken literally, as suggesting that God has the same characteristics, emotions, and habits as humans? There were, in fact, several popular books in the Middle Ages that vested God with physical dimensions of awesome proportion. If these descriptions were to be taken as metaphors, symbols, or

mere figures of speech, how were they to be interpreted and under-
stood? Maimonides was also disturbed by passages in the rabbinic litera-
ture that describe God as weeping and praying. In response to this,
Maimonides stated: "Anyone who is led to believe that God has a body
is a heretic!" Still, in the thirteenth century Rabbi Abraham ben David
(Rabad), one of the leading rabbis of France, defended the belief that
God has anthropomorphic and anthropopathic qualities, and criticized
Maimonides' views as inconsistent with Jewish tradition.

Maimonides explains that these descriptions are not essential characteristics of God. God does not have an outstretched arm, a face, anger, or
compassion. Such descriptions are the result of our perception of events
in the world, whose cause we attribute to God. When we believe in
God, we say He "lives." When we see the world, we say God "creates" or
"acts." When we sense that God rewards some and punishes others, we
say He is "merciful" or "judging." We see only the effect and not the
cause. We do not know whether God's essence includes life, action,
mercy, or judgment. Those are human attributes and cannot be the same
as God's attributes. To hold otherwise would be to make God like us,
and that would be idolatry. God acts in His own unique way, and the
consequences of His actions are described in human terms. If we say
that this is similar to the action of a hand or an action done with anger
or compassion, we confuse the effect with the cause. Maimonides warns
that we should not confuse human and divine actions by attributing to
God what are merely human physical or emotional characteristics: the
biblical and talmudic passages that speak of God in human terms are not
meant to be taken literally. They are mere figures of speech, since "the
Torah speaks *as if* in the language of the sons of man." The transcendent
God is by nature above that. Maimonides explains that biblical anthropomorphism is necessary to convey a sense of God's existence, actions,
and providence. The anthropopathic expressions convey God's moral attributes and the myriad ways in which He governs the universe.

Maimonides' conception of the transcendent God gained acceptance
and replaced many of the more popular views. Maimonides' God is the
hidden God of the rabbinic tradition taken to extremes. He professes
that there can be no real relationship between God and man, since God
is unique, incorporeal, and transcendent. There is nothing that God and
man share, inasmuch as man is corporeal and rooted in the physical

world. There can be no relationship between two beings that share nothing in common. In an attempt to refine and purify the rabbinic conception of God, he removes God so far from humanity that there is almost no human contact with Him. Maimonides attempts to destroy the paradox inherent in the rabbinic view that God is both remote and near by concluding that, since God cannot be both, He must be one or the other. His philosophic consistency led him to the conclusion that God must be remote and inaccessible.

The common term for God among Maimonides' philosophic contemporaries was not the biblical and traditional name of God, YHVH (known as the Tetragrammaton, which was pronounced *"Adonai."* God was designated as *bilti baal tachlit* (translated from the Arabic term *la nihaya,* "one who has no limit"), *sibbat kol ha-sibbot* ("the cause of all causes"), and *shoresh ha-shorashim* ("the root of all roots"). Philosophers such as Maimonides stressed the impersonal aspect of God to emphasize His differentness. For them, the personal God of the Bible was how ancient Israelites imagined their God. For those who could live in the rarefied atmosphere of philosophy, it was hard to see how one could attribute personality to God without diminishing His greatness.

Maimonides introduced the idea that humans project onto God those qualities we see as ideal or desirable. As people recognize that these are human notions of perfection, they can realize that they are "inventing" God. This does not mean that God's very existence is invented as much as it means that our perception of God's attributes is created in our own image. The intellectual challenge posed by Maimonides was to abandon the naive, idolatrous ideas that we have about God in favor of clear, unalloyed rational thinking about the transcendent cause of existence. He was faced with the challenge of explaining how his new conception of God could be reconciled with the biblical portrayal of the personal God.

THE *SEFIROT* AND THE FEMININE ASPECT OF GOD

Maimonides widened the abyss separating God and man. The challenge then became to reestablish a relationship between man and the unknowable God. That challenge was met by the Kabbalah, the medieval

Jewish mystical tradition which originated in Provence and Spain in the early thirteenth century. The Kabbalists believe that Maimonides preserved God's transcendence at the expense of His personality and immanence. The Kabbalah sought to introduce a new notion of spirituality without appearing to be new. The very term "Kabbalah" means "that which is received," or "tradition." Kabbalah claims to be part of the unbroken transmission of the Oral Torah going back to Sinai.

In most respects the Kabbalists accepted Maimonides' theory of a unique and unknowable God. However, they found it difficult to understand how one could dispense with the idea of a personal God. The God of philosophy was hardly one to whom a Jew could pray. Nevertheless, there was little disagreement on the notion of the absolute impersonality of God's essence.

The Kabbalists' solution to the dilemma was to introduce a distinction between the hidden and revealed aspects of God. The hidden, infinite aspect of God is called "the Infinite" (*Eyn Sof,* "without end"). This name was understood as the proper one for the hidden aspect of God. It suggests that God exists without implying anything about His character. According to the Kabbalists, God should be called *It* rather than *He* although there is no neuter gender in the Hebrew language. Actually, because of the great sublimity and transcendence of God, no name at all can be applied to "the Infinite." The name *Eyn Sof* conveys only that God is unlike anything we know. According to these mystics, *Eyn Sof* is not the proper object of prayers, since *Eyn Sof* has no relationship with His creatures. The personal aspect of the hidden God is mediated by the ten *Sefirot,* ten infinite yet knowable aspects of His being. There are, therefore, two natures of God—the infinite, unknowable essence and the ten discernible aspects.

The word *Sefirot* originally meant "numerals," and was taken from the earliest Hebrew text on the nature of numbers and letters, *Sefer Yetzirah* (The Book of Formation). *Sefirot* is a generic term that means that the aspects of God's being, or the instruments of God's activity, can be counted. There are ten *Sefirot* just as there are ten cardinal numbers. Some Kabbalists explain that the word comes from the Hebrew root *sapper,* "to tell," implying that these aspects tell us about God. Others have suggested that it derives from the Hebrew word for sapphire, since the *Sefirot* illuminate our knowledge of God like a precious and radiant gem.

There have been a variety of attempts to translate *Sefirot* into English. They have often been called "spheres," "radiances," or other occult terms. The *Sefirot,* however, are numerically identifiable symbols of the various aspects of God's being or activities. A more faithful English rendition would be "calculi," a word that signifies both a means of reckoning and the use of symbols. Since there is no good English translation of *Sefirot,* the use of the original Hebrew term is still preferable.

The *Sefirot* are the bridge across the abyss, the connective tissue between the infinite God and the finite world. They are the link that makes it possible to maintain God's absolute unity while preserving the relationship between God and man. They, and not *Eyn Sof,* are the object of human prayers. By differentiating between *Eyn Sof* and the *Sefirot,* it is possible to say that God is incorporeal, immaterial, and unchangeable while still adhering to the traditional notion of the personal God. All anthropomorphic and anthropopathic references and the traditional notion of an active, personal God refer to the *Sefirot.* All the statements that imply corporeality, composition, and change in God refer to the *Sefirot,* not to *Eyn Sof.* The *Sefirot,* not *Eyn Sof,* is the God of the Bible. Therefore, a Kabbalist can justifiably claim that "*Eyn Sof* is nowhere mentioned in the Bible." The Bible refers only to the *Sefirot,* the knowable God, not the hidden God.

The theory of the *Sefirot* is an attempt to explain how the infinite God can have a relationship with the finite world and how an unknowable God can be known by man. The relationship of *Eyn Sof* to the *Sefirot* can be illustrated by drawing an analogy between the soul and the body. The soul, which is invisible and unknowable, dwells within the body. Although there is only one soul in each body, the soul acts through a variety of physical organs. The soul is, therefore, the essence that uses the "instruments" of the body for its activity. The manner in which the soul is connected to the body is still a mystery. Nonetheless, we claim to know that there is a soul even if it remains inscrutable because of its incorporeal nature.[15] Likewise, *Eyn Sof* dwells within the *Sefirot,* which are the instruments by which God relates to the world.

The most accessible of the *Sefirot* is the tenth or last *Sefirah,* which is designated *Shekhinah* or *Malkhut* (kingship). The archetype employed in the *Shekhinah* symbolism is feminine, and this *Sefirah* is described as the feminine aspect of divinity. The paternal symbolism of God in rabbinic Judaism is replaced by a maternal one. This queen-and-mother archetype stresses divine nurturance and the accessibility of God. It is the part of the deity that comes close to man and bonds with him. The *Shekhinah* is the divine lover with whom the mystic unites in symbolic matrimony and sexual imagery. It is the providential and powerful aspect of divinity which rules over the world, sustains it, and judges it. The femininization of God stresses intimacy, while the masculinization stresses distance.

The Kabbalah introduced a deeply mythical understanding of God that preserved His transcendence but deepened His accessibility through the invention of archetypes and symbols that personalized Him. The kabbalistic theory grew in popularity among large segments of world Jewry following its inception in Spain in the thirteenth century. It captured the imagination of many medieval Jews in Italy, Poland, the Ottoman Empire, and North Africa until the end of the seventeenth century, when it was challenged by new theories, including those of Baruch Spinoza.

BARUCH SPINOZA AND NATURE AS GOD

Baruch (Benedict) Spinoza (1632–77), a descendant of Marranos (the Jews who converted to Christianity in fifteenth-century Spain and Portugal), is arguably the first modern Jewish thinker. He built on the foundation laid by Aristotle, Maimonides, and others to teach that God is the source of all reality. The essence of God is unknowable except for two infinite and unique attributes, which he called thought and extension. Earlier philosophers had called God "pure form," by which they meant that God was a pure thinking being whose ideas were the forms that emanated upon the world. They believed that God was free of all matter, which had its own independent existence apart from God. God's ideas then emanated upon matter, which took their form. This theory meant that forms were ideas that came from God and were, therefore, pure and good. Matter, however, which had no cause and certainly was inferior to God's forms, was passive and was acted upon by the pure ideas. Matter was inferior and, therefore, not divine.

Spinoza was the first figure in Western thought to teach that God is identical with nature and can, therefore, be found in the world. Spinoza attributes to God the essential attributes of thought and extension, which mean "form" and "matter" respectively. This means that "not only individual thoughts are traceable to God as their source, but also individual extended things can be traced directly to God."[16] The statement that God is extension or matter—not only thought or form, as the medieval philosophers argued—is Spinoza's unique contribution because it means that God Himself is material.[17] Other philosophers had posited a dualism between God and matter that suggested that goodness and ideas come from God whereas matter is independent of God and brings about physical existence and evil. Never before had any Jewish philosopher claimed that God was both form and matter.

Spinoza taught that human beings, themselves composed of mind and body, are therefore modes of divine thought and extension. Since God is the cause and source of all things, which are merely modes of the attributes of thought and extension, everything must exist within God. If God is both form and matter, there is no dualism between the spiritual and the physical realm, between ideas and things, between God and human beings. Everything, including God, has the same nature—mind and extension—and all existence is therefore homogeneous and animate. The homogeneity of all existence and the belief that all existence is animate lead to the conclusion that God is all and the universe is one living being.

This God is wholly impersonal and incapable of revealing anything to the world. Spinoza's God is not the God of the Bible. Spinoza, who was excommunicated by the Jewish community of Amsterdam for these views, was accused of being an atheist. Far from it: he was the consummate rationalist who took the God of Aristotle and Maimonides to its logical destination. His pantheistic, impersonal, and material God who is identified with all existence represents the end of the medieval philosophical tradition. At the same time, his radically unknowable God hints at the beginning of modern secular doubt about the existence of the personal God of the Bible.

Following Spinoza, Jewish thought diverged in two directions. First, Jewish conceptions of God were not limited by the traditional constraint of belief in a personal God. It was now possible to claim that Judaism tolerated even the most extreme formulations of belief in God. Second, agnosticism was made intellectually respectable as a Jewish approach to God, since the unknowability of God was no longer a scandalous tenet.

HASIDISM AND THE GOD WITHIN US

In the Ukraine, around 1735, Israel ben Eliezer, known as the Besht (an acronym for Baal Shem Tov, "Master of the Good Name"), a popular folk preacher and healer, gathered a following of devotees to a new religious teaching that was based, in part, on the Kabbalah. This discipline, Hasidism (Pietism), involved a technique for achieving union with the divine and liberation from the vicissitudes of this world. The central teaching of the Besht is that man can achieve oneness with the divine through ecstatic prayer and transcendence of the material world.

Hasidism promoted a new human ideal, the Hasid. As opposed to the scholar, the Hasid is illuminated with the presence of God and becomes intoxicated with God through ecstatic prayer. Hasidim were panentheists, believing that the perception of the world as a separate reality is incorrect and that the world exists only within God, the sole reality. They believed that only God is real, that this world is merely an illusion and not truly real. Hasidic teaching asserts that there is nothing that truly exists except God's being. In hasidic language, all the phenomena of the world are only vessels that contain the divine light but have no independent reality of their own. The world is really a veil that, if removed, leaves only divinity.

Nothing exists in the world independent of God. Everything that exists can be elevated back to its divine source. There is little room in this conception for anything but God: "One should know that everything in the world is infused with the Creator, may He be blessed. Every product of human thought is the result of His providence." The beauty of the world lies not in the things of this world but in God, the source of all beauty. The task of the Hasid is to elevate the divine sparks, to raise everything back to its source, to transcend the partial and seek the absolute. Things in this world do not really matter except as they are man-

ifestations of God. Beauty does not really exist in the world other than
as a concretization of divinity in human form. Everything is a vessel for
the divine essence:

> If one should notice a beautiful woman, he thinks: What is the cause
> of her beauty? Is it not true that if she were to die, she would not have
> this appearance? If so, her beauty comes from the divine power that suf-
> fuses her. He gives her the beauty and complexion. Thus, the source of
> her beauty is the divine power. Why, then, should I be drawn to the par-
> tial when I can unite with the source of all the universe?

Every Hasid must raise the sparks, must elevate everything to its
source, must transcend the partial for the whole, must see the divine
essence in every material thing. Every object that vibrates internally
with the *Sefirot* must be raised back to its source. True worship of God is
the pursuit of the essence within the vessel, the divine within the
worldly, the spiritual within the material.[18]

One of the more daring formulations of hasidic belief in God is that
of Shneur Zalman of Liadi (1745–1813), the founder of Habad-
Lubavitch Hasidism. Shneur Zalman was the leading disciple of the
maggid Dov Baer of Mezritch, the successor to the Baal Shem Tov. The
hasidic movement he founded takes its name from *habad*, a Hebrew
acronym for *hokhmah* (wisdom), *binah* (understanding), and *daat* (knowledge)—the three upper *Sefirot* a Hasid aspires to mystically and whose
qualities he seeks to emulate intellectually. Lubavitch is the name of the
town in White Russia where Shneur Zalman established his community
of followers.

In his major writing, the *Tanya,* Shneur Zalman offers the theory that
there is nothing real in all of existence other than God and that all that
exists is within God. This radical theology—known as acosmism, or
"world-denying" mysticism—is mistakenly thought to be more typical
of Hinduism than eighteenth-century Lithuanian Judaism. The universe
and all existence are the intellectual expression or speech emanating
from God's mind. It might appear to be different from God but in reality
it is nothing more than a dressing for God's essential being. Nothing exists except as a thought of God's mind. We might perceive things to exist

as separate substances, but our perception is incorrect. Nothing exists but God and all that is exists within God. Our sense of the separate existence of the universe is an illusion.

For Shneur Zalman, the phenomena we perceive are not real except when we perceive them. The only reality is God. The world is nothing more than a transparent shell for God, but the shell itself is only a perceptual illusion. The world is nothing and meaningless in relation to God, and it is a mistake based on our limited understanding and perception of God to believe that the world is real. God is all-encompassing reality, including within itself everything that we know of as existence. The goal of the Habad-Lubavitch Hasid is to recognize the difference between illusion and reality. This can be achieved through knowledge that the ritual and religious obligations of Judaism are expressions of divinity that must be performed scrupulously. At the same time, the Habad-Lubavitch Hasid must transcend the limits of human existence by annihilating his sense of self and separateness from God. This can be achieved through a meditative process in which one consciously concentrates his mind toward understanding his insignificance in relation to God.

MODERN JEWISH BELIEFS

Modern Judaism is defined by the Orthodox, Conservative, Reconstructionist, and Reform denominations. Orthodox Judaism accepts the sacred myth of belief in God as it was formulated by rabbinic Judaism. For many non-Orthodox Jews, God is what we would normally identify as that which we "love with all our heart, with all our soul, and with all our might."[19] It might not be what the ancestors called God. God is that reality or absolute to which we subordinate other concerns and which commands our "most fateful decisions." God for moderns is "a Reality that qualitatively transcends us, one that nevertheless impinges upon us by its commanding presence."[20]

Eugene Borowitz, one of the preeminent contemporary Jewish thinkers, is regarded as the leading religious philosopher of Reform Judaism. Borowitz is critical of the drift away from spirituality in American Judaism. He sees the effort to answer the question "What is God?" in modern terms as the search for our ultimate concern—using the term of Paul Tillich, a twentieth-century Protestant theologian—or what Borowitz calls "our existential absolute." Borowitz argues for a return to belief in the "transcendent Other." By transcendence, he means a being that is independent and beyond us, which lures us through religious awe to emulate its character by arousing within us "love," and which has such compelling and commanding power that we would freely accept its standards as a covenant. Borowitz's God is an "axial reality far more elemental than mind or feeling or unconscious or self but one undergirding them and thereby endowing them with unique worth."[21] To avoid association with many of the negative connotations of the word "God," Borowitz calls God "the Transcendent," or "transcendent reality." This does not mean that God specifically commands us or wants us to do anything in particular. It does mean that, insofar as we acknowledge the Transcendent, we are free to follow the duties that our awareness of God implies.

Borowitz explains his experience of the transcendent Other in terms of overcoming his innate modern skepticism about the presence of God. Rather than accept the radical doubts about God and values, Borowitz unabashedly affirms belief in God: "I find this Ultimate to be of such superlative quality as to lift me far above myself in aspiration and, often, in consequent action. I am surprised, grateful, honored, commissioned by this intimacy with the Other that I and our people call, let me say it, God."[22]

The Conservative movement issued a statement of principles of Conservative Judaism, *Emet ve-Emunah,* in 1988. In it, Conservative Judaism's understanding of God is presented not as a belief in a specific notion of God but rather as the very act of asking the right questions about God: "Does God exist? If so, what sort of being is God? Does God have a plan for the universe? Does God care about me? Does He hear prayer? Does God allow the suffering of the innocent?"[23] In this regard, Conservative Judaism "affirms the critical importance of belief in God, but does not specify all the particulars of that belief."[24] Still, the manifesto recognizes a plurality of God concepts.

For Conservative Judaism, belief in God means faith that a supreme, supernatural being exists and has the power to command and control the world through His will. What is the basis for believing in God? The

Conservative movement teaches that God's existence can be known from the testimony of Scripture, the fact that there is something rather than nothing, the vastness and orderliness of the universe, the sense of command that we feel in the face of moral imperatives, the experience of miraculous historical events, and the existence of phenomena that seem to go beyond physical matter, such as human consciousness and creativity. All of these perceptions are encounters that point beyond us. They reinforce one another to produce an experience of, and thus a belief in, a God who, though unperceivable, exists in the usual sense of the word.[25]

Some modern Jewish thinkers have attempted unsuccessfully to remove the notion of God from Judaism without destroying the edifice of Judaism. For example, Mordecai Kaplan, the founder of Reconstructionism, the fourth movement among the contemporary Jewish denominations, views God as a process and a power, not as a being or entity. God is "a power that makes for salvation," meaning that God is the impulse for goodness that exists within human beings and societies. According to Kaplan, the inclination to justice, goodness, and peace is God itself. God is neither a being nor the sacred element in the everyday world. God is indistinguishable from goodness, virtue, and creativity. God is also a function of the "natural religious impulse" within human beings that generates the discoveries and creativity that give rise to human meaning. This naturalist God is every bit as real for Kaplan as the supernatural God was for his predecessors. This is not a supernatural or a personal God but a natural power which, according to Kaplan, literally exists.

The hasidic idea that God is that force which gives a vitality to the world without which nothing could exist has had appeal to secular as well as observant Jews. In fact, the teachings of Hasidism were reinterpreted by Martin Buber (1878–1965), one of the most noted Jewish thinkers of the twentieth century. The idea that God is most accessible within the world led Buber to conclude that hasidic teaching, stripped of its Orthodox practice, held out a possible answer for modern men and women who were searching for spiritual meaning. He taught that God could be experienced in the world when we free ourselves from the habitual and mundane, and recognize that God is present at every moment and in every place. He taught that there is no rung of being on which we cannot find the holiness of God everywhere and at all times.

Although he was born in Vienna, the cultural capital of western Europe, Martin Buber was raised in Poland in the traditional home of his grandfather, a noted rabbinic scholar who introduced him to the study of Judaism. Later, Buber returned to Vienna where he attended university, then continued his studies in Berlin. He developed interests in philosophy, Zionism, and the teachings of Hasidism. In 1923, he published *I and Thou,* one of the most important works of twentieth-century existentialist philosophy. In 1938, he fled Nazi Germany and settled in Israel where he taught at the Hebrew University of Jerusalem until his death. He was active in Jewish education and in efforts to bring about reconciliation between Arabs and Jews.

Buber's philosophical views evolved over a lifetime. His early thinking about God, reflected in his writings on Hasidism, was pantheistic.[26] He believed that God is the inner unity which is both present in and the true essence of everything in the world. Buber's later theism saw God as the "Eternal Thou" who is realized in every true and profound encounter between ourselves ("I") and another person ("Thou"). Buber's God is a distinctly other being who is experienced personally and who has always been experienced by humans since ancient times. God is the Eternal Thou who gives meaning to each personal encounter between humans. God is both wholly other and present in the world in the experience of human relationships. When two people truly experience each other, God is there. He can only be experienced through other persons: "Man cannot reach the divine by reaching beyond the human."[27] He is an eternally present being who evokes awe and love in those who experience Him. God is the all-encompassing presence who addresses humanity through the experience of living in the world. Buber maintained that God is not a being in whom one believes and speaks about in the third person but rather a being to whom one speaks directly. Martin Buber's God "is the Being that may properly only be addressed, not expressed."[28] God does not watch over individuals or command law, nor can he be sought after through rituals. Buber was a religious humanist who did not believe that God reveals a message or law to humanity; He reveals only a presence.

Rabbi Abraham Joshua Heschel (1907–72) was the scion of several important hasidic figures, including the Maggid of Mezritch, Levi Isaac of Berditchev, and Abraham Joshua Heschel of Apt. He was educated in traditional Jewish learning but was also immersed in the major streams of Western philosophy. In 1938, he was deported from Germany by the Nazis and, within two years, arrived in the United States. Steeped in the hasidic traditions of European Jewry, his ideas had a great impact on Jewish religious thought in America. He taught briefly at Hebrew Union College in Cincinnati but his later career revolved around the Jewish Theological Seminary in New York, where he exerted a profound influence upon several generations of Conservative rabbis. He was a pioneer in the civil rights movement and in the anti–Vietnam War movement.

According to Heschel, God is not a philosophic idea but a powerful and mysterious presence who reaches out to us through the world. All of creation consists of continual marvels which make commonplace deeds into spiritual adventures. Everywhere in the world, Heschel sees God reaching out to us. It is not we who are in search of God; it is God who is in search of us. What meaning is there to the life of a Jew, asks Heschel, if it is not to acquire the ability to feel the taste of heaven?[29] We respond to God's reaching out with our answer: prayer. We reach out to God in prayer, but God is also reaching out to us. The awareness of God occurs in the moment when one stands face to face in "radical amazement" with the natural order or when we are overwhelmed by the experience of God's love and care for the individual and the world. The experience of God is so fundamental and deep that it is beyond conceptual or rational analysis. The dynamic presence of God is also felt in the Hebrew prophets' moral passion, which they based on God's absolute call for righteousness.

Buber and Heschel have presented important new perspectives on the sacred myth of Judaism. Buber's version of the sacred myth chooses immanence over transcendence. We can draw the transcendent to us and infuse the sacred into the everyday. This is a spirituality of immanence. We can see the transcendent in nature and in other human beings, the profane can be made sacred, Israel can live as a sacred people among other nations, the holiness of the Sabbath can be applied to life throughout the week, and we can overcome evil through our deeds. The sacred myth, according to Heschel, invites us to be drawn toward God's transcendence, which lifts us out of the mundane into the sacred. It is a spirituality of transcendence. We can overcome the polarities by choosing God over nature, the holy over the profane, Israel over the other nations, the Sabbath over the other days of the week, and good over evil. We can choose transcendence over immanence. Buber and Heschel represent the two existential approaches of modern Jewish belief.

In Judaism, the search for understanding God never reaches a final destination. Judaism seeks absolute answers to "What is God?" but those answers are never final. What matters is the search and the struggle to define the transcendent source of being and to understand its place in our lives. Each generation, each person, will understand God differently. But each generation will wrestle with the question. Most important, each of us must arrive at our own answers, just as those who came before us. We must improve upon their answers, just as they improved upon the answers of those who came before them. We must reach outside of ourselves to find our answers, to gain the faith that replaces uncertainty. At other times, we need only look around to find the faith that was always there inside. We need to hear the voice within us that speaks to us and offers us assurance. Hannah Senesh, the Jewish Hungarian resistance fighter who was captured and killed by the Nazis when she parachuted behind enemy lines, composed a prayer that speaks of this certainty:

My God,
My God,
I pray that these things never end——
The sand and the sea,
The rush of the waters, the lightning of the heavens, the prayer of the soul.

2

Human Destiny

What does it mean to be a human being created "in the image of God"? The sacred myths of Judaism about the purpose and meaning of human existence begin with this enigmatic and challenging premise. Jews have wrestled with the basic questions about human destiny in many ways. In this chapter, we will look at some of their attempts to define the spiritual dimension of human life; the ethical imperative; what can be learned from the stages of life; and strategies for strengthening our awareness of the transcendent element in our daily life. We will find here a uniquely Jewish approach to spirituality.

The Jewish view of human destiny begins with the belief that God created the first human being in His own image. Each individual is the earthly representation of God, and all people participate equally in this noble stature. Each person is also unique. As Martin Buber said, "In every man there is something precious which is in no one else." This belief shapes and determines every Jewish approach to explain the nature and purpose of human life. Everything has a purpose, and the purpose of human life is to refine the image of God within us. Anything that strengthens the divine image is called "holy"; anything that detracts from it is "unholy."

Human destiny is the call to view all moments in life as opportunities to reach beyond the mundane to find higher meaning and significance. The Jewish view of human destiny challenges us to nurture and cultivate the divine image implanted within each of us. When we fail to seek the transcendent dimension in life, we weaken the bond between ourselves and God. The image of God, the divine spark, is within each of us. This requires that we look at other people as "holy" and at our own lives as opportunities to strengthen the divine image.

The spiritual dimension of Judaism is the emphasis on strengthening the image of God, the divine spark, wherever it might be found within our world. All human actions, behaviors, habits, and attitudes are directed toward calling us to the transcendent or bringing the transcendent into the world. Jews believe that all of human life can be understood as the spiritual process of experiencing God within the world. To experience the divine within the world is to realize God's presence. Ultimately, to know yourself is to know God.

THE IMAGE OF GOD

According to the Torah, Adam, the first human, was created in the image of God. The Torah explains that man is the pinnacle of creation and bears an intentional likeness to God. Man is endowed with the authority to govern the earth and its creatures:

> And God said, "Let us make man in our image, after our likeness. They shall rule the fish of the sea, the birds of the sky, the cattle, the whole earth, and all the creeping things that creep on earth." And God created man in His image, in the image of God He created him; male and female He created them. (Genesis 1:26–27)

The midrash gives several explanations as to why the Bible refers to "our" image and "our" likeness in the plural. After all, was not God the sole creator? One rabbi said that it referred to God's own heart, with which He took counsel. Another view suggested that God was assisted in the creation of man by His ministering angels in heaven. A third offered the opinion that God, who saw the future havoc men would wreak, invoked the aid of His own attribute of mercy in His decision to create the world.

Other rabbinic writings held that "in our image, after our likeness" means that Adam was created in the image of the dignity of God.[1] Rashi (Rabbi Solomon ben Isaac of Troyes, France, 1040–1105), the preeminent Bible commentator, explained that the "image of God" refers to our ability to understand and think, which distinguishes us from all other creatures. Maimonides took the "image of God" to mean that we are created with an intellect, the only feature God and human beings have in common.

According to rabbis of the talmudic era, there were differences of opinion as to why only one Adam was created. Some argued that this was to accentuate the importance of each individual. Others said that it was to establish a measure of human equality by attributing common ancestry to all human beings. Another suggested that the creation of a solitary man points to one solitary God as creator. Yet another maintained that human worth and distinctiveness are insured when so many different individuals can be traced back to the father of all humanity:

> Man was created alone in order to teach you that if anyone causes a single soul to perish from Israel, Scripture imputes to him the destruction of the entire world; and if anyone saves alive a single soul in Israel, Scripture imputes to him the saving alive of the entire world. Again, [man was created alone] for the sake of peace among men, that one might not say to his fellow, "My father was greater than yours"; and that heretics might not say, "There are many ruling powers in heaven." Another reason: To proclaim the greatness of the Holy One. For if a man strikes many coins from one die, they all resemble one another; in fact, they are all exactly alike. But though the King of kings, the Holy One, Blessed be He, fashioned every man from the die of the first man, not a single one of them is exactly like his fellow. Hence, each and every person should say, "The world was created for my sake."[2]

Other rabbis explained that man was originally created along with woman as an androgynous being, one that had both male and female gender characteristics. This interpretation, which does not imply that the rabbis accepted homosexuality or bisexuality, showed how Adam and Eve were both created in the image of God:

> R. Jeremiah ben Eleazar said: When the Holy One created Adam, He created him hermaphrodite [i.e., androgynous], as is said, "Male and fe-

male created He them . . . and called their name Adam" (Genesis 5:2). R. Samuel bar Nahman said: When the Holy One created Adam, He made him with two fronts; then He sawed him in half and thus gave him two backs, a back for one part and a back for the other part.³

The rabbis concluded that the creation of human beings is the very purpose of the creation itself. There is no one other than a human being who can perfect or destroy the world. Humans must live with the consequences of their dominion over the earth, for there is no one else to clean up after them. According to one midrash:

> When the Holy One created the first man, He took him and led him around all the trees of the Garden of Eden, and said to him: Behold My works, how beautiful, how splendid they are. All that I have created, I created for your sake. Take care that you do not become corrupt and thus destroy My world. For once you become corrupt, there is no one after you to repair it.⁴

THE SOUL

Since the talmudic era, Jews have believed that the image of God in human beings refers to the spiritual dimension of human existence. Judaism posits the existence of a spiritual realm beyond the individual that animates and energizes the life of the soul. The body is formed from the earth, but the soul is from God. This view of the human being is summarized in a traditional formulation included in the daily prayers: "The soul You have given me is pure, my God. You created it, You formed it, You breathed it into me, and You preserve it within me. You will also take it from me, and You will restore it to me in time to come. So long as this soul is within me I acknowledge You, Lord my God and God of my fathers, Master of all creation, Lord of all souls. Praised are You, Lord, who restores the soul to the lifeless, exhausted body."

In the Torah there is no idea of body and soul as two distinct and different aspects of a human being. A living man or woman is seen as a unified organic being, described in Hebrew as *nefesh*. *Nefesh* refers to human life in general and to human character in particular. According to the Bible, the first human, Adam, was created as a living being (*nefesh chayah*). Genesis describes the actual creation of Adam as the singular act of bringing all of him into existence at once: "The Lord God formed man from the dust of the earth. He blew into his nostrils the breath of life, and man became a living being" (Genesis 2:7). The Hebrew word *nefesh* is also used to refer to human feelings and experiences. This is how it is used in the verse "You shall not oppress a stranger, for you know the feelings [*nefesh*] of the stranger" (Exodus 23:9).

The Bible also uses the term *ruah* (spirit) and *neshamah* (breath) to describe human life. *Ruah* refers to the spirit or breath, the power that comes from outside the body and causes life as its visible manifestation. In the Book of Job, God is described as the source of life and human vitality: "In whose [i.e., God's] hand is the life [*nefesh*] of every living thing, and the breath [*ruah*] of all mankind" (Job 12:10). The Bible uses *neshamah* as a synonym for the living human organism: "The Lord God formed man from the dust of the earth. He blew into his nostrils the breath of life [*nishmat chayim*], and the man became a living being" (Genesis 2:7).

There is no differentiation, however, between the body, *nefesh, ruah,* and *neshamah* in the Bible. They all refer to the living, breathing, feeling human being created by God. The human being is a monistic or unified being consisting of one integrated nature. There is no notion in the Bible of any dualism or dual nature—such as body and soul—in the human being. The Bible contains no mention of a separate soul.

During the rabbinic era, the dualistic view of human nature replaced biblical monism as an expression of the strong spiritual bias of the rabbinic sages. This followed from rabbinic Judaism's view of the world as polarized between God and the mundane, holy and unholy, and soul and body. The sages adopted the idea that the human being was composed of two distinct entities—soul and body. Further, not only did man have two natures, but these derived from two dissimilar types of existence: the soul was from heaven and the body was from the earth.

The rabbinic teachings distinguished between the soul and the body in all animals, human beings, and even angels. Every being has these two natures. An animal's body and soul are both material and derive from the earth. An angel's body and soul are entirely ethereal and come from heaven. The human body comes from the material realm of the earth while the human soul is from the heavens. Therefore, a human being's two natures consist of an animal body and an angelic soul: "All created beings that were created from heaven [i.e., angels], their soul and body are from heaven; all creatures that were created from the earth [i.e., animals], their soul and body are from the earth, except man, whose soul is from heaven and his body is from the earth."[5]

In this view, the status of the human being is intermediate between angels and animals. His divine soul is his salvation while his earthly body is the source of wrongdoing. The importance of this theory is that it suggests that a human being is capable of being angelic or bestial depending on which of his two natures he actualizes. He is able to achieve transcendence through the exercise of his soul or degradation through the actions of his physical body. This soul–body dualism is not biblical but rabbinic and shows a decided bias against animalistic, physical pleasure in favor of spiritual pursuits that connect the soul to God. This does not imply that the rabbis had disdain for the body, even within this hierarchy of values. Care of the body, as home to the soul, was regarded as a virtue. Hillel the Elder spoke of the care of the body as an act of piety.[6]

The rabbis explained that the soul is related to the body as God is related to the world: "As the Holy One fills the entire world, so the soul fills the entire body. As the Holy One sees but is not seen, so the soul sees but is not seen. As the Holy One sustains the entire world, all of it, so the soul sustains the entire body. As the Holy One is pure, so the soul is pure. As the Holy One dwells in chambers that are innermost, so the soul dwells in chambers that are innermost. Therefore let him [i.e., man] who has these five characteristics come and praise Him who has these five characteristics."[7]

The human soul, according to the medieval Jewish thinkers, consists of *nefesh, ruah,* and *neshamah.* The Kabbalists, however, believed that while *nefesh* is innate, *ruah* and *neshamah* are acquired. *Nefesh* is the soul that gives life, the physical force common to all living beings. *Ruah* is a higher faculty that enables a person to rise above limited physical existence and achieve religious transcendence. It is the religious instinct in humans that leads Jews to contemplative Torah study and religious living. The *neshamah* is something greater which can be conferred only by God. It is the state of being that can only be achieved as the result of great spiritual accomplishment.

The *nefesh,* closely related to the body, is similar in substance and existence to the material world, whereas the *neshamah* is similar to the divine world. The Jewish mystics, who accepted the concept of the dualism of body and soul common to most medieval thinkers, also accepted a dualism of *nefesh* and *neshamah.* The body is composed of the natural elements of heaven (air), earth, and water, while the soul is made directly by God, who places it in the body. One midrash retells the creation story as a description of the formation of a human being. It reinterprets the creation of man in the "likeness" as referring to the creation of the body from the elements heaven, earth, and water, not to the image of God. Only the soul is created in the "image of God." Together, God and the natural elements create the human being "in our likeness." The soul is the spiritual and eternal part of a human being, but the body does not live on:

> When the Holy One, Blessed be He, created the world, the basis of all was water and from water everything was sown. The Holy One, Blessed be He, made three craftsmen who would carry out His plan in this world. They were: heaven, earth, and water. By means of these three, everything in the world was created. God called upon each of these three to fashion the beings necessary for this world.
>
> To the water, He said: "Bring forth the earth which is below you; go and gather into one spot." This was done, as it is written: "Let the water be gathered" (Genesis 1:9). To the earth, He called and said: "Bring forth the creatures from within you, animals, beasts, and the like." It was done immediately, as it is written: "God said, 'Let the earth bring forth every kind of living [*nefesh*] creature' " (Genesis 1:24). To the heavens, He called and said: "Place yourselves between the [upper] and [lower] water." And they did, as it is written: "God made the expanse" (Genesis 1:7).
>
> By means of these three, the entire work of creation was completed, each one according to its kind. When the sixth day arrived, they were ready to create as on the previous days. The Holy One, Blessed be He, said to them: "None of you alone is capable of creating this creature [i.e., man] as with the other creatures which came to life so far. All of you, join together with Me, and let us make man! You cannot make him by yourselves. The body will belong to the three of you, but the *neshamah* belongs to Me!"
>
> Thus, He called to them and said: " 'Let us make man' (Genesis 1:26),

you and Me. I will make the *neshamah* and you will make the body." And so it is, that the body is from these three [elements], craftsmen in the work of creation, while the *neshamah* was given by the Holy One, Blessed be He, who joined with the others in this. " 'In our image, after our likeness' (Genesis 1:26) means that man should be worthy of us.

"Through the body which is from you, he will know you and resemble you. And with that which is taken from Me, the *neshamah,* he will separate himself from mundane affairs and his cleaving and desire will be for holy and divine matters. Moreover, the body which is taken from you three will not have permanent existence, just like you. How is he like you? He is like the other creatures which you brought forth, since he is dust like all the other creatures. But the holy *neshamah,* which I gave him, not the body, will grant him eternal existence and through it he will resemble Me."[8]

The Zohar, the most important book of the Kabbalah, explains the functions of the three souls:

> The purpose of the *nefesh* is to sustain the body by drawing it toward the observance of the commandments. The commandments sustain the life of the body and are described as "our life and the length of our days." *Nefesh* sustains life by leading humans to deeper understanding of the reasons for the commandments and to religious inspiration. *Neshamah* can only enter the body and complete the soul when God deems the individual worthy because of the accomplishments of *nefesh* and *ruah.* [*Nefesh* causes] sustenance of the body by means of religious observance which it arouses. The [purpose] of *ruah* is to arouse [the body] to Torah and to guide it in this world. And if one is deserving, the *nefesh* through religious observance and the *ruah* through involvement in Torah, an exceptional benefit [*neshamah*] immediately descends upon it from above according to his actions.[9]

Nefesh serves the nutritive and preservative function for the body. Here, the Zohar defines the performance of Jewish ritual observances as the real cause of human survival. The religious actions of man are motivated by the *nefesh,* and they in turn preserve his physical existence. *Ruah* is the faculty that motivates us to understand the deeper, spiritual meaning of the Torah beyond the merely physical observance of the commandments. If we perfect our understanding of the Torah on this deeper level, we achieve a greater spiritual station, *neshamah*. The *neshamah* is attainable only by followers of the Torah who lead exemplary lives. This is the soul that enables us to achieve insight into the Torah and that leads to religious communion with God and, ultimately, immortality.

The souls are hierarchically arranged in us, beginning with *nefesh,* and the higher soul is attainable only after the lower soul has been acquired. "*Nefesh* is the lowest awakening. It is attendant to the body which it nourishes. The body clings to it as it, in turn, clings to the body. If it reaches its fulfillment, it becomes a throne upon which the *ruah* is installed as a result of the awakening of the *nefesh*. . . . After these two are arranged, they are disposed toward acquiring *neshamah,* and the *ruah* becomes a throne for the *neshamah,* which is installed upon it."[10]

The *neshamah* is the spiritual aspect of the human soul that links it to the divine world. The description of the *neshamah* in relation to the other faculties of man is indistinguishable from descriptions of the relationship of *Eyn Sof* to the other *Sefirot*. "This *neshamah* is hidden, above all else, and the most sublime."[11] We can, therefore, be conceived as a structure parallel to and analogous with the *Sefirot*. The soul in us is what the essence of *Eyn Sof* is to the *Sefirot*. The connection between us and the *Sefirot* is even deeper because the soul originates within the *Sefirot* and creates an essential connecting link between the divine realm and us. The important element in this notion is that one who has the correct insight into this relationship is able to direct the activities of the *neshamah* toward union with the *Sefirot*.

The Jewish mystic believes that the boundaries between his inner world, the outer world in which he lives, and the realm of divinity can be traversed easily. He sees the soul as the vehicle that links heaven and earth. The mystic is especially conscious of the power of actions that can elevate the soul from its bodily home to its heavenly origins. For the Kabbalist, this is the goal of Judaism.

THE ETHICAL IMPERATIVE

The biblical system of ethics should be understood in relation to the ancient Near Eastern religions from which it diverged. The fatalistic world-view of the other ancient religions saw the world as heading toward continuing enslavement to the capricious passions of the gods. The Exodus from Egypt and the Sinaitic Torah provided a contrasting perspective in which freedom and righteousness supplanted slavery as the basic human condition.

The slavery the Israelites experienced in Egypt was a form of political bondage common in the ancient Near East. The revolt against the oppression and the Exodus from Egypt led to the replacement of slavery with the covenant between God and Israel. This was the first time in recorded human history that the notion of positive freedom was introduced as a political and religious idea.[12] Whereas the Egyptians understood freedom as license, the Israelite idea of positive freedom was understood as the replacement of slavery by a moral law.

The Torah incorporated this new notion of freedom within its legal code and extended the rights and protections of freedom to all Israel: women (including widows), children, and non-Israelites as well. Even though the institution of indentured servitude was permitted in Israel, it was no longer arbitrary or permanent slavery. For example, the rules governing Israel decreed that a Hebrew slave must be freed after six years (Exodus 21:2). Other regulations abolished Hebrew slavery altogether (Leviticus 25:39–43). The Sabbath laws required that not only must an Israelite cease from labor on the seventh day, but he must also ensure that his non-Israelite workers and his work animals rest on that day (Exodus 23:12). The reason given for these measures is that you should "remember that you were a slave in the land of Egypt and the Lord your God freed you from there with a mighty hand and an outstretched arm; therefore the Lord your God has commanded you to observe the Sabbath day" (Deuteronomy 5:15).

The covenant at Sinai demanded righteousness as the price of freedom. The Israelites were to be "a kingdom of priests and a holy nation," which meant a kingdom of equals without a human king and a righteous people following God's law. Many sections of the Torah delineate the demands of right conduct for Israelites and their responsibilities to other men, women, children, orphans, slaves, and non-Israelites. The commanding God of the Bible demands fidelity to His laws because they are God's own ways. Just as God is just, so Israel should be just.

The classical biblical prophets, Amos, Hosea, Micah, Isaiah, and Jere-

miah—whose activities spanned the eighth to sixth centuries B.C.E.—
expressed a "breathless impatience with injustice."[13] The various
prophets leveled harsh and relentless rebukes against the indifference to
evil they witnessed among their contemporaries. They were not interested in beauty but truth, not equity but justice, not compromise but
moral absolutism. Amos condemned the rich for their exploitation of
the poor. Hosea condemned the entire society for idolatry. Isaiah chas-
tised his contemporaries for their sinfulness. Jeremiah condemned his
entire society—ordinary men, prophets, priests, and kings—for greed,
oppression of the less fortunate, and social injustice.

The prophets were "champions of immutable justice,"[14] who demanded absolute and uncompromising righteousness throughout Israelite society. This is expressed throughout the Prophets. Micah said,
"He has told you, O man, what is good, and what the Lord requires of
you: Only to do justice and to love goodness, and to walk modestly with
your God." Amos warned, "Seek good and not evil, that you may live,
and that the Lord, the God of hosts, may truly be with you, as you think.
Hate evil and love good, and establish justice in the gate."

The prophetic approach to justice was grounded in the belief that
God is the only source of moral law. There is no autonomous moral law
which can be arrived at independently by human beings. Only God can
create, ordain, and decree what is right and what is wrong. That is why
moral violations are treated as sins against God, not merely as infractions
of the law.[15] Morality derives not from the self-evident rightness of behavior but from God's personal and intimate pathos or concern for the
world.[16]

Some rabbis tried to distill the 613 *mitzvot* or commandments to a
summary creed. In a playful interpretation of biblical passages, several
anonymous rabbis attempted to reduce the entire body of Jewish teachings to its irreducible core. One sage declared that King David reduced
the entire body of *mitzvot* to eleven ethical principles: (1) moral action,
(2) moral speech, (3) honesty with oneself, (4) honesty to others, (5) not
harming others, (6) not blaming others, (7) despising evil action in others, (8) respect for God-fearing people, (9) courage, (10) avoiding usury,
and (11) refusing bribes. Next, another rabbi claimed that Isaiah reduced
the essence of the *mitzvot* to six principles: (1) moral action, (2) moral

speech, (3) avoiding ill-gotten gains, (4) refusing bribes, (5) shunning violence, and (6) ignoring temptation. Another rabbi stated that the prophet Micah reduced them to the three principles of justice, mercy, and humility. The last contestant argued that the prophet Habakkuk had the final word when he said that the cardinal principle is faith (*emunah*).[17] Although most of the participants in this exercise reduced the *mitzvot* to ethical precepts, the final word suggested faith in God. Nevertheless, the preponderance of rabbinic opinion favored the centrality of ethics in Judaism.

The medieval Jewish philosopher Moses Maimonides was influenced by the ethical teachings of Aristotle. In particular, he followed the doctrine of the "golden mean," which sees moral goodness as moderation. Some Muslim and Jewish pietists within medieval society equated moral goodness with indifference to the material world and spiritual apathy to worldly things. These pietists stressed holy poverty, asceticism, and piety as the antidote to the pitfalls of complete freedom and license. Maimonides, on the other hand, believed that true piety lies in the middle ground between license and asceticism: "The proper actions are moderate actions, the mean between the two extremes, both of which are wicked—one by excess, the other by insufficiency."[18]

Maimonides cited the virtues of prudence, graciousness, courage, self-respect, modesty, and patience as examples of the golden mean. The relationship between proper actions and the correct virtues must be reinforced by education and practice. There is no virtue in spiritual extremism or moral excess, which he understood as deviations from the mean. Such extremism is the result of a sickness of the soul that can only be remedied by a corrective tendency in the opposite direction of the extreme.[19]

Maimonides, however, also approved of certain forms of spiritual extremism for religiously exceptional individuals. Singular individuals had traditionally been permitted in Judaism to practice acts of "supererogation" (*lifnim mi-shurat ha-din*). This refers to the performance of unspecified religious acts that go beyond what is required by Jewish law but are not specifically prohibited. In rabbinic Judaism, such individuals were

called "pious" (Hasidim). Maimonides permitted supererogation of a
particular virtue as an antidote to its corresponding vice. For example, a
person who is gluttonous should cultivate self-denial. However, he prohibited the practice of spiritual extremism through asceticism, which he
viewed as sin.

The Jewish system of values, which distinguishes between virtues and
vices, is evident throughout every period in history. The Book of
Proverbs identifies the seven moral sins of pride, lying, violence, evil intent, evil action, false testimony, and contentiousness (6:16–19). The
midrash adds the major sins of not studying Torah, not performing *mitzvot,* despising those who perform *mitzvot,* despising teachers of Torah,
obstructing someone from performing the *mitzvot,* and denying the divine origin of Torah, belief in the afterlife, and the existence of God.[20]
Other sources named the vices of pride, envy, anger, lust, gluttony, greed,
lethargy, or sadness as cardinal sins.

Certain vices are singled out for particular condemnation. Spreading
rumors (*lashon ha-ra*) is regarded as the moral equivalent of murder. Gra-
tuitous or baseless hatred (*sinat chinam*) is such a grave offense that it is
cited as the reason for the destruction of the Second Temple. Unfair
economic advantage and fraud are likened to encroaching upon a
neighbor's property (*hassagat gevul*). The duty to protect the rights of animals is extended to preventing any infliction of unnecessary pain on
them (*tzaar baalei chayim*), which leads to a prohibition against hunting
for sport. Jews are cautioned against partisanship and factious dissension
within the Jewish community and against pursuing divisive controversy
unless it is a matter of great significance and serves a moral purpose
(*machloket le-shem shamayim*).

Providing fairly for the needs of the less fortunate members of the
community is regarded as a fundamental virtue. This is called righteousness (*tzedakah*), not charity, and implies a financial obligation of each individual, regardless of one's economic status, to others. In biblical times,
a person was expected to contribute at least one-tenth of his earnings or
wealth to the poor (Numbers 18:21). At the time of conversion, a convert is to be told of the very great significance of the laws of *tzedakah.*[21]
Maimonides declared *tzedakah* to be the most important of the commandments one is obligated to perform.[22]

The rabbinic attitude to wealth is appreciative of what money can provide even as the rabbis caution against excessive materialism. Wealth is defined not as accumulation but as the pleasure that comes from self-sufficiency: "Who is rich? He who is satisfied with his portion."[23] One tradition maintains that excessive wealth is the source of anxiety rather than pleasure: "The more you get, the more you fret."[24] Personal wealth is not regarded as the private possession of the one who has accumulated it: the poor as well as the employees who contribute to the financial success of the owner are considered as having a right to a portion of the proceeds.[25] Sigmund Freud, who viewed the charitable instinct as distinctively Jewish, observed wryly: "It does not pay to be a rich man if one is a Jew; other people's unhappiness will make it impossible to enjoy too much one's own wealth."

Rabbi Israel Salanter (1810–c.1880) founded the Musar movement for the moral regeneration of the Jewish people. Salanter emphasized the importance of social ethics in contrast to the prevailing tendency within Lithuanian Judaism, which emphasized personal piety and Talmud study. A singular devotion to Talmud study, not social ethics, as the most valuable of human endeavors was the norm in the community. Salanter believed that the human desire for pleasure is a drive that leads a person toward violation of the commandments. Although many physical pleasures are permitted by Jewish law, ultimately the human desire for pleasure pulls in the direction of sin. The antidote to this slippery slope is the fear of divine punishment. While he believed that the desire to serve God is a noble and inspiring virtue, the fear of divine punishment is a more potent factor in motivating a person to avoid sin. Unlike his teachers, the Gaon of Vilna and Rabbi Hayyim of Volozhin, who believed that Torah study leads to moral behavior, Salanter thought that fear of punishment guarantees moral behavior.

Salanter developed a series of techniques designed to foster effective moral education based on the fear of divine punishment. These included the study of ethical precepts through a vocal and melodious recitation of the moral literature in a melancholy, singsong voice—accompanied by groans and tears—in a state of powerful emotional excitement. He encouraged the repetition of ethical aphorisms and the creation of ethical parables drawn from everyday experience.[26]

Another technique Salanter developed was based on the importance of self-scrutiny and awareness of one's own moral weaknesses. It involved setting modest ethical goals for oneself and anticipating the challenges one was likely to face. He believed deeply in the ability of a human being to change and improve his personality through behavior modification and character training (*tikkun ha-middot*). He elevated moral traits to the status of religious commandments, thereby giving legal force to character improvement. Thus self-examination and identification of one's own character faults become positive *mitzvot*. He recommended two techniques for moral self-improvement: "subjugation of the wicked impulse" and "correction of the wicked impulse." Although it is better to correct than to conquer the wicked impulse, both these techniques should be employed, he counseled, in different situations and at various stages.[27] Salanter was a strict ethical behaviorist who believed that the substitution of a moral virtue for a vice could be achieved by consciously displacing a negative attitude, tendency, or behavior and replacing it with a positive one.[28]

Later on, Rabbi Salanter distinguished between the "bright" and "dark" forces or powers in the human personality. The dark forces are stronger than the bright ones, stimulated easily by external stimuli and buried deeper in the human soul. The bright forces are those conscious emotions, attitudes, and ideas that are often overtaken by the unconscious or dark forces. In his view, the dark forces may erupt in anyone at any time and for any reason, causing a sudden change in one's conscious patterns of life. His prescriptions for "correction of the wicked impulse" are directed at the unconscious and can be achieved, in his view, by repeatedly inducing a state of "excitement." During this state—which can be brought on by chanting, repetition of ethical aphorisms, and self-examination—one becomes agitated and aroused about one's shortcomings. After repeated exercises such as this, the unconscious is tamed and the desired change may occur gradually on the conscious level.[29]

Modern Jewish views on ethics were shaped decisively by the views of the German philosopher Immanuel Kant (1724–1804). Kant believed that metaphysical knowledge—that is, knowledge of the suprasensual world—was not possible. Therefore, knowledge of God was impossible and essentially a matter of faith. As humans, we do not rely on God to determine what is right or wrong. Rather, we believe that there is an independent moral law that has the same degree of absolute certainty as Newtonian physics had during Kant's era. The moral law, according to Kant, can be found in ordinary moral consciousness, the innate understanding of moral goodness which is evident in ordinary people. Although Kant might be faulted for a naive belief in ordinary human goodness, he did argue persuasively for the inherent and self-evident reasonability of morality.

Kant taught that self-evident moral truths, such as honesty, become categorical or universal truths. What a person regards as right, not only now but in all cases, is a categorical imperative, an absolute and self-evident duty: one knows and therefore ought to do the right thing. Kant held that ethics are categorical imperatives which arise from self-evident truths that cannot and need not be justified by having a divine origin. He believed in the "autonomy of the moral agent," that is, in the ability of an ordinary person to know what is right and wrong. He rejected the notion of a divinely ordained moral law in favor of the ability of a human being to use autonomous human judgment to reach sound ethical conclusions. Human reason, not God, is the source of moral authority.

The implication of Kantian philosophy is that ethics are no longer subject to external authority such as the revelation of the Torah. The human being becomes the ultimate arbiter of morality. This profound change in Western philosophical thinking also inevitably influenced a revolution in Jewish thought. The consequence for Jewish Kantians was the emergence of the idea that human consciousness, not Torah or tradition, is the ultimate moral authority and that humans are autonomous moral agents who need not turn to biblical or rabbinic authority for guidance. His influence was powerful among German Reform Jews and other emancipated Jews who wanted to conceive Judaism as a religion of ethics based on reason, not revelation.

Hermann Cohen (1842–1918), a leading follower of Kant, was the first in a long line of Jewish intellectuals who argued that the essence of Judaism is ethics and all of Judaism must be seen as directed toward the aim of creating a universal, moral code of human conduct. Although such a claim was made by Orthodox and liberal Jewish thinkers alike, this understanding of Judaism became central to the belief of the Reform movement.The Orthodox proponents of Kantian ethics also interpreted all of Jewish civilization retroactively as fitting this tendency. Liberal Jewish thinkers used ethics as the criterion to evaluate which of those elements of the Judaism they inherited should be preserved. If a particular aspect of Judaism did not seem to promote the idea of Judaism as ethics, it was ignored.

The equation of Judaism with ethics was a profound transformation. It reduced a complex civilization with its own sacred myths, belief system, symbols, rituals, and sense of destiny to one fundamental principle. This led to the theory, first introduced by nineteenth-century Reform Jewish thinkers, that there was a single identifiable "essence" of Judaism, an irreducible core that defines what is and what is not worth preserving. The essence they chose was ethics. Much of Reform Judaism throughout the twentieth century can be understood as an effort to define Judaism's essence in terms of universal ethics while justifying the existence of the Jews as a particular group.

The emphasis on ethics created a dilemma because it removed the raison d'être for the continuation of Judaism. If ethics were universal, what did it matter that Jews had a national talent for ethics or that Judaism was the first civilization to incorporate an ethical code? Society values progress and gladly disposes of archaic ideas when better ideas appear. In modern society, Judaism has no monopoly on ethics, and no religion by itself has a monopoly on ethical sensibilities. One does not need to be Jewish to live ethically.The idea that the essence of Judaism is ethics easily led to the notion that the fulfillment of Judaism lies in its own disappearance through the full participation of Jews in the non-Jewish world.

The Jewish emphasis on ethics can be clearly observed in the legacy of East European Jewry to American Jewish immigrant culture, which included not only religious traditions but the popular ideal of *mentshlichkeyt. Mentshlichkeyt* is the Jewish notion of what it means to be a decent, upright person. It is the subject of much of Yiddish theater and American Jewish literature. Irving Howe, the literary critic, described immigrant Jewish culture in America as a rich and complicated ethic that remains embodied in the code of *mentshlichkeyt,* a readiness to live for ideals beyond the clamor of self, a sense of plebeian fraternity, an ability to forge a community of moral order even while remaining subject to a society of social disorder, and a persuasion that human existence is a deeply serious matter for which all of us are finally accountable. Not that these strengths were unique to the immigrant Jews or that there is any reason to suppose they might not survive the immigrant milieu; but for many children and grandchildren of the [New York Lower] East Side, it was through this world that one first came to glimpse a life worthy of the idea of man.[30]

Yiddish culture sees the moral challenge as central to being human: "A man is called a man because he struggles" (*a mentsch heyst a mentsh vayl er mentsht zikh*).[31] The central contribution of the Yiddish usage of *mentsh*—literally, "a man"—is the distinction it stresses between what human beings are and what they could be.[32] The secular traditions of Yiddish culture in Europe and North America preserved the strong Jewish ethical emphasis even when they dispensed with the religious tradition from which it had originated. *Mentshlichkeyt* is the central theme of much of American Jewish literature, including the fiction of Saul Bellow, Bernard Malamud, Cynthia Ozick, Grace Paley, Henry Roth, Philip Roth, and Isaac Bashevis Singer. Although it is impossible to reduce Judaism in its various manifestations solely to a concern for ethics, it is unimaginable to portray Judaism without this central value.

THE STAGES OF LIFE

Rabbinic Judaism believed that human growth and development are directed toward nurturing the divine image in humans. This involves pursuing a life of Torah study, moral conduct, marrying and creating a family, and continuing to grow throughout adulthood. The stages of life and the tasks associated with each stage were defined by the rabbis:

Judah ben Tema used to say: At the age of five, one is fit for Scripture; at ten, for Mishnah; at thirteen, for [fulfilling the] precepts; at fifteen, for Gemara [i.e., Talmud study]; at eighteen, for the bridal chamber; at twenty, to pursue [a calling]; at thirty, for the peak of strength; at forty, for understanding; at fifty, for counsel; at sixty, for mature age; at seventy, for a hoary head; at eighty—a sign of exceptional strength; at ninety—bent [beneath the weight of years]; at a hundred—as one that is already dead, who has passed away and ceased to be in this world.[33]

The rabbis viewed marriage as an indispensable part of life, although they spoke from an entirely male perspective:"When a man is without a wife, he lives without joy, without blessing, without good."[34] Marriage and procreation were regarded as obligatory to propagate the human species.[35] The age of eighteen was considered the ideal time for marriage. In the view of the rabbinic sages, a man who did not marry by early adulthood was someone whose energies were more likely to be distracted by sex than directed toward the pursuit of Torah and *mitzvot.*

Some rabbis debated whether the importance of Torah study was so great that it was more important than marriage for a scholar. Which should take precedence? The rabbis generally answered that Torah had precedence unless a scholar's single status would distract him from his studies. Others disagreed and decided that marriage had precedence: "Our masters taught: If there is a question whether to study Torah or take a wife, a man should first study Torah and then take a wife. But if the man cannot live without a woman, he may take a wife and then study Torah. R. Judah said in the name of Samuel: The ruling is: A man must first take a wife and then study Torah. R. Yohanan retorted, With a millstone around his neck, is he expected to study Torah?"[36]

The rabbinic tradition was written by men for men, and so its perspective is one-sided. Marriage is a responsibility that a man should assume only after he has provided a foundation for his and his family's basic needs of food, shelter, and livelihood. "A man should first build a house and plant a vineyard, and only after that take a wife."[37] The rabbis noted that love and marriage are more than mutual attraction between a man and a woman. Rather, they are the result of God's determining the proper human match. God is the ideal matchmaker. Many believed that "a man's marriage partner is from the Holy One."[38] Others stated that the difficulty of matching partners is so great that it can be done only by God. This gave special status to the *shadchen,* the East European Jewish matchmaker who acted as God's agent in arranging the right marriages. The rabbis stated that "pairing a man and woman is as difficult as the splitting of the Red Sea [during the Exodus from Egypt]."[39] Rabbi Akiva said that "when a husband and wife are worthy [i.e., through *mitzvot*], the [divine] Presence abides between them; when not worthy, fire [i.e., strife] consumes them."[40] The rabbis cautioned that a man should always try to marry into a better family than his own. He should investigate a future wife's brothers because it is likely that their character will be an important predictor of what sort of children they will have. The reason: "Most children take after their maternal uncles."[41]

The fifth commandment states the primary responsibility of children to their parents: "Honor your father and your mother, that you may long endure on the land which the Lord your God is giving you" (Exodus 20:12). The relationship between children and parents is analogous to the relation between the people Israel and God.[42] All rabbinic prescriptions regarding filial responsibility stem from this analogy and from the implicit authority of parents and necessary gratitude of the child. Maimonides ruled that honor implies that a son should not stand or sit in his father's customary place, contradict his father's words, or call him by his first name.[43] Still, in recognition of the inevitable and even necessary conflict between parents and children, one rabbinic sage stated that the most difficult of all *mitzvot* is the fifth commandment.[44] According to the Talmud, parents' responsibilities include noninterference with the legitimate decisions of adult children regarding marriage, their choice of location for advanced studies, and emigration to Israel. The adult child must still assume responsibility for the welfare of his aging parents.

The Jewish family traditionally meant the extended or three-generation family. The nuclear family refers to the two-generation household. Fathers are obligated, according to rabbinic Judaism, to support their children and educate their sons, teach them a trade, and even teach them how to swim.[45] The father has legal responsibility regarding performance of the *mitzvot* for daughters until age twelve and sons until age thirteen. In the Sephardic tradition, the father recites the following blessing on the day of his son's bar mitzvah: "Blessed is God for releasing me from responsibility for this child's deeds!" (*Barukh she-petarani me-onsho shel zeh.*)

The rabbis regarded divorce as necessary under certain circumstances. These include physical impairments (e.g., contagious disease, inability to produce children, male impotence) that prevent fulfillment of the marriage vows or cause feelings of physical repulsion, inability or unwillingness to maintain marital relations or to provide reasonable maintenance, spousal abuse, infidelity, and intentionally misleading the spouse into violation of certain *mitzvot.* The rabbis were concerned about the complex social dynamics in marriages between previously divorced persons. They recognized that divorced persons are not free of memories of their former spouses. They said that "when a divorced man marries a divorced woman, there are four yearnings in the bed."[46]

The rabbis were not ascetics who avoided the pleasures of life. They saw all of creation as a source of human delight as long as the pleasures were permitted by Jewish law and did not detract from devotion to learning Torah. The rabbis taught that the world was created for the sake of procreation.[47] The denial of human marital sexuality is equivalent to the destruction of human life.[48] When one sees beautiful things in nature, one is to recite the following blessing: "Blessed be He who has such in His world."[49] When one sees a good-looking person, one is to say: "Blessed be He who has created beautiful creatures."[50] When one notices the renewal of nature in the spring, one should say: "Blessed be He who has His world lack nothing and who has created in it goodly creatures and goodly trees for the joy of mankind."[51] A righteous person is a person who thanks God for everything he eats, drinks, sees, hears, and enjoys.

According to the rabbis of the talmudic era, the creation of a human being is regarded as another creation of the world. The human being is conceived in the image of God and leads a beatific existence in the womb. During this period, the embryo learns the entire Torah from God. At the moment of birth, however, an angel arrives and strikes him on his mouth, and he forgets everything. Life after birth is a process of relearning, rather than learning, the entire Torah that the embryo once knew: "[During the period of gestation] light burns above its head, and it gazes and is able to see from one end of the world to the other. There is no time during which man abides in greater happiness than durnig those days. At that time, he is taught the entire Torah, all of it. But as he comes into the air of the world, an angel appears, strikes him on his mouth [creating the indentation on his upper lip known as the philtrum], and makes him forget the entire Torah."[52]

The soul of an infant is pure at birth. When the child is born, an angel charges it to live according to the teachings of Torah: "The embryo does not leave the womb until it is made to swear an oath. What is the oath it is made to swear? Be righteous, be not wicked; even if the entire world, all of it, tells you, 'You are righteous,' consider yourself wicked. Always bear in mind that the Holy One is pure, that His ministers [i.e., angels] are pure, and that the soul I placed in you is pure; if you preserve it in purity, well and good; but if not, I will take it from you."[53]

When does life begin? One rabbinic legend states that the soul enters the body at conception, which is, therefore, the beginning of life.[54] According to other rabbinic sages, the embryo is merely a chemical morass until forty days from conception.[55] Thus life is seen to begin sometime between conception and forty days later. Abortion is prohibited under rabbinic law because it is understood as the taking of life. Under certain circumstances, however, it is permitted by rabbinic Judaism, particularly when the life of the mother is in jeopardy. Most sages required that the jeopardy to the mother be vital to her physical well-being. Others regarded nonvital threats to the mother as valid reasons to permit abortion under some circumstances.

The birth of a child is seen as a partnership between the father, the mother, and God. The interdependence among the three is fundamental: "No man can come into being without a woman, and no woman can come into being without a man, and neither of them can come into being without the Presence [of God]."[56] The rabbis suggested that a couple's obligation to reproduce was fulfilled only when they had at least one child of each gender.[57]

The Kabbalists were deeply interested in questions of human destiny. It is a fundamental axiom of Jewish mysticism that whatever exists in the world must first exist, in divine form, in the divine realm. Nothing can exist unless it has its "root" in the *Sefirot*. A human being is defined as the composite of its body and soul. Therefore, if the body is created by its father and mother, the soul must also be produced by a similar union. Since the soul comes from heaven, the "parents" of the soul must also

reside in the divine realm. The father and mother of the soul are, therefore, the masculine and feminine aspects of God within the realm of the
Sefirot.

Once the *nefesh* is generated by the union of the masculine and feminine aspects of God, it resides in the realm below the *Sefirot.* The number of *nefashot* (plural of *nefesh*) rapidly multiplies as the union of the
masculine and feminine aspects of God produces further offspring. All of
these come to live in a realm of spiritual beings, called the "treasury of
souls," which is located between the world of the *Sefirot* and the domain
inhabited by human beings. This realm contains the forms produced by
the *Sefirot* but none of the matter that characterizes the world in which
we live.

The *nefesh* has a rich and colorful existence within this realm. Since it
is the progeny of the *Sefirot,* it has something of their nature. The spiritual structure of the *nefesh* at this level is androgynous: it contains elements of the masculine and feminine forces that produced it. It has, at
this point, an indeterminate gender because it contains both genders in
equal measure and balance. Only later, when the soul is ready to enter
the body, does it separate into its masculine and feminine components.
Each half of the soul enters a different body, one half determining that
its host will be a man; the other, a woman. Some Kabbalists believed that
this occurred forty days after conception, while others maintained it occurred at the moment of birth.

The birth of a human being and the formation of human character
are the results of processes that begin in the realm of the "treasury of
souls." The mystics believed that the original nature of the human soul is
a harmonious balance between contradictory masculine and feminine
forces. The unity is disturbed by the necessary descent of the soul into a
human body. On one hand, birth represents a loss of the original unity
of the soul when it is separated from its heavenly abode. On the other
hand, the soul cannot accomplish its destiny except by living in a human
body.

Each soul yearns to reunite with its original mate and to recapture the
unity of their existence before entering the world. This is the highest
form of human love, according to the Jewish mystics, because it is the
spiritual attraction of one soul for its mate. Each soul has one specific

destined mate, its "other half," with which it was once united. Left to their own devices, men and women wander aimlessly in search of their destined partners. This idea, which is found originally in the *Symposium* of Plato, is known as "Platonic love." Platonic love is not asexual love, but rather the spiritual attraction of one soul for its original mate. This concept was adopted by many medieval writers, including the author of the Zohar. Only God, the architect who designed the different roads on which these souls travel, can match the destined partners correctly. Truly, these are marriages made in heaven. True love, then, is the love between two destined "soul mates" and their reunion. This becomes the goal for each person to pursue.

DEATH AND AFTERLIFE

The Bible contains no consistent theory about life after death. Genesis 3:17–19 states that the sin of Adam and Eve caused mortality with no continuation of life after death:

> To Adam He said, "Because you did as your wife said and ate of the tree about which I commanded you, 'You shall not eat of it,' cursed be the ground because of you; by toil shall you eat of it all the days of your life. Thorns and thistles shall it sprout for you. But your food shall be the grasses of the field; by the sweat of your brow shall you get bread to eat, until you return to the ground—for from it you were taken. For dust you are, and to dust you shall return."

This passage, like later ones ("If a man dies, can he live again?"—Job 14:14), suggests that life ends at the time of death. Other sections, particularly in the prophetic writings, suggest that there is an afterlife in which all the dead descend to a region in the depths of the earth called Sheol. This region is also called *kever* (the grave), *bor* or *shachat* (the pit), and *avadon* (the wasteland).[58] It is a place of darkness and gloom where all the dead share the same unhappy fate. The dead already waiting in Sheol greet the newcomers with warnings of what they will find: "Worms are to be your bed, maggots your blanket" (Isaiah 14:11). Only the Book of Ecclesiastes, which was one of the last biblical compositions, offers a hopeful prediction about the destination of the individual after death: "The spirit of man returns to God, who gave it" (12:7). Later rabbis disagreed whether death was a punishment for Adam's sin[59] or an inevitable stage in human destiny.[60]

The only explicit biblical reference to the afterlife comes from the very late Book of Daniel: "Many of them that sleep in the dust of the earth shall awake, some to everlasting life and some to reproaches and everlasting abhorrence" (12:2). This suggests that by the Second Temple period, when Daniel was composed, there was a belief that the good will be rewarded and sinners punished after death. The very question of whether there is an afterlife became a contentious issue in Second Temple Judaism. The Sadducees, the priestly nobility, many of whom were biblical literalists, did not believe in an afterlife. The Pharisees, the predecessors of rabbinic Judaism, who believed in the existence of the separate soul, subscribed to the theory of the afterlife. It was their view that later came to predominate in Jewish belief and was expressed in the credo "All Israel has a portion in the world-to-come."[61]

The rabbis of the talmudic era believed that reward for *mitzvot* and punishment for violation of them do not happen during life but after death. The individual is accountable in the afterlife, "the world-to-come" (*olam ha-ba*), for the preponderance of his actions. The world-to-come, in fact, is seen as more important than this world: "This world is like a vestibule before the world-to-come. Fix yourself up in the vestibule, so that you may enter the banquet hall."[62] This is not meant to diminish the importance of earthly life, especially when it is directed toward moral renewal: "Better one hour spent in repentance and good deeds in this world than the whole life in the world-to-come."[63]

Life in this world is preparation for the world-to-come. Whatever a person accomplishes in this world determines his fate in the next. Once a person has died, there is no opportunity to change one's destiny. "In this world, he who is twisted can be made straight, and he who lacks something can have it made good. But in the world-to-come, he who is twisted cannot be made straight, and he who lacks something cannot have it made good."[64] This is the meaning of Hillel's popular aphorism "If not now, when?"[65] Rabbinic thought emphasizes the immediacy of life and action and the danger of postponing change. Although reward and punishment are deferred until the world-to-come, destiny is determined by one's actions in this world according to the principle of measure for measure. The rabbinic sages warned that one should not perform *mitzvot* to acquire reward in the afterlife. The observance of *mitzvot* should be for their own sake because they are the proper exercise of God's commandments. This is expressed in the rabbinic aphorism "Be not like servants who serve their master in the hope of receiving a reward; be like servants who serve their master with no expectation of receiving a reward."[66]

The rabbinic sages in the first century B.C.E. developed the theory of the afterlife in new and original directions. They maintained that for the first year after death, the soul remains in a state of limbo in which it has a tenuous relationship to the body, but increasingly it severs its ties with the body. During this period, the soul may have consciousness but no power of speech. There was significant disagreement as to whether the soul is aware of events in the world.

According to the rabbis, the righteous receive their reward in the afterlife in the celestial Garden of Eden, while the wicked are punished in Gehenna or Gehinnom. This applies equally to Jews and non-Jews. Rabbi Yohanan ben Zakkai said that "there are two ways open before me, one leading to the Garden of Eden and the other to Gehinnom."[67] The notion of the Garden of Eden as paradise is based on the idea that there is a heavenly Garden of Eden besides the earthly one described in Genesis. Gehinnom is the name of a valley south of Jerusalem where pagan rituals of sacrifice, including the incineration of children, were conducted in ancient times (2 Kings 23:10). It came to represent the antithesis of Israelite religious practices. Later on, the name Gehinnom was applied in rabbinic literature to a place of horror where the wicked were punished after death.

The rabbis portray the heavenly Garden of Eden as a spiritual place unlike anything known on earth. It is a timeless place where the righteous are freed from the cares of this world and from physical sensations, living in a rapturous state of intimacy with God. "Rav had a favorite saying: The world-to-come is not at all like this world. In the world-to-come, there is no eating, no drinking, no procreation, no commerce, no

envy, no hatred, no rivalry; the righteous sit with crowns on their heads
and enjoy the radiance of the [divine] Presence."[68]

Rabbinic teaching generally suggests that the wicked will be con-
signed to Gehinnom for twelve months following death, after which
they are annihilated forever. Rabbi Akiva, however, said that the wicked
suffer in Gehinnom for one year, after which time they are purged of
their wickedness and are permitted to join the others in the Garden of
Eden.[69] Traitors to the Jewish people and those who egregiously violate
Jewish religious teachings remain in Gehinnom permanently and endure eternal suffering.

There were considerable differences of opinion in the Middle Ages
about the nature of Gehinnom, or hell. The rationalists and philosophers, such as Maimonides, denied the existence of hell. Maimonides
held that the punishment for a wicked soul was to be "excised," or
denied continued existence: the soul simply ceased to exist. For traditionalists and mystics, the destiny of the wicked was portrayed in
dark, purgatorial strokes. A popular medieval text, *Tofet ve-Eden* by the
Hebrew poet Immanuel of Rome, a younger contemporary of Dante,
described the horrors he was shown on a tour through Gehinnom:

> We journeyed thence, and lo, there were pits full of serpents, poison-
> ous and flying, hundreds and thousands of lions and leopards were dying,
> and round about angels of death with their swords were plying, and tor-
> rents of mighty waters in floods were lying, making the hearts of onlook-
> ers gasp with sighing. . . . And as we journeyed thence, we saw a man
> with his right hand and tongue all slit; they had made of him a target,
> against which with darts from brazen bow they hit, so that thereby to the
> earth his very gall, pouring forth, did flit. Now, placed upon an iron grid,
> he would of roasting endure the pang; again, in bitter waters they would
> immerse him with a clang; then again, him upon a wooden gallows they
> would hang; at another time with stones at him they would bang.[70]

Medieval midrashim depicted the Garden of Eden and Gehinnom as
each containing seven departments. Each soul is assigned to the appropriate location, depending on its merit or the severity of its wickedness.

Maimonides believed that the Garden of Eden and Gehinnom were
metaphors, not actual places. The Garden of Eden meant the "bliss of the

soul," which it achieves through intellectual communion with God. Maimonides maintained that immortality is achieved not only through moral action but primarily through intellectual accomplishment. Immortality is possible only for the individual who so perfects his intellect that he thinks philosophically about God and His attributes perpetually. Ultimately, according to Maimonides' negative theology, the philosopher who meditates about God becomes the only candidate for immortality. Such an individual will have developed such a pure conception of God that his ideas become synonymous with the thought of God. When a philosopher achieves this state, he is thinking God's eternal ideas and his thoughts achieve identity with God's thought. Thus, it is not necessarily he who is thinking but God thinking through his mind. Immortality is the eternal endurance of the divine intellect within the individual. For Maimonides, Gehinnom was a metaphor for the absence or deprivation of intellectual immortality.[71]

The Jewish mystics believed that one who acquires the *neshamah,* the third stage of the soul, achieves immortality. This soul comes from God and therefore returns to it. In an elaborate parable, the Zohar describes the destiny of the *neshamah* in the course of life and after it leaves this world:

A king has a son whom he sends to a village to be educated until he shall have been initiated into the ways of the palace. When the king is informed that his son is now come to maturity, the king, out of his love, sends the Matron, his mother, to bring him back to the palace, and there the king rejoices with him every day. In this wise, the Holy One, be blessed, possessed a son from the Matron, that is, the supernal holy soul. He dispatched it to a village, that is, to this world, to be raised in it, and initiated into the ways of the King's palace. Informed that His son was now come to maturity, and should be returned to the palace, the King, out of love, sent the Matron for him to bring him into the palace. The soul does not leave this world until such time as the Matron has arrived to get him and bring him into the King's palace, where he abides forever. Withal, the village people weep for the departure of the King's son from among them. But one wise man said to them: "Why do you weep? Was this not the King's son, whose true place is in his father's palace, and not with you?" If the righteous were only aware of this, they would be filled with joy when their time comes to leave this world.[72]

Death is not a tragedy in most instances, according to Jewish mystics. It is the return of the soul to its source. There is death for the body but not for the soul, since the soul, not the body, is the essence of man. In fact, the death of a righteous person is approached with a certain anticipation: "At the moment when the soul of a righteous man wants to depart, there is happiness. The righteous man is confident in his death that he will receive his reward."

According to the Kabbalah, Adam's sin in the Garden resulted in contamination of all human beings with sin. This idea was based on the kabbalistic teachings that all of existence is tainted by the impurity of the snake that tempted Eve. The contamination of sin is transmitted in each of us and we struggle throughout our lives to overcome it. The Kabbalist Ramhal (Moshe Hayyim Luzatto, 1707–46) taught that the purpose of death is to cleanse the body from the inherited sin of the first Adam by freeing the soul from its prison.

According to Kabbalah, changes begin to occur thirty days before a person's death. At night while he is sleeping, his soul ascends to heaven and makes tentative forays into the afterlife. There, it is introduced to its next abode and becomes acquainted with this realm. Man begins to lose awareness and control of his soul during this period as the connection between it and the body weakens.

During this period before death, his shadow begins to disappear. The shadow is equated in Jewish mysticism with the astral body (*tzelem*). The astral body is a nonphysical projection of an individual's physical self. Just as the soul comes from without, the physical body is said to have an independent spiritual existence before it becomes a real body. Before birth, the astral body lives in the heavenly treasury known as "the heavenly Garden of Eden." Man is born with the physical manifestation of this astral body, which is sometimes described as the "image [*tzelem*] of God." The astral body stays with man during his lifetime and becomes a garment woven from his deeds that accompanies his soul to the grave. The astral body may also hover over a man and serve as a protecting angel during his lifetime. The connection between the actual body and the astral body is weakened as death approaches and the latter prepares for its separate journey.

On the day of death the soul and the body together undergo a preliminary reckoning. On that day, God judges man according to his actions while he was alive. At that moment man is especially vulnerable to the forces of evil in the world and to great terror and anxiety about his fate. Although modern Judaism has dispensed with much of the mythology of rabbinic and medieval Judaism, the Jewish mystical tradition is replete with descriptions of heaven and hell, consuming fires, vicious snakes, and threatening demons. These mythological images are taken as real phenomena that await the sinner after death:

> Woe to those who are ignorant of and do not pay attention to the ways of Torah. Woe to them when the Holy One, blessed be He, brings man to judgment for his actions and his body and soul stand in testimony on his account before they separate. That very day is the day of reckoning, the day on which the record books lie open and the forces of judgment stand ready. At that moment, the serpent takes his place ready to strike him and all his limbs tremble. The soul departs from the body and takes flight, not knowing where it is heading or where it will land. Woe for that day, a day of anger and contention.[73]

Before a man dies he has a visionary encounter with Adam, the first man. Adam asks him why he is leaving the world and how he will depart. He replies: "Oh, it is because of your sin that I am about to depart this world." Adam then responds: "My son, I violated just one commandment and was punished for it. Look how many sins you committed and how many commandments of your Master you have violated!"

At the moment of death, man also sees close relatives and friends who have already died. They appear to him lifelike and inviting. If he is destined for the afterlife, they greet him cheerfully. If he is destined for perdition, they do not acknowledge him unless they themselves are condemned. In this case they utter, "Woe, woe!" In either case, once he has died, his relatives lead him to view heaven and hell, and leave him at the appropriate destination. As a person is being laid to rest in the grave, he is confronted by all the deeds he has committed in his lifetime. All human words and actions have an existence independent of man which may yet return to haunt him. The Zohar describes graphically how these appear alongside the coffin at the graveside:

When he is being carried to his grave, [his words and deeds] appear and walk before him. Three heralds, one before him, one to his right and one to his left, announce: This man who rebelled against his master and against heaven, earth, the Torah and its commandments—look at his deeds, look at his words! He ought never to have been created! Then all the dead are stirred up against him from their graves and say: "Woe, woe—that he should be buried among us!"[74]

During the seven-day mourning period, the soul travels back and forth between the grave and its home, and participates as a mourner over its own body. For the first twelve months after death, the soul possesses consciousness and remains in constant contact with the body; it is even believed to return to it at times.[75] The soul of the deceased passes through many trials before it reaches the heavens. If the soul is not worthy of the afterlife, it may be "tossed around as a rock in a sling" and transmigrated into another body.

Transmigration of souls (*gilgul nefashot*)—the recycling of a soul from one deceased person into another body—was the subject of great concern and disagreement among Jewish mystics. One school of thought maintained that transmigration was a form of punishment; a second school saw it as an opportunity to repair sins committed in a previous life. There is agreement that there can be transmigration only of the *nefesh* or *ruah*, not the *neshamah*, which is immortal. Transmigration may occur as both opportunity and punishment. By contrast, mortal sins often require the complete obliteration of the offending soul without the possibility of any afterlife or ultimate resurrection in messianic times. Transmigration is an act of divine mercy that saves the soul from extinction and provides it with a second chance.

A righteous individual may undergo transmigration to complete commandments that he or she did not fulfill in the previous life or to correct actions that were not according to Jewish norms. This form of return may also provide the occasion for a pious person to contribute to the welfare of humanity a second time or to bring additional goodness to the world. Souls can have no more than three transmigrations, except for righteous people, whose returns are not limited. On the other hand, transmigration is also a form of punishment for offenders, especially

those who transgress sexual norms. Even a man or woman who chooses
to be childless may suffer transmigration for not having fulfilled the biblical injunction to "be fruitful and multiply." Some mystics even suggested that under dire conditions a soul may be resurrected in the body
of an animal as a form of punishment. The alternative to transmigration
is Gehinnom, the cleansing fire that purges and punishes but does not
necessarily destroy the soul. Transmigration is clearly preferable to perdition. A sinful soul that has no hope of reward may be condemned to
trials of fire and purgatory. Although many Jewish theologians, such
as Maimonides, objected to the idea of an inferno or purgatory for
souls, and others denied that there are such beliefs in Judaism, many
Jewish mystics held to a belief in the fiery extermination of unworthy
souls.

THE QUEST FOR SPIRITUALITY

Hasidism conveys some of the most significant modern Jewish spiritual
teachings about human destiny. Hasidism was founded by East European
Jews and continues today as a religious revival movement among ultra-
Orthodox Jews. It is founded on the premise that true spirituality arises
out of the heart of the individual and goes beyond the prescribed religious formulas. The following story is told by the founder of Hasidism,
the Baal Shem Tov:

> A villager, who year after year prayed in the Baal Shem's House of
> Prayer in the Days of Awe, had a son who was so dull-witted that he
> could not even grasp the shapes of the letters, let alone the meaning of
> the holy words. On the Days of Awe his father did not take him to town
> with him, because he did not understand anything. But when he was
> thirteen and of age according to the laws of God, his father took him
> along on the Day of Atonement, for fear the boy might eat on the fast
> day simply because he did not know any better. Now the boy had a small
> whistle which he always blew when he sat out in the fields to herd the
> sheep and the calves. He had taken this with him in the pocket of his
> smock and his father had not noticed it. Hour after hour, the boy sat in
> the House of Prayer and had nothing to say. But when the Additional
> Service commenced, he said: "Father, I have my little whistle with me. I

want to sing on it." The father was greatly perturbed and told him to do
no such thing, and the boy restrained himself. But when the Afternoon
Service was begun, he said again: "Father, do let me blow my little whistle." The father became angry and said: "Where did you put it?" And
when the boy told him, he laid his hand on his pocket so that the boy
could not take it out. But now the Closing Prayer began. The boy
snatched his pocket away from his father's hand, took out the whistle and
blew a loud note. All were frightened and confused. But the Baal Shem
went on with the prayer, only more quickly and easily than usual.[76]

Genuine spirituality is to be found not in the prescribed formulas of
institutional religion but in the "heart-knowledge" each individual possesses and the human desire to achieve *devekut,* communion with God.
While Hasidim believed in the importance of observing the *mitzvot,*
learning Torah, and praying with devotion, they believed that there was a
deeper spiritual realm of listening to the world as the song of God. The
disciples of the Maggid of Mezritch, for example, noted that their
teacher went to the pond every day at dawn and stayed there for a little
while before returning home again. One of his students explained that
he was learning the song with which the frogs praise God. The idea of
being rather than actively pursuing is central to hasidic spirituality. The
maggid once explained to his students that the best way to learn Torah is
to cease to be aware of oneself and become an ear that hears what the
universe is constantly saying within you. The truest appreciation of
Torah is hearing what you yourself are saying. Another hasidic master,
Rabbi Pinhas of Koretz, used to say, "A man's soul will teach him," and
explained that there is no person who is not constantly being taught by
his own soul.

Each human being has a vocation in life and a specific and unique
calling. The hasidic teacher Baruch of Medzibozh said that the world
needs each and every human being because every person has the mission to make something perfect in this world. That mission is unique to
the individual, who must fulfill his or her own personal destiny. Before
his death, Rabbi Zusya of Hanipol said, "In the next world they will not
ask me: 'Why were you not Moses?' They will ask me: 'Why were you
not Zusya?'"[77] The emphasis on responsibility of the individual is what

distinguishes the Jewish belief in human destiny. There are no alternatives to accepting the burden of responsibility and accountability for one's own destiny. Rabbi Pinhas of Koretz explained that God created only one Adam to teach us that we should assume responsibility for our lives "as though there were only one person on earth—yourself!"[78]

3

Good and Evil

If God is good, and human beings are created in His image, how do we explain the existence of evil and suffering in the world? The sacred myths of Judaism answer this perennial question in terms of human freedom and responsibility. The first impulse is often to answer the question by explaining that there is a cause-and-effect relationship between human action and human destiny. God has planted in us His own image and has given us complete freedom to choose right or wrong. We are not destined to a particular fate from birth but shape our destiny through our actions. This myth implies that suffering is the result of our own wrong actions and choices.

The sacred myth of good and evil makes clear that this is only a partial answer. In a world replete with misery, the innocent suffer along with the guilty. Why is it that good people should also be victims of a fate that only the wicked deserve? The sacred myth explains that we are unable to satisfactorily answer that question. The suffering of the innocent is a mystery that only God can answer. But He does not.

Jewish views on sin and human nature differ significantly from those of Christianity. Paul (d. ca. 65 C.E.), the apostle of Jesus, was a Jew who

shaped early Christian thought. His views on sin, which formed the
basis of Christian teaching, differed dramatically from those of rabbinic
Judaism. Paul and Augustine (354–430), the early Church Father, taught
that man was innately sinful as a result of Adam's disobedience of God,
and that this condition was transmitted to all newborns. Christianity
holds that humans are sinful by nature and cannot change their fate except through faith in Jesus, whose sacrifice atones for human sinfulness.
While human nature cannot escape sinfulness, salvation through faith
can free us from punishment. Sin is intrinsic and inevitable, and salvation entails an act of grace through the special agency of a divine inter-
cessor. In Christianity, sin is a fact of birth, whereas in Judaism, sin is a
matter of choice.

THE IMPULSE FOR GOOD AND
THE IMPULSE FOR EVIL

The rabbis taught that man has two impulses—one for good (*yetzer ha-
tov*) and one for evil (*yetzer ha-ra*). The dual nature of the human being
means that a person is neither inherently good nor bad but is, or becomes, what he does. The rabbis did not believe in original sin but
taught that the impulse to sin is present from birth. The impulse to sin is
a human capacity, not the defining characteristic of human nature.

According to the rabbis, the evil impulse does not arise within a
human at conception but first appears at birth and predominates during
childhood and early adolescence. Children are viewed as particularly
subject to the evil impulse, which causes them to be attracted to mis-
chief, trouble, and violation of the commandments:

> Antoninus asked Rabbi [Judah I, the Patriarch], "At what time does
> the impulse to evil gain mastery over a person—at the time of his con-
> ception or at the time he is born?" Rabbi: "At the time of his concep-
> tion." Antoninus: "If so, he would have kicked his way out of his mother's
> womb. Accordingly, the impulse to evil must gain mastery at the time of
> birth."
> Subsequently, Rabbi used to say: This is one thing that Antoninus
> taught me, and Scripture supports him, for it is said, "At the door
> [through which the newborn child issues], sin crouches" (Genesis 4:7).[1]

The impulse for good, moral action is an acquired characteristic which cannot be relied upon until a boy is at least thirteen. Until then, a boy tends toward violation of the *mitzvot,* disregard for morality, and impulsive behavior. A child is depicted as lacking in religious, moral, and social sensibilities; he must be guided carefully until he reaches the age when he can be trusted to exercise good judgment on his own:

> The sages said: The impulse to evil is [at least] thirteen years older than the impulse to good. It begins growing with a child in the mother's womb and comes out with him. If the child is about to profane the Sabbath, it does not deter him; if the child is about to take a life, it does not deter him; if the child is about to commit an act of unchastity, it does not deter him. Only at the age of thirteen is the impulse to good born in a child.[2]

The rabbis had a realistic and honest appreciation for human nature. While they did not view human nature as evil, they had few illusions about human character. Their candid and blunt descriptions of human personality appealed to people struggling with genuine human dilemmas. Despite the rose-colored image of rabbinic saintliness, the rabbis were the first to adopt a realistic appraisal of human motivation and behavior, which they acknowledged in themselves as well. They regarded the good impulse as a less potent and less influential force in human personality than the evil impulse. Generally, they saw the good impulse as passive, with little power or influence over human conduct. The evil impulse was considered a more potent source of energy:

> When a man stirs up his passion and is about to commit an act of lewdness, all parts of his body are ready to obey him. On the other hand, when a man is about to perform an act of piety, all his parts become laggard, because the impulse to evil in his innards is ruler of the two hundred and forty-eight parts of his body, whereas the impulse to good is like a man confined in a prison.[3]

The rabbis acknowledged that the evil impulse is the active, dynamic part of the human soul which is responsible for action. It is impossible for a person to serve God with the good impulse alone because it lacks the vitality necessary for religious action. The evil impulse is libido, the impulse for vibrancy and life which drives the human being. The rabbis saw this as the male gender-specific trait that impelled a man to succeed in the world. This trait results in competitiveness, anger, lust, and jealousy but may be channeled into more positive directions. The rabbis suggested that this warriorlike tendency in a human being can have productive as well as unproductive outcomes. In their view, the productive outcome occurs when a man channels this energy into love, home, family, and work. They believed that the evil impulse is not evil per se, but a tendency to evil that can also lead to human creativity and achievement:

> R. Samuel bar Nahman said: The words "Behold, it was good" refer to the impulse to good, and the words "Behold, it was very good" (Genesis 1:31) refer to the impulse to evil. But how can the impulse to evil be termed "very good"? Because Scripture teaches that were it not for the impulse to evil, a man would not build a house, take a wife, beget children, or engage in commerce. All such activities come, as Solomon noted, "from a man's rivalry with his neighbor" (Ecclesiastes 4:4).[4]

The evil impulse was also seen to be stronger in men of great religious virtuosity. The rabbis of the talmudic era often discussed the sexual temptations that perplexed them and their contemporaries. They wrestled with temptation and acknowledged its real power over them. In many instances, when they came face to face with sexual temptation, they admitted their readiness to submit to their evil impulse, until, at the last moment, they found the ability to resist. One such legend is associated with the great sage Abbaye, who doubted his own ability to resist:

> Abbaye, hearing a certain man say to a woman, "Let us get up early and go on our way," said to himself: I will follow them to keep them from doing what is prohibited. He followed them through meadows a distance of three parasangs. As they were about to separate, he heard them say, "The company is pleasant, but the way is long" [i.e., they held back from sexual union]. Abbaye said: If I were in their place, I could not have restrained myself. And in deep anguish he leaned against the bolt in a doorway. An elder came and recited the tradition: "The greater the man, the greater his impulse to evil."[5]

The rabbis recognized the power of the human libidinous instinct and did not think there was anything unnatural about it. This led them to write in the *Sayings of the Fathers*: "Who is a hero? One who conquers his own [evil] impulse."[6] They did not deny the existence of the evil impulse, nor did they hold sentimental illusions about human nature. They acknowledged that the challenge to maintain oneself on the straight path was a difficult one. They believed that it could be met by an honest understanding of human character and by a discipline that might guide an individual through difficult choices. An individual's character was seen as a matter of choice—not fate, destiny, or nature.

Medieval Jewish thinkers also were concerned with the problem of human motivation and behavior. Bahya ibn Pakuda, the eleventh-century Spanish Jewish philosopher who wrote *The Duties of the Heart*, believed that the evil impulse is locked in a lifelong struggle with the human intellect. He saw the greatest weapon against the *yetzer ha-ra* as the exercise of reason and judgment over emotion and impulse. This naive faith in the ability of reason to conquer the basic impulses shows the intellectual bias of medieval Jewish philosophers generally. The evil impulse in a person tries to subvert the individual's rational judgment, which is the only weapon effective against it: "The [evil] impulse is not satisfied with defeating you once or even a hundred times."[7] The evil impulse causes a host of problems, including undermining belief in the immortality of the soul after death, the oneness of God, the necessity of prayer, the divine origin of the Torah, the validity of Jewish law, the doctrine of reward and punishment, and other tenets of Jewish belief that he considered essential.

Moses Maimonides offered his own unique perspective on the subject of the evil impulse. Jewish thinkers had long debated whether it was better to be so pious as to have never been tempted to sin or to have been tempted but to have successfully conquered the urge. Whereas the earlier rabbinic sages viewed the virtuous man as the one who "conquered his [evil] impulse," some of Maimonides' medieval philosophical predecessors preferred "the pious man" who was above temptation to begin with by virtue of his exercise of reason over passion.

Maimonides explained this apparent conflict by saying that the rabbinic sages were referring to *hukkim,* or commandments that do not have an apparent reason behind them, whereas the philosophers were referring to *mishpatim,* or rational commandments such as the prohibitions against murder and theft. Thus, a pious man is the one who conquers his impulse to violate commandments that do not have apparent reasons but is above temptation when it comes to self-evident ones. Maimonides, however, viewed the *hukkim* or nonrational commandments not as matters of morality but, in a more limited sense, as matters of religion. Thus, he concludes that morality and virtue are related only to the *mishpatim* or rational commandments. In this regard, Maimonides concurred that the virtuous man is "the pious man" who is above temptation.[8]

There were Jewish thinkers in the Middle Ages who indeed believed in original sin. A Jewish pietistic movement appeared in the Rhineland between 1150 and 1250, and became known as Ashkenazic Hasidism (Hasidei Ashkenaz, not to be confused with eighteenth-century Polish-Ukrainian Hasidism). Adherents of Hasidei Ashkenaz redefined the concept of the pious person in a way that differs from the rabbinic ideal: they believed in an ascetic renunciation of the things of this world.[9] Their ideology was based on a deeply pessimistic attitude to life and in the belief that the only hope for a victory of good over evil lay in the ultimate arrival of the Messiah. As one metaphor of the Hasidei Ashkenaz stated: Man is a rope whose two ends are pulled by God and Satan, and, in the end, God is stronger.[10] The Hasidei Ashkenaz believed that the original sin Adam committed led to a transmitted sinfulness which contaminated all human beings. This is strikingly similar to the teaching of original sin in Christianity and is probably the result of Christian influences on Jewish thinking.

No Jewish movement showed a greater sensitivity to human motivation and behavior than did Polish-Ukrainian Hasidism. The teachings of eighteenth-century Hasidism acknowledged that the power of the evil impulse was the greatest force in the human personality. Rather than fight it, the hasidic teachers counseled that libidinous impulses be recognized and appreciated for what they are, the sole source of all human energy and creativity. They could and should be redirected, sublimated, and channeled in the direction of proper behavior.

Hasidic teaching was based on the belief that God could be approached through the ordinary physical acts of eating, drinking, conducting business, and engaging in sex—all activities inspired by the evil impulse. The Hasidim were fond of quoting Proverbs 3:6: "In all our ways, know Him!" This verse lends support to the idea of worshiping God through all the human senses. The opportunity to worship is not restricted to the traditional avenues of prayer and study. Every waking moment, even those apparently mundane moments of eating, drinking, and satisfying other bodily urges, become opportunities for achieving holiness, depending on how we fulfill them. Martin Buber sums up the hasidic approach:

> He who still harbors the evil impulse has a great advantage, for he can serve God with it. He can gather all his passion and warmth and pour them into the service of God. He who has no evil impulse cannot give perfect service. What counts is to restrain the blaze in the hour of desire and let it flow in the hours of prayer and service.[11]

This doctrine of sublimation and transferring the "blaze" of the evil impulse toward worshiping God is central to hasidic teaching. This led to the idea of "worshiping God with the evil impulse" as an essential element in human religious expression. For Hasidism, the evil impulse is primarily related to sexual desire. Hasidism counsels not surrender to the evil impulse but rather the transformation of the impulse toward the passionate worship of God. This technique flirts with danger because it advises taking the temptation of the evil impulse to the brink and then, suddenly, changing direction and sublimating the impulse toward a permissible outlet. The Baal Shem Tov once said: "A man should desire a woman to so great an extent that he refines away his material existence."[12] This does not mean that the Hasid should capitulate to the desire but rather that the desire should be experienced and nurtured up to the point of temptation. Then, at the last moment, the desire should be channeled back to a spiritual climax, at which point the Hasid recognizes that the true object of his desire is communion with God, the source of all yearning.

What matters is the proper spiritual intention (*kavanah*) that one adopts even while performing the most routine and mundane acts. Hasidism taught that evil is only that which is "not yet good." There is no such thing as an evil thought. Hasidism called libidinous thoughts "strange thoughts" and recognized that these thoughts intrude routinely upon a man during the course of a day, especially during prayer. They regarded these thoughts not as evil but rather as opportunities to capture the passion and energy of the libido and redirect it toward passionate, even erotic, prayer. For Hasidism, nothing is inherently impure unless it is allowed to manifest itself in impure action. All thoughts are permissible as long as they become opportunities to direct the psychic energy implicit in the thought in a morally acceptable direction.

COMMANDMENTS AND TRANSGRESSIONS

The rabbis viewed the human being as possessing the capacity to do good or evil. Performing a *mitzvah* was identified with doing good, and a violation of a *mitzvah,* called an *averah* (transgression), was synonymous with doing evil. The rabbis assumed that an individual would constantly strive for good but was likely to have many lapses. The goal of rabbinic Judaism is to work toward perfection even while anticipating failures. The rabbis believed that it was reasonable to expect that an individual would do more *mitzvot* than *averot* and tip the scales in favor of goodness. Human destiny was a matter of choice, not of fate, and the destiny of an individual was never regarded as irreversible, even up to the moment of death.

In rabbinic thought, the purification of the human soul through study, worship, and good deeds is the path to the world-to-come. This does not lead, however, to a negative estimation of the physical aspects of human life. It serves to promote the view that the soul must regulate the activities of man. The rabbis held that each individual's ultimate destiny was linked to the accumulated effect of his or her deeds, for better or for worse. A *mitzvah* contributes positively to the account of human deeds while an *averah* diminishes the effects of good deeds. An *averah,* a deed in violation of Jewish law, is also equated with sin (*hett*), the moral quality that is the result of an *averah.* Sin refers to the moral status of the action but not to the character or nature of a human being. Nevertheless, the individual takes on the status of his or her actions and the cumulative effect of those acts determines one's fate in the afterlife.

It is difficult to be considered a sinner according to the rabbis. A human being is not a sinner by nature and a person has many opportunities to correct the course of his own behavior. One sage said that a man who commits a particular *averah* is forgiven up to four times for the same offense before his actions tip the scales against him.[13] But the rabbis also maintained that the accumulated effect of many *averot* will shape a person's very character and change his own nature from good to evil. Repetition of specific patterns of behavior will reinforce that behavior for good or for evil. The rabbis expressed this in the formula "The reward for a *mitzvah* is another *mitzvah* and the reward for an *averah* is another *averah.*"[14]

The rabbis asserted that a person must be as scrupulous in avoiding a minor *averah* as with performing a major *mitzvah* because every infraction lowers the threshold between minor and major violations. "When a man violates an easy precept, he will in the end violate a grave precept."[15] They understood that any improper behavior is conducive to more serious improprieties. "If you have lapsed into a transgression, worry not so much about that transgression as about the one that will come after it."[16] Since the rabbis believed that infractions are not punished immediately, the absence of punishment can reinforce immoral behavior and lead ultimately to a complete breakdown of moral order. Therefore, they drew the line clearly by stressing the importance of fulfilling all *mitzvot* with equal gravity.

The totality of human action also determines the fate of the world and tips the scales in the direction of good fortune or suffering:

> R. Eleazar son of R. Simeon said: The world is judged by the majority [of its deeds], and an individual is likewise judged by the majority [of his deeds, good or bad]. A man should therefore always regard himself and the world as half-meritorious and half-guilty. If he performs one good deed, happy is he, for he has tilted the scale both for himself and for the entire world, all of it, toward the side of merit; if he commits even one transgression, woe to him, for he has tilted the scale both for himself and for the entire world, all of it, toward the scale of guilt, as is said, "But one sinner destroyeth much good." On account of a single sin this man has committed, he has destroyed for himself and for the entire world much good.[17]

Human deeds have real power to shape one's destiny. One's ultimate reward or punishment depends neither on character, predestination, nor accident. Destiny depends entirely on the accumulated effect of a person's own actions, for which he or she alone is responsible. Rabbinic Judaism stresses personal accountability for actions and the opportunity to change one's destiny at any point through changes in behavior. The rabbis often referred to the fear of sin as the force that motivates a person to good behavior. This suggests a less than noble estimation of human nature and stresses the negative consequences for improper behavior. Often, it is not the impulse to do good that drives a person, but the fear of sin or retribution.

Although rabbinic Judaism stressed knowledge and understanding of Torah as a human virtue, many sages emphasized the primacy of correct behavior over learning. In a series of analogies, the rabbis illustrated that proper behavior is the foundation of all other human achievements:

> R. Hanina ben Dosa said: He whose fear of sin takes precedence over his learning—his learning will endure. But he whose learning takes precedence over his fear of sin—his learning will not endure. . . . He used to say: He whose [good] works exceed his learning—his learning will endure. But he whose learning exceeds his [good] works—his learning will not endure. . . . Rabban Yohanan ben Zakkai was asked, "How would you describe a man who is both learned and fearful of sin?" He replied, "He is a craftsman who has the tools of his craft in his hand." "And the man who is learned but does not fear sin?" He replied, "He is a craftsman who has no tools of his craft in his hand." "And the man who fears sin but is not learned?" He replied, "He is no craftsman, but the tools of his craft are in his hand."[18]

REPENTANCE AND CHANGE

Rabbinic Judaism promoted the idea that human change for the better is possible at any point in life. The rabbis called this *teshuvah* (turning), the phenomenon of human self-improvement in the direction of performing the *mitzvot*. *Teshuvah* is necessary, according to the talmudic rabbis, when one has turned away from God by violating the *mitzvot*. *Teshuvah* means turning back to God and cleaving to Him through the *mitzvot*. A human being is capable of changing the course of his or her own destiny at any point in life, even at the moment of death. Change should be a routine, regular, and continuous part of human life. This is critical because a person may die suddenly without the opportunity to anticipate one's own death and perform *teshuvah*. A continuous commitment to *teshuvah* is a hedge against dying before one has achieved moral goodness. A person must be ready at any moment to stand in final judgment and account for his or her actions to God:

> When R. Eliezer said, "Repent, even if only one day before your death," his disciples asked him, "Does any man know what day he will die?" R. Eliezer: "Then all the more reason that he repent today. For should he die tomorrow, his entire life will have been spent in repentance. . . ." Regarding this, Rabban Yohanan ben Zakkai said: The matter may be illustrated by the parable of a king who invited his servants to a banquet without designating the precise time. The wise ones among them adorned themselves and sat at the entrance to the palace, for they said, "Is anything lacking in a royal palace?" The foolish went to their work, saying, "Can there be a banquet without preliminary preparation?" Suddenly the king called for his servants: the wise entered his presence adorned, while the foolish entered his presence wearing their soiled [working clothes]. The king rejoiced in welcoming the wise but was angry with the foolish. "Let those who adorned themselves for the banquet, sit, eat, and drink," he ordered. But let those who did not adorn themselves for the banquet remain standing and watch."[19]

There is no obstacle to human change at any point in life. In fact, rabbinic teaching encourages a person to be receptive to *teshuvah* throughout life since we never lose the capacity for change and growth. We reinvent ourselves at every point in life. The rabbis emphasize the ultimate importance of living in the present moment as if it were decisive for the course of one's destiny:

> R. Simeon ben Yohai said: Even if a man is perfectly righteous all his life, but rebels in the end, he annuls the [good] deeds he had previously performed, as is said, "The righteousness of the righteous shall not deliver him in the day of his transgression" (Ezekiel 33:12). And conversely, even if a man was completely wicked, but then resolved on penitence, his wickedness is never mentioned to him again, as is said, "Nor shall the wickedness of the wicked cause him to stumble when he turns back from his wickedness" (ibid.).[20]

The rabbis reaffirmed that "the gates of repentance are always open, and he who wishes may always enter."[21] A person is held to account solely for his own behavior, but it is impossible to prevent one who has evil intentions from acting on them. His peers should stand out of the way of someone who is intent on committing a sin, but his good intentions should be given encouragement and support. The rabbis offered the advice that "if a man comes to defile himself, others should not stand in his way; but if he comes to purify himself, he should be helped."[22] The rabbis were confident that a person who seeks to accomplish *teshuvah* will also receive divine assistance. "So great is the power of a return in *teshuvah* that as soon as a man meditates in his heart to vow penitence, it soars up at once [to God]."[23]

The rabbis accorded great respect to one who engaged in sincere *teshuvah*. They even debated whether it was better to have sinned and repented than never to have sinned or had the impulse to sin at all. Some believed that a person who never had to undergo *teshuvah* was inferior to the person who successfully confronted his mistakes and temptation but overcame them: "In the place where the penitents stand, even the wholly righteous are not permitted to stand."[24]

Teshuvah is regarded as one of the greatest gifts of God. The rabbis were concerned with the sincerity of the person who engages in *teshuvah*: "How is one to tell whether a penitent is genuine? R. Judah said: When the penitent has the opportunity to commit the same sin once and once again, and he refrains from committing it."[25] It is not acceptable to commit an infraction with the knowledge that one can atone for it afterward. In such a case, repentance is not possible. *Teshuvah* is only possible if the act was committed without the intention to make up for it later. "He who says, 'I will sin and then repent, I will sin and then repent,' will be given no opportunity to vow penitence."[26] Moreover, he who sins and causes others to sin is not given the opportunity to repent.[27]

The medieval Jewish philosophers developed elaborate practices of repentance based on their understanding of human nature. Saadya Gaon, for example, explained that there are many ways in which the motivation for repentance may occur. A person might experience genuine remorse during the commission of a sin or even years afterward. He might become anxious about the possibility of punishment awaiting him or might experience setbacks in his life as signs of impending punishment. He might also experience a deathbed conversion. Saadya regarded the latter as the least noble form of *teshuvah*. He described the four stages of *teshuvah*: The repentant sinner should (1) abandon the sinful act, (2) express grief and feel remorse, (3) plead with God for forgiveness, and (4) renounce and avoid repeating the sin when the opportunity presented itself again.[28]

The Hasidei Ashkenaz subscribed to a theory of penitence that had its roots in medieval Christian penitentiary doctrine. They taught that there are four categories of *teshuvah*. First, *teshuvah* meant that when the opportunity to repeat the initial sin presented itself again, it was not repeated. Second, *teshuvah* could mean that one would establish specific practices in order to prevent and avoid repeating the same sin. Third, *teshuvah* involved incurring a degree of self-mortification in proportion to the amount of pleasure one had derived from the initial sin. Fourth, *teshuvah* entailed torturing and inflicting pain on one's body for particularly egregious sins.[29] Hasidei Ashkenaz believed deeply in the practice of equanimity or self-abnegation in which the practitioner cultivates the ability to withstand pain and to be indifferent to pleasure. This leads to the renunciation of worldly pleasures. They would subject themselves to bitter extremes of temperature, sleeping on the floor, and other forms of bodily pain as forms of self-punishment. They did not, however, adopt sexual abstinence as part of their regimen.[30]

FREE WILL

The rabbis believed that humans possess absolute free will to direct their own actions, while, at the same time, for every action there is ultimately a consequence. According to one rabbinic view, God determines before a person is born what his physical characteristics, intelligence, and financial status will be. All human characteristics are predetermined, except for behavior and moral action. God does not decide whether in the course of a person's life that person will become righteous or wicked. The "fear of heaven," the rabbinic term for the moral impulse in a human being, is entirely within the control of the individual:

R. Hanina bar Papa expounded: The name of the angel in charge of conception is Night; he takes each drop [of semen] and places it before the Holy One, saying to Him, "Master of the universe, what is this drop to become, a strong man or a weak man, a wise man or a fool, a rich man or a poor man?" But he does not say, "A righteous man or a wicked man?" R. Hanina added: "Everything is in the hands of Heaven except the fear of Heaven."[31]

Although the rabbis of the talmudic era taught a theory of complete human freedom and responsibility to choose a course of action, some sages held that God has prior knowledge of what action will occur. The leading proponent of that paradoxical view was Rabbi Akiva, the great sage of the second century. Akiva said, "Everything is foreseen by God, but the right to choose is given to man."[32]

The belief in free will was a central tenet in the philosophy of Moses Maimonides: "Free will is bestowed on every human being. If one desires to turn toward the good way and be righteous, he has the power to do so. If one wishes to turn toward the evil way and be wicked, he is at liberty to do so."[33]

Maimonides recognized that the doctrine of individual accountability for one's actions was meaningless unless one has complete freedom to choose:

> If God had decreed that a person should be either righteous or wicked, . . . or if there were some force inherent in his nature which irresistibly drew him to a particular course . . . how could the Almighty have charged us through the prophets: "Do this and do not do that, improve your ways, do not follow your wicked impulses," when, from the beginning of his existence his destiny had already been decreed or his innate constitution irresistibly drew him to that from which he could not set himself free? . . . By what right or justice could God punish the wicked or reward the righteous?[34]

At the same time, Maimonides believed in divine omniscience. If God is omniscient, does that not imply that God knows what we will do before we do it? Maimonides' answer was that divine omniscience is perfect and can therefore know only perfect things. If God can know only perfect things, He cannot know us as individuals or our actions, since we are finite, transient creatures. Maimonides believed that God's perfect knowledge extends only to knowledge of the human species, which is an eternal idea, and not to the transient individuals who make up the species.

Maimonides concluded that God is not interested in our specific actions. Our actions reflect our moral character. Our moral character determines whether we pursue truth and goodness or falsehood and wickedness. Therefore, moral actions ultimately shape whether we are able to perfect our souls and achieve the intellectual knowledge of God. We have complete choice in this regard and the consequences are entirely within our hands.

SUPERSTITION AND EVIL

During the Middle Ages, Jewish philosophers such as Maimonides taught that evil was the result of human free choice to sin. Sin diverted our moral strength and damaged our intellectual abilities. Sin made it impossible for us to be receptive to God's continuous emanation or overflow of goodness upon the world and upon our minds. The philosophers believed that human moral goodness influenced God by strengthening the connection that links God and the world. Moral action reinforces the bond and evil severs it. Evil, however, does not exist independently as a real force in the universe. There is no realm of evil or dark force lurking in the world to subvert goodness. The universe, governed by God, is a good, moral universe in which there is no inherent evil. Evil is the result of human action that causes the interruption and cessation of God's continuous and sustaining emanation upon the world. Moral actions produce a form of immunity from persecution and suffering by strengthening the link between human beings and God. Sin brings about an estrangement from God's goodness which results in the loss of protection from harm. Thus, evil is the exposure to the potentially disastrous consequences of our own moral behavior.

The Kabbalists disagreed with Maimonides' view of evil. They believed that whatever exists in this world, first exists within God in its most ideal, sublime, and universal form. They perceived evil to exist in the world, and they attributed the source of evil to God Himself. They did not believe that God was evil; rather, He contained the root of evil in perfect measure along with other perfections, including the root of goodness. Just as the *yetzer ha-tov* has its root within God, so too does the *yetzer ha-ra*. The earliest Kabbalists described this "root" within God variously as "the quality whose name is evil," "the left hand of the Holy One, blessed be He," and "the forces of strict judgment," and found it personified in the *Sefirah* known as Judgment (*din*) or Power (*gevurah*).

The Kabbalists described evil in various ways. First, they saw evil as the offshoot of the *Sefirah* Judgment or Power. The *Sefirah* Judgment can be drawn in either of two directions. It can be tempered by the *Sefirah* Mercy, which produces a balance and harmony between the antithetical forces of Judgment and Mercy. These two *Sefirot* are the extremes of pure divine love and severe divine judgment, which need to be balanced by each other. But if the two *Sefirot* are not harmonized, either one might predominate and produce an excess of divine love or severity. The excessiveness or imbalance of one *Sefirah* over the other is the source of disequilibrium within the world. The result of excessive Judgment is cosmic imbalance, which manifests itself in the appearance of evil in the world, resulting in death, conflict, and catastrophe. The Kabbalists likened this to a river that overflows its banks or a bottle that is filled too high. Although the source is pure and beneficial, the superabundance produces tragic consequences and evil takes on a life of its own. This independent existence of dark and demonic forces, which originated within the pure divine realm, is a paradoxical formulation of the reality of evil. The Kabbalists saw evil as a real, substantive force that has broken off from the realm of God and has its own power and presence in the world. This is what they called "the other side" (*sitra ahra*) or Satan, the realm of evil outside God.

Other Kabbalists believed further that a separate realm of ten evil *Sefirot* emanate directly from the *Sefirah* Judgment. These *Sefirot*, sometimes called the "left emanation," are engaged in a constant struggle with the ten *Sefirot* of goodness for control over the world. The Jewish Gnostics who subscribed to this mythology of evil believed that the evil *Sefirot* prevailed in the creation of the world. This view is a radical departure from rabbinic theology, which saw creation as entirely good.

According to the Jewish Gnostics, we must overcome the inherent contamination of the world by defeating the power of the evil *Sefirot* and
restoring the ten *Sefirot* of goodness to their proper role over the world.

This mythology saw the world as divided sharply between forces of
good and evil, each fighting the other in a battle to the death for domination over the world and the human soul. This deeply dualistic and
pessimistic view produced a rich mythology about Lilith, the legendary
first wife of Adam. She is portrayed as a seductress who tempts men into
producing demonic offspring with her. She and her evil male consort
Samael produce demons, devils, and beasts. They persecute men and
tempt them to do evil. Kabbalah portrays the terrible fate that awaits
those who succumb to the "left emanation."

Kabbalah taught that the original creation of the world was disrupted
by Adam's sin, which caused the world to be governed by Judgment or
the "left emanation." This view, strikingly similar to Christian teaching,
saw the "sin of first Adam" as disrupting the flow of divine goodness and
causing the world to be subjugated to the domination of evil. Thus, the
original sin of Adam is transmitted from one generation to the next and
taints each person with the "contamination of the snake." Although this
view is deeply pessimistic, the Kabbalah also teaches that the possibility
of moral goodness still resides within each person and affirms that
human goodness can overcome cosmic evil. The Kabbalists believed that
within the deepest evil in the world lies a spark of holiness which, if
nurtured, can grow into a flame of goodness capable of overtaking and
consuming the powers of darkness.

Although this tenet that evil dominates the world was central to the
teachings of some Kabbalists, it never became the predominant Jewish
belief. It contradicted too thoroughly the sacred myth of Judaism that
God in His goodness created a good world. No matter how deeply the
Kabbalists held to their negative estimation of the world, they maintained that it was possible to overcome and ultimately defeat evil
through proper mystical actions and rituals. They saw themselves as
champions of goodness against evil and were deeply confident in the ultimate victory of goodness. The practice of kabbalistic rituals in the battle against evil frequently entered the repertoire of folk practices in
Judaism. The invocation against the evil eye ("no evil eye," or *keyn ayin*

ha-ra, pronounced *keneyna hora* by Yiddish-speaking Jews) is one of the vestiges of this tradition. Other forms of superstition and magic entered East European Jewish folklore through contact with Christian Slavic folk traditions, which shared a fearful, pessimistic view of the world. No matter how superstitious Jewish folklore traditions might have been, they were centered on kabbalistic teachings that emphasized the opportunities of overcoming the dark forces of the world. Still, the Kabbalists held to their belief in original sin, hell, and the existence of demonic powers in the world.

WHY DO THE INNOCENT SUFFER?

There is no more fundamental problem in religion than why bad things happen to people who do not seem to deserve them. The Torah implies that a person's fate is a direct consequence of his actions, measure for measure. The biblical concept of proportionate cause and effect is depicted in the narratives of the early patriarchs. For example, Jacob's theft of his father's blessing from Esau is requited in the deception about his intended bride, Rachel.[35] Whatever goes around, comes around and there is no escaping the effects of one's actions. On the other hand, the Torah also suggests that we might receive beneficial treatment from God because of the meritorious behavior of our ancestors. God remembers His love for our ancestors and treats us more favorably than we might otherwise deserve. Whatever occurs to us must somehow be the result of our own behavior or the merit of our ancestors.

The Torah's explanation for human suffering proved insufficient for later generations. The rabbis portray God as a demanding judge who holds the righteous to account for their minor misdeeds while giving credit to the wicked for their few good deeds. In their view, ultimate reward and punishment are reserved for the afterlife. If reward and punishment are reserved for the world-to-come, is there a correlation between action and destiny during life? The rabbis were troubled by the question of God's justice. If God is just, how is it possible to explain the suffering of righteous people or the success of wicked people during their lifetime? Rabbi Akiva explained that the righteous might pay in this life for their few misdeeds so that they will be rewarded in the afterlife for their merits. The wicked will prosper in this world for their few good deeds but in the afterlife will surely be punished:

> R. Akiva said: The Holy One is exact with the righteous as well as with the wicked, searching out the very depths of their being. He is exact with the righteous, holding them to account for the few wrongs they committed in this world, in order to lavish bliss upon them and give them a goodly reward in the world-to-come. On the other hand, He lavishes ease upon the wicked and rewards them in this world for the few good deeds they performed in order to requite them in the world-to-come.[36]

Some rabbis believed in inherited merit and guilt. They saw the suffering of children as punishment for the misdeeds of their fathers and the success of the wicked as reward for the goodness of their fathers. This view suggests that individual retribution—reward or punishment—is not limited to the afterlife but is transmitted to the next generation. This is a form of retribution directed at the parent as a warning against the consequences of his own actions upon his children. It is intended to warn the parent that while he might escape punishment in this life for his misdeeds, the punishment will fall upon those he loves most. We inherit the world our parents leave, as our children will inherit the world we leave them.

According to one rabbinic legend, Moses asked God:

> Master of the universe, why is it that some righteous men prosper while others suffer adversity, some wicked men prosper while others suffer adversity? The Holy One replied: Moses, the righteous man who prospers is a righteous man who is the son of a righteous man; the righteous man who suffers adversity is a righteous man who is the son of a wicked man. The wicked man who prospers is a wicked man who is the son of a righteous man; the wicked man who suffers adversity is a wicked man who is the son of a wicked man.[37]

Other rabbis believed that suffering was a test of a person's faith and confidence in God. God would only test a saint because He knows that a sinner would not stand the test. Therefore, the righteous suffer because God favors them.

"The Lord testeth the righteous" (Psalm 11:5). R. Jonathan said: Your potter does not test defective vessels because if he gives them a single rap [to test them], they break. Which vessels does he test? The sound ones, which even if rapped many times will not break. So, too, the Holy One does not test the wicked—only the righteous.[38]

The Kabbalists were especially troubled by the premature death of children. How can a child be held liable for his own actions? Does this imply that a child dies for the sins of his parents? The Kabbalists explained that the death of children is an anticipation of sins they would have committed. Their premature death is an early gathering that plucks them while their life is still in full bloom and before the flower withers on the branch. This is seen as an act of divine mercy that entitles them to reward in the afterlife they would not merit if they lived their full life.

The Book of Job is the most significant treatment of the issue of suffering in the Hebrew Bible and in all of world literature. The concept of proportionate cause and effect is insufficient to explain Job's suffering. The narrative of the book establishes unequivocally that Job was a righteous man who was meticulous in offering sacrifices to God on behalf of his family. The antagonist in the account, Satan, is an angel who argues with God that Job's piety is superficial and that under duress Job would abandon his devotion to God. God accedes to the challenge and in one day all of Job's wealth, along with his ten children, is wiped out. In the face of such disasters, Job declares: "The Lord has given and the Lord has taken away; blessed be the name of the Lord" (Job 1:21). Next, Job is afflicted with disease. His wife urges him to curse God. Still, he resists and rebuffs his wife: "Should we accept only good from God and not accept evil?" (Job 2:10). Only when Job's three friends, who ostensibly come to comfort him, reaffirm their belief that suffering is punishment for sin does Job begin to protest his innocence.

Job questions why an innocent man would suffer. Could it be that God punishes the righteous for their few iniquities so that they will ultimately be rewarded and exempted from further retribution? Could it be that God is testing Job's devotion and piety? Neither answer satisfies Job. Suddenly God's voice is heard, addressing Job directly—vindicating him before his friends as a righteous man, but chastising Job for his hubris in claiming to know and judge God's ways. The answer is not the one we expect concerning divine justice and morality. Instead, God demands a change in perspective on the part of man, an acknowledgment of the limits of human knowledge and ultimately of man's insignificance in the scope of the universe. God speaks to Job from within the tempest and chastises him for trying to understand the incomprehensible ways of God:

> Then the Lord replied to Job out of the tempest and said:
>
> Who is this who darkens counsel,
> Speaking without knowledge?
> Gird your loins like a man;
> I will ask and you will inform Me.
>
> Where were you when I laid the earth's foundations?
> Speak if you have understanding.
> Do you know who fixed its dimensions
> Or who measured it with a line?
> Onto what were its bases sunk?
> Who set its cornerstone
> When the morning stars sang together
> And all the divine beings shouted for joy?
>
> Who closed the sea behind doors
> When it gushed forth out of the womb,
> When I clothed it in clouds,
> Swaddled it in dense clouds,
> When I made breakers My limit for it,
> And set up its bar and doors,
> And said, "You may come so far and no farther;
> Here your surging waves will stop"?
>
> Have you ever commanded the day to break,
> Assigned the dawn its place,
> So that it seizes the corners of the earth
> And shakes the wicked out of it?
> It changes like clay under the seal
> Till [its hues] are fixed like those of a garment.
> Their light is withheld from the wicked,
> And the upraised arm is broken.

> Have you penetrated to the sources of the sea,
> Or walked in the recesses of the deep?
> Have the gates of death been disclosed to you?
> Have you seen the gates of deep darkness?
> Have you surveyed the expanses of the earth?
> If you know of these—tell Me. (Job 38:1–18)

God's answer to Job is the classical answer of Judaism to the question of human suffering. God is transcendent and His nature is unknowable. We can relate to Job's anguish and loneliness. God's silence about the fairness or injustice of his fate leaves him in a state of religious despair. Trust in God can never again be taken for granted. Yet the voice within the tempest strangely brings Job the desolate peace of a man who accepts his fate and the abyss between human and divine understanding. The very existence of God as creator of the universe gives our lives meaning. The only way to make life bearable when we cannot find answers is to recognize that some answers are beyond us. This is also the conclusion of the rabbinic tradition: "Rabbi Yannai said, '[The reason] why the guilty prosper or the innocent suffer is not within our grasp.' "[39]

Job meets a face of God that is awesome, remote, and terrifying; it is beyond the categories of human experience. Job, however, emerges from his trials a wiser man. Never again will he expect life to provide him with predictable answers. Job learns from his experience because he is open to what God can teach him. Although this story does not offer easy answers about human suffering, it points to the human capacity that ever astounds us—the ability to continue life after tragedy and even to grow in compassion and wisdom. The story of Job inevitably brings us back to the world of human activity, the only arena in which we can live.

Can we accept the idea that there is no sufficient answer to the question of human suffering in the Holocaust? Some religious traditionalists have argued that our sins are so overwhelming that we have eclipsed God and caused God to withdraw from us. Modern Hasidism continues to see mass suffering as a form of divine retribution for sins and as a form of punitive divine withdrawal (*hester panim*, "hiding His face") from the Jewish people. Hasidic survivors of the Holocaust frequently see the destruction of their own families as divine retribution for their own sins and the collective sins of the Jewish people.[40] They often single out the violation of the *mitzvot,* which they equate with the growth of non-Orthodox Judaism—including Zionism—and assimilation as the reason for divine retribution in the Holocaust. Some Christian theologians take a similar tack in positing a collective punishment for Jews.

These extreme theological positions horrify us with their willingness to view innocent victims as object lessons for a fundamentalist agenda. The rabbis took the myth of sin and punishment to its limits and beyond in an effort to find answers to unanswerable questions. We cannot accept the traditional rabbinic explanation that the victim's supposed guilt is the cause of his suffering. This explanation becomes obscene when confronted with the murder of six million men, women, and children.

For many contemporary Jewish theologians, the traditional notion that an active personal God is responsible for reward and punishment is obsolete. The view of one modern Jewish theologian, Richard Rubenstein, is that God is dead. If God is not dead, at least belief in God is dead. To the writer and Holocaust survivor Elie Wiesel, God's silence at Auschwitz and every other killing site is an ongoing challenge to God's goodness. In his play *The Trial of God,* Wiesel invokes the Jewish tradition of convening a *bet din,* or rabbinical court, and charging God as the defendant. He wants to force God to answer out of the silence that intensifies despair. In the void between the extreme positions of Rubenstein and Wiesel, we realize that humanity as a whole has to assume full responsibility for those tragedies that result from human actions or the failure to act.

The mystery of how God could have permitted the Holocaust remains inexplicable. The only viable explanation is that the Holocaust, and all evil, pose a challenge to us all. When confronted by evil, we must oppose it without compromise, without temporizing, without hesitation. All evil challenges us for a response that sees each victim or potential victim as created in the image of God. Only the absolute conviction that he who saves one life saves the entire world can offer meaning in the face of absolute evil. The certainty that evil challenges us to total and uncompromising moral action is rooted in the imperative to mend the world through resistance to evil.[41]

Jewish thinkers today reject the view of blaming the victim or looking for the source of evil in human sin. In a much broader sense, however, the rabbinic emphasis on human responsibility for the evils of the world still pertains. Human beings are ultimately responsible for the actions of their own governments. In the Holocaust, there were perpetrators, collaborators, and bystanders, as well as governments that failed to act to end the atrocities. There were also heroic individuals who resisted the Nazis at great personal risk. Although we cannot ultimately explain why evil persists, we can agree on the human imperative to actively resist it. We are responsible for the world and for each other. Still, the vexing spiritual question remains, "Why did God not intervene to prevent the suffering?" This is a question we cannot presume to answer, but within a purposeful universe we cannot avoid the asking.

4

The Chosen People

> Now then, if you will obey Me faithfully and
> keep My covenant, you shall be My treasured
> possession among all the peoples. Indeed, all
> the earth is Mine, but you shall be to Me a
> kingdom of priests and a holy nation.
>
> (Exodus 19:5–6)

The crucial turning point in the destiny of the Jewish people occurs at
the moment when Moses relays God's message to the people assembled
at the foot of Mount Sinai. To this offer of a covenant, "All the people
answered as one, saying, 'All that the Lord has spoken, we will do' " (Exodus 19:8). The books of Exodus and Leviticus go on to record the
commandments and rules of conduct for the people pledged to represent God in the world.

The sacred myth of the chosen people is born in the covenantal relationship between God and Israel. It is a pact that is eternally and recip-
rocally binding. In it, the people Israel collectively assume a calling to
make God known to the world, to bear witness to the one God and His
unity through adherence to His laws. In turn, the people are rewarded
as God's "treasured people" (*am segulah*), connoting a relationship of
special intimacy and knowledge of God.

The belief in chosenness implies an exclusive relationship based on
mutual love. The prophets view the relationship between God and Israel
as a marriage. When they castigate the people during the period of the
monarchy for their lapses into idolatry, the prophets compare Israel to

an adulterous wife who violates her marriage vows. They remind the people of God's loving devotion in delivering them from slavery in Egypt and in revealing to them His Torah. Conversely, the Hebrew psalms call out to God to help his favored people "for His own Name's sake" and in remembrance of the original covenant between God and our ancestors. The special vocation of the chosen people is reflected in the traditional liturgy as well. The *Aleinu* prayer begins by thanking God for choosing the people Israel for this special destiny and ends with the hope that the day will arrive when all people will recognize the supremacy of the one, true God.

The fulfillment of the mutual and reciprocal responsibilities of the covenant relationship defines the destiny of the Jewish people. Yet this belief has itself been redefined and reinterpreted in every generation throughout Jewish history. How is it possible for the universal God of all humanity to choose and favor one people above all others? In North America today, how can we value equality, tolerance, and religious pluralism, on one hand, while believing that God favors the Jews and has reserved for us a special destiny, on the other hand? The very term "chosen people" has sometimes become associated with notions of superiority, exclusiveness, and intolerance. Because the belief that Israel is God's chosen people is laden with many implications, Jews have found it necessary to constantly redefine what this means.

Jews have often believed that the Jewish people possess a special genius or talent, residing in each one of us, that makes us essentially different from every other people. Is there something mystical in the Jewish people that makes Jews distinct? Some point to Jewish spirituality, the indefinable sense of inner identity as a Jew, the sense of camaraderie shared by Jews around the world, the ability to identify certain people and their character traits as Jewish, and the disproportionate success of Jews in certain fields as proof of the unique character of the Jewish people. So strong is the consciousness of uniqueness that even Jews who do not think of themselves as religious are often reluctant to sever their ties to the Jewish people or its destiny.

Today, as Jews have gained unprecedented acceptance in modern societies, the tendency toward universalism has weakened the sense of a particular Jewish identity. Many Jews feel we are no different from any other people, nation, or ethnic group, although we have our own unique religion, history, culture, community, homeland, and folkways. Jewish universalists point out that while the Jews once believed we were God's chosen people, such a notion has no place in today's egalitarian world. Jews continue to wrestle with the contradiction between their belief in the special destiny of the Jewish people and the belief that all people are created in the image of God.

The distinctiveness of the Jewish people has long been a central pre-occupation of Jews and non-Jews. The Jewish people is one of the few to have endured continuously since ancient times and to have adapted effectively to changing circumstances. No other people has maintained its devotion to its ancestral homeland while also developing methods of preserving its identity throughout a centuries-long diaspora. The persistence of Judaism since antiquity, despite repeated efforts to eradicate it, demonstrate a durability that both provokes and mystifies its enemies. To Jews and non-Jews, the survival and longevity of the Jewish people are nothing short of a miracle.

The terms "Judaism" and "Jew" are first used around the beginning of the first millennium C.E. There is no word in the Bible for what we call Judaism; the religion is variously referred to as the "teachings" (*Torah*), "commandments" (*mitzvot*), and "laws" (*hukkim* or *mishpatim*). In the Torah, the Jewish people are called Hebrews (*ivrim*) and Israel (*yisrael*). *Ivrim* refers to the migration of Abraham and his clan from the Tigris–Euphrates region to the land of Canaan. The word *yisrael* literally means "you have striven with beings divine" and refers to the acquired name of the patriarch Jacob, who wrestled with the mysterious figure at Peniel (Genesis 32:29). Both the people and the homeland came to be known by this name, Israel. Following the establishment of the kingdom of Judah during the First Temple period, Judeans were called *yehudim,* which was soon translated as Jews.[1]

The biblical homeland was known by its two principal provinces—Israel and Judah. Following the Roman conquest of the region in the first century B.C.E., it was renamed in Latin as Palestina. The Romans chose to name this area after the Philistines, ancient Roman trading partners on the Mediterranean coast, to indicate that they did not recognize it as a Jewish homeland. The use of the name Palestine was revived by the

British colonialists after World War I and, more recently, by the Arabs living in the area west of the Jordan River. The Arab Palestinians today have no connection with the Palestine of Roman days. The Romans called Judah—the area of primary Jewish settlement in Palestine—Judea, and the Israelite inhabitants Judei. The words "Jews" and "Judaism" entered Western languages during the Roman occupation. They were not originally the terms Jews used to designate themselves and their religion.

THE SACRED MYTH OF THE CHOSEN PEOPLE

The sacred myth of the Jewish people begins with the account of how God chose the Jewish people from among all the nations of the ancient world to be His special people. At first, God chose Abraham who, alone among his contemporaries, recognized that there was one God who ruled the universe. God commands Abraham, "Go forth from your native land and from your father's house to the land that I will show you" (Genesis 12:1). God requires that he abandon all that is familiar to him and leave his homeland to settle in the land of Canaan, later called the Land of Israel, and that he worship the true God. God promises him that he and his descendants will be God's chosen people. After Abraham purchases land, God promises Abraham and his descendants that they will possess the entire Land of Israel. The promise occurs, however, when Abraham is ninety-nine years old and Sarah is eighty-nine. God announces to Abraham that Sarah will soon give birth to Isaac, despite their advanced age:

> When Abram was ninety-nine years old, the Lord appeared to Abram and said to him, "I am El Shaddai. Walk in My ways and be blameless. I will establish My covenant between Me and you, and I will make you exceedingly numerous." Abram threw himself on his face; and God spoke to him further, "As for Me, this is My covenant with you: You shall be the father of a multitude of nations. And you shall no longer be called Abram, but your name shall be Abraham, for I make you the father of a multitude of nations. I will make you exceedingly fertile, and make nations of you; and kings shall come forth from you. I will maintain My covenant between Me and you, and your offspring to come, as an ever-

lasting covenant throughout the ages, to be God to you and to your off-spring to come. I give the land you sojourn in to you and your offspring to come, all the land of Canaan, as an everlasting possession. I will be their God." (Genesis 17:1–8)

God requires that Abraham be circumcised as the sign of the covenant. Every Jewish male child since then is welcomed into this people through the *brit milah,* the ritual circumcision ceremony that harks back to God's covenant with Abraham. Subsequently, God reiterates the promise to Isaac, Jacob and his sons, and Moses. God expands the covenant in each new formulation, leading up to the revelation at Mount Sinai. Finally He formulates the covenant as the Ten Commandments and subsequent laws which He dictates to Moses as he leads the people through the Sinai wilderness on the way to the Promised Land.

At each step in the course of Abraham's life, God promises him a destiny that appears highly unlikely. How can a one-hundred-year-old man give a child to a ninety-year-old woman? The fact that Sarah does give birth is meant to prove that God is directing these events and that He is more powerful than nature. Moreover, these phenomena are the first evidence that God is directing the course of events in a very unnatural way, with an end and a purpose in mind. Not only does God make the barren woman conceive, which is against the laws of nature, but He further redirects the course of history. He promises Abraham that his second-born son, Isaac, rather than Ishmael, his firstborn, will continue the line and transmit the covenant. This goes against the ancient law of primogeniture, which guarantees the firstborn the primary right of inheritance. The biblical narrative tells the sacred myth of how God chooses to direct affairs toward a preconceived outcome and to not allow the natural course of events to unfold. In each generation from Abraham to Moses, God chooses the unlikely hero to be His champion. Isaac is chosen by God over Ishmael. Jacob is chosen over Esau to be the bearer of this promise.

At each stage along the way, God's intervention in history results in his renewing His choice of Abraham and his descendants for a special destiny. The covenant is articulated as a contractual relationship between God and Israel that involves mutual and reciprocal obligation and is predicated on performance of God's laws. If Israel accepts the Torah, God will guarantee a special status to it among all the peoples of the world.

In Deuteronomy, the final book of the Torah, which reiterates God's charge to Moses, the covenant is presented in a slightly different light. Here it appears as a gracious and freely given gift from God which is the fulfillment of a promise. There is no suggestion that the covenant is conditional upon Israel's proper behavior:

> For you are a people consecrated to the Lord your God: of all the peoples on earth the Lord your God chose you to be His treasured people [*am segulah*]. It is not because you are the most numerous of peoples that the Lord set His heart on you and chose you—indeed, you are the smallest of peoples; but it was because the Lord loved you and kept the oath He made to your fathers that the Lord freed you with a mighty hand and rescued you from the house of bondage. (Deuteronomy 7:6–8)

Later biblical passages stress the voluntary choice of Israel's participation in the covenant. Their own agreement places a higher burden upon them because they themselves have taken on the demanding responsibilities of moral and ritual practice. They have no excuse for not living up to these responsibilities and carry a burden of accountability for them. When Joshua, Moses' successor, later assembles the tribal elders at Shechem, he reminds them of their promise to worship no other gods: "You are witnesses against yourselves that you have by your own act chosen to serve the Lord" (Joshua 24:22). The people respond with agreement and Joshua renews the covenant in writing. This covenant between God and Israel is a living commitment that is continually renewed and reaffirmed.

Still, Israel is an unlikely choice for this task, just as each of the forefathers was an unlikely choice to carry on his father's line. God chooses the small, insignificant people despite their apparent low status.

Further, the covenant is not an individual relationship but involves the people in its entirety. It emphasizes especially the social responsibilities of the Jewish people to seek justice and create a lawful society. This is a relationship with God established by the Jews as a people, not just Jewish individuals.

The covenant implies the inherent superiority of the Torah and the moral superiority of the Jewish people. It also appears to be fragile and susceptible to cancellation for nonfulfillment of its conditions.

The sacred myth of chosenness has been reflected in the rituals of Judaism. The religious festivals—Passover, Shavuot, Sukkot, and the Holy Days, Rosh Hashanah and Yom Kippur—start with the blessing over wine, which begins: "Blessed are You, Lord our God, King of the universe, who has chosen us from among every nation, exalted us above every language, and sanctified us by Your commandments." God distinguished the people Israel from other national groups and made them a "kingdom of priests and a holy nation" by virtue of the unique religious and moral practices of Judaism. A similar blessing is made whenever a Jew is called to read from the Torah in public: "Blessed are You, O Lord our God, king of the universe, who has chosen us from among all peoples and has given us Your Torah."

The notion of chosenness as uniqueness and superiority emerges in the more popular forms of expression in Judaism. The *Amidah,* the central prayer in Jewish liturgy, conveys this forcefully in its festival version: "You have chosen us from among all peoples, You have loved us and taken pleasure in us, and have exalted us above all tongues. You have sanctified us by Your commandments, and brought us near to Your service."

The *Aleinu* prayer, composed during the Second Temple period, expressed popular Jewish triumphalism. The prayer clearly states that God created differences between Jews and non-Jews, and the destiny of the Jews differs from that of other peoples: "It is for us to praise the Lord of all, to proclaim the goodness of the creator of the world. He did not make us like the nations of the earth, and did not fashion us like the tribes of the earth. He did not make our portion like theirs, nor did He make our destiny like that of the multitudes who bow down to vanity and emptiness and pray to a god who cannot redeem them." In the Middle Ages, the phrase "who bow down to vanity and emptiness and pray to a god who cannot redeem them" was removed by Christian censors, who read this as an affront to Christianity.

Not all rabbinic authorities accepted the idea that Israel was inherently preferable over any other people. Some sages asserted that Israel was not God's first choice; rather, He chose Israel only because they freely accepted the moral responsibility the Torah demands. Israel was God's final choice as the only nation that had the spiritual willingness to accept God. One midrash tells a tale about how God offered the Torah to several nations, including Edom and Ishmael, who rejected it because its moral requirements were alien to their own cultures. In Jewish tradition, Esau is the ancestor of Edom, the forerunner of Roman Catholicism, and Ishmael is the ancestor of the Arabs. Thus, this passage implicitly asserts Israel's moral superiority over these two dominant cultures. Finally God turned to Israel, who accepted the Torah with no questions asked:

> When He who is everywhere revealed Himself to give the Torah to Israel, He revealed Himself not only to Israel but to all the other nations as well. At first God went to the children of Esau. He asked them: Will you accept the Torah? They said right to His face: What is written in it? He said: "Thou shalt not murder." They replied: Master of the universe, this goes against our grain. Our father, whose "hands are the hands of Esau" (Genesis 27:22), led us to rely only on the sword, because his father told him, "By thy sword shalt thou live" (Genesis 27:40). We cannot accept the Torah.
>
> Then He went to the children of Ammon and Moab, and asked them: Will you accept the Torah? They said right to His face: What is written in it? He said: "Thou shalt not commit adultery." They replied: Master of the universe, our very origin is in adultery, for Scripture says, "Thus were both the daughters of Lot with child by their father" (Genesis 19:36). We cannot accept the Torah.
>
> Then He went to the children of Ishmael. He asked them: Will you accept the Torah? They said right to His face: What is written in it? He said: "Thou shalt not steal." They replied: Master of the universe, it is our very nature to live off only what is stolen and what is got by assault. Of our forebear Ishmael, it is written, "And he shall be a wild ass of a man: his hand shall be against every man, and every man's hand against him" (Genesis 16:12). We cannot accept the Torah.
>
> There was not a single nation among the nations to whom God did not go, speak, and, as it were, knock on its door, asking whether it would be willing to accept the Torah.

At long last He came to Israel. They said, "We will do and hearken" (Exodus 24:7).[2]

Another midrash takes a more jaundiced view of Israel's willingness to accept the Torah. The midrash recognizes that the covenant is maintained not only by the free choice of a willing people, but also by the implicit threat of punishment should they not accept their obligation. Israel is God's choice and the people are compelled to agree. In explaining the meaning of the word "under" in the verse "And they stood *under* the mount" (Exodus 19:17), R. Avdimi bar Hama said: "The verse implies that the Holy One overturned the mountain upon them, like an inverted casket, and said to them: If you accept the Torah, it is well; if not, your grave will be right here."[3]

A LIGHT UNTO THE NATIONS

The biblical prophets introduced the notion that Israel is chosen to demonstrate to other nations the superiority of God's Torah. Until the sixth century B.C.E., Israel paid little attention to the religious life of other peoples. Then, growing military and political pressure and religious influences from the neighboring Assyrians and Babylonians provoked the prophets to denounce these forces and argue for the superiority of Israel's moral and monotheistic teachings. The prophet Isaiah believed in the universality of the ethical and monotheistic teachings of Israel. If the Torah was true, why should it be limited to Israel? Isaiah broadened the convenantal responsibility to include a new obligation to reach out to other nations and disseminate God's teachings. The Torah was the possession of Israel, but the message of God is universal.

Isaiah describes Israel metaphorically as God's servant and draws from this relationship the new responsibility of a universal mission of Israel. In Isaiah's speech, God calls Israel to serve as His agent to bring His message to other peoples: "For He has said: 'It is too little that you should be My servant in that I raise up the tribes of Jacob and restore the survivors of Israel: I will also make you a light of nations [*le-or goyyim*], that My salvation may reach the ends of the earth' " (Isaiah 49:6).

Judaism has viewed Israel's responsibility as being "a light *of* nations," namely, an exemplary people who show their devotion to the one, living God by example. In fact, during much of the Middle Ages the belief in the superiority of the Jewish religion over others provided Jews with a significant measure of consolation. The hostility of Christianity and Islam was regarded by Jews as part of the price they had to pay for being the people of the covenant. This allowed them to endure the abuse of Christians and Muslims while retaining an inner conviction that their truth was God's truth.

Judah Halevi, the eleventh-century Spanish-Jewish poet and philosopher, was the author of *Kuzari,* one of the most popular Jewish books of all time. He believed that God's choice of the Jews involved the bestowing of a special quality upon the people as a whole. This quality, the "divine influence," is a real entity that resides within the collective people and individual Jews. It is transmitted from parents to children and confers special characteristics upon the people Israel. First, they have a special capacity for prophecy, which was evident at Sinai where the entire population heard God utter the Ten Commandments. Second, Israel is the "heart of humanity," which means that the Jewish people are a kind of barometer of the human condition. Whatever happens to humanity, happens to Jews, only more so. While Jews have a greater inclination than others to seek God, they also are more susceptible to moral failings that bring about divine retribution. Third, the Jewish people have a greater moral responsibility than other people because they are the heart of mankind. They have the duty to be a "light *of* nations" and bring God's teaching to the nations of the world.

This view of the inherited distinctiveness of the Jewish people was emphasized a century later in the Zohar, the leading text of the Kabbalah. According to Kabbalah, there are several gradations of the human soul. The lowest part of the soul, *nefesh,* is common to all living beings, while only Jews have a *neshamah,* the higher soul. This idea could be misconstrued as claiming the genetic superiority of Jews. Rather, it means that one can achieve *neshamah* only by following the Torah.[4] Still, we find reflected here the trend in Judaism that sees Jews as unique by virtue of an essential quality, whether it be an inherent divine influence or potential access to a higher soul. In the popular folklore of East European Jewry, this became known as the *yiddishe neshomeh*—the uniquely

Jewish soul—which implies that a person is compassionate, modest, generous, caring, and spiritually sensitive.

There is another equally authoritative tradition in medieval Judaism that sees chosenness as a feature of Jewish behavior but not as an innate characteristic. In the tenth century, Saadya Gaon stated that the defining characteristics of Jewish peoplehood is extrinsic, namely, possession and fulfillment of the laws of the Torah: "Our nation is a nation only by virtue of its laws."5 Take away the Torah and the Jewish people does not exist. Moses Maimonides goes even further than Saadya in maintaining that if one does not follow the Torah, one is not even considered a member of the Jewish people. Jewishness is not unconditional but requires the affirmation of certain beliefs, knowledge of God, and practice of the Torah laws. After explaining that the foundations of the Torah include ethics, knowledge of and belief in one God, and observance of the commandments, Maimonides declares: "Anyone who destroys one of these foundations which I have explained to you has left the community of Torah adherents."6 Jewishness, let alone chosenness, is entirely conditional. If one violates this condition, one is considered an Israelite sectarian and is excluded from the community. "Israelite sectarians are not like Israelites at all."7 The Israelite sectarian is considered anathema to the Jewish people, such that it is forbidden to speak with him or return his greeting. "We are not bidden to mourn them on their deaths."8 For Maimonides, to whom knowledge of God is a central commandment, the Jews were chosen to know, worship, and follow God: "God sent Moses our Master to make out of us 'a kingdom of priests and a holy nation' through the knowledge of Him."9

Chosenness was sometimes seen as innate and inherent in the Jewish people; at other times, Jewish thinkers believed that chosenness required Jews to regularly reaffirm the covenant and the duties that go with it.

The belief that the covenant implied responsibility to live by the commandments of the Torah and to be "a light of nations" was reinterpreted by modern Jewish thinkers. The greatest challenge to chosenness as a central tenet of Judaism came with the opportunity for Jews to integrate as individuals within modern societies. It became difficult to reconcile Jewish uniqueness with the case for social and political acceptance. Reform Judaism was one of the first modern responses to this

challenge. In the eighteenth century, the founders of the Reform movement began to play down the role of the commandments and exalt the
ethical dimensions of Judaism. The change in emphasis within Reform
Judaism was evident in the renewed attention paid to the role of the
Jewish people as "a light *of* nations." In order to highlight this role, the
expression was changed to "a light *unto* the nations." Such a subtle shift
stressed that Israel was not only to be a moral exemplar but to see its religion as missionary, with morality as the Jewish mission.

Early Reform thinkers believed that Judaism is a set of universalistic
teachings which have made great contributions to Western civilization.
They introduced the "mission-people" concept as a new twist on the
chosen-people concept. The mission-people concept places the responsibility on Israel both to live up to the ethical demands of the covenant
and to disseminate these ethical teachings to the world. In dropping the
ethnic and ritual dimensions of Judaism, the proponents of the mission-
people concept sought to turn Judaism into a universal ethical culture.
Isaac Mayer Wise, a leading twentieth-century American Reform rabbi,
thought that Judaism had a real chance to become America's religion of
choice if it were recast as the purest form of ethical monotheism, without any ethnic component.

The Reform reinterpretation of the chosen-people concept as the
mission-people concept has come to mean that the Jews are not chosen
by God, but rather choose to embrace a social gospel—that Jews have a
higher calling to solve the injustices in modern society. But having
spread this social gospel, what is the need, we might ask, for the continued existence of the Jews and Judaism? Rabbi Leo Baeck, German Reform rabbi and Holocaust survivor, provided one answer: Jews possess a
special genius for ethical monotheism which keeps the idea alive even
today. Were the Jews and Judaism to disappear, ethical monotheism
would lose its irreplaceable advocate and might itself disappear.

Nevertheless, the Reform belief that the Jewish people are missionar-
ies for ethics has not proved sufficient to explain why Judaism and the
Jewish people should continue to exist, and it provides no impetus for
the transmission of Judaism. Ethical ideas are the intellectual property of
all people and of none exclusively. It is no surprise that many Jews disaf-
filiate with Judaism and the Jewish people when they have been raised

to believe that Judaism is reducible to certain universal truths. For if that is all that Judaism is about, it is easy to dispense with the medium and yet preserve the message. The mission-people concept soon disappeared, but the idea persisted that Jews should hold and be held to a high standard of ethical practice and exert considerable effort on behalf of social justice.

In 1975, Reform Judaism made a decisive break with its own past and restored much of what its predecessors had eliminated, including an emphatic statement about the importance of tradition, peoplehood, and the Hebrew language. Reform Judaism now reaffirmed belief in chosenness, peoplehood, and certain *mitzvot* but continued to insist that the exalted station of the Jewish people is a product of its ethical religion. This ideological shift reflected the shift back to traditional beliefs within the Reform movement as well as an increasing recognition of the importance of Israel and peoplehood in modern Jewish life.

Among the four religious denominations of American Judaism, the more traditional ones—Orthodox and Conservative Judaism—continue to advocate a belief in chosenness rooted in the notion of religious obligations, the *mitzvot,* that define the specifically Jewish way of life. Only the Reconstructionist movement rejects the idea of the chosen people. This reflects the position of the founder of the movement, Mordecai Kaplan, who vehemently opposed the idea that God chooses one people over another. God, for Kaplan, was the impulse for goodness that resides in human beings, not a transcendent being with a capacity to choose. Moreover, the belief in the distinctiveness and difference of the Jewish people contradicted Kaplan's sense of American democratic egalitarianism. Reconstructionism, however, introduced the new notion that Jews are "called to God's service." This means that Jews have a religious responsibility to live and act in the world according to the teachings of Judaism. It is the Jews who are called but it is not necessarily God who is calling. Thus, the Jewish people is the "choosing people" rather than the "chosen people."

Jews have always understood their continued existence as rooted in a higher purpose than ethnicity. No other people feels compelled to justify itself in this way. We can only see this as the attempt to explain living in two cultures—Jewish and Western secular—simultaneously. But at-

tempts to define Jewishness more universally through modernizing the
sacred myth of chosenness often fail to provide a rationale for continued
Jewish distinctiveness and survival.

WHAT IS SPECIAL ABOUT BEING JEWISH?

Even as strong a critic of the Jewish religion as Sigmund Freud believed in the persistence and distinctiveness of the Jewish people. Although he never believed in the notion of chosenness, his views on
Jewishness might be considered a secular version of the sacred myth.
Freud believed that his "Jewish nature" was responsible for providing
him with the characteristics of freedom from intellectual prejudices and
the willingness to take points of view contrary to majority opinion. He
identified these as the two characteristics that had become indispensable
to him in his life's work. He defined his Jewishness as consisting of
"Many obscure emotional forces, which were the more powerful the
less they could be expressed in words, as well as a clear consciousness of
inner identity, the safe privacy of a common mental construction."[10] The
distinctive Jewish characteristics, the "clear consciousness of inner (Jewish) identity," according to Freud, include the Jewish predilection for in-
tellectualism and penetrating beneath the surface of things, the penchant
for self-criticism, intolerance for pretense and conventional thinking,
and a strong ethical and charitable orientation.[11] Ironically, as the
founder of identity theory, Freud introduced the concept of modern
Jewish identity based on Jewish values. But his theory of Jewish identity
is untenable because he explains the distinctiveness of the Jewish people
in terms of wholly secular values. In the end, the values of secular
Jewishness lead to assimilation and the loss of any distinctive Jewish
identity.

Some Jewish thinkers of the late nineteenth and early twentieth centuries believed that a revived national definition of the Jewish people
could provide a coherent system of meaning for modern Jews. Ahad
Haam ("One of the People"), the pen name of the Russian Zionist
Asher Ginzburg, and other Cultural Zionists, such as the Russian Hebrew writer Hayim Nahman Bialik, had tremendous love for the spirit
and vitality of the Jewish people even if they had doubts about tradi-

tional Jewish belief and practice. They sought to identify the "genius of the Jewish people," which had given rise to a distinctive religious culture.

Ahad Haam believed that the Jewish people possessed a "national spirit" which was characterized by a commitment to the prophetic ideals of absolute righteousness. The Jewish people had survived throughout history by virtue of their national spirit and will to live, which was based on dedication to the fundamental and abiding principle of doing what is uncompromisingly right—not by virtue of belief in God. But over time Judaism had become encrusted with rituals, observances, and a law that threatened to stultify the moral sensibilities of the Jewish people. His views on ethics and ritual were similar to those of Reform Judaism, although his views on peoplehood differed fundamentally from those of Reform.

Ahad Haam thought that the only way to preserve the national spirit of the Jews was to return to the ancestral Land of Israel and to establish a homeland based on the prophetic ideals of absolute righteousness but freed from the constraints of Jewish law. He promoted the creation of a spiritual and cultural center for the Jewish people in the Land of Israel. He was concerned not with politics or the goal of statehood but rather with solving the spiritual dilemma of modern Judaism. Such a spiritual and cultural center would serve as a model for the revival of the Jewish national spirit in the Diaspora as well. Unlike the political Zionists, Ahad Haam did not want the homeland, if it ever became a state, to be a state like other states. Cultural Zionism contributed to the idea that Israel should be an ideal Jewish state, not in terms of religious practice, but in terms of absolute morality and prophetic righteousness. A new, spiritual Jewish culture could then take root in its own language, Hebrew, and lead the way to a renaissance of Jewish life in Israel and throughout the Diaspora.

The idea that Cultural Zionism can provide a reason for continued Jewish existence remains appealing but elusive. By necessity, the State of Israel has been shaped by serious political and military challenges as much as by ideals of justice. While Jews living throughout the world have been inspired by Israel, this is more often by virtue of its military strength and successes in immigrant absorption than its exemplary cultural achievements. Cultural Zionism has had significant impact on world Jewry by making the study of the Hebrew language an important part of Jewish education. It never succeeded, however, in establishing the "spiritual center" that would create a modern, secular Hebrew culture throughout the Diaspora.

Martin Buber viewed Judaism as neither a religion nor a nationality but as a spiritual process of "striving for an ever more perfect realization of three interconnected ideas: the idea of unity, the idea of the deed, and the idea of the future."[12] The idea of unity is the Jewish tendency, according to Buber, to perceive the context in which phenomena occur, not just the individual phenomenon; to see the forest, not just the trees. This culminates in "the idea of the world-creating, world-ruling, world-loving God" and in our history of ever seeking a more integrated and unified idea of God.[13] The idea of the deed means that human action should arise out of the sense of absolute freedom and responsibility to do what is right unconditionally. Judaism values the deed done not to gain reward but because it is right. The idea of the future is that of striving to create a more perfect world even if its achievement remains constantly on the horizon, always out of reach.

For Buber, Judaism had lost its spirit and become ossified in a law that substitutes ritual for the immediacy of religious experience. He saw the renewal of the Jewish spirit in the revitalization of the ideas that once animated Jewish life. He believed the ideal Jew is one who is moved by these three ideals. "Only when Judaism again reaches out, like a hand, grasping each Jew by the hair of his head and carrying him, in the tempest raging between heaven and earth, toward [the ideal symbolized by] Jerusalem . . . only then will the Jewish people be ready to build a new destiny for itself where the old one once broke into fragments."[14]

New understandings of what it means to be a Jew have reshaped the belief in chosenness. Franz Rosenzweig (1886–1929) was raised as an assimilated Jew in Germany but moved to embrace Judaism in its various manifestations. Rosenzweig, who resisted all attempts to categorize him or reduce Judaism to a formula, presented one model of a contemporary Jew: the ideal Jew is a person who sees no distinction between being human and being Jewish. Jewishness is something inexplicable, something fundamentally personal that arises out of one's deepest self, an identity at the core of one's being which extends to every facet of one's life. Being Jewish is the very essence of one's humanity and radiates outward into every sphere of life. He rejected identification with Orthodoxy, although he was himself observant, because he objected to reducing Judaism to a set of duties. He saw the Orthodox emphasis on the *mitzvot* as reductionism. He rejected Reform Judaism because, in his view, it reduced Judaism to a set of ideas about ethics and monotheism but disposed with the *mitzvot*. Finally, he rejected Zionism for reducing Judaism to a notion of a national task, that of creating a homeland for the Jews. Jewishness, for Rosenzweig, does not start with an identification with one of the Jewish "recipes."

Rosenzweig eschewed simple formulas except for one that he saw as the starting point for every modern, secular, assimilated Jew who is drawn to Jewishness: "Nothing Jewish is alien to me." The modern Jew lives at the periphery of Judaism and yet inexplicably feels drawn toward the center. The ideal Jew for Rosenzweig was the one who embraces the totality of Jewish experience and then sets about filling in the gaps in his or her Jewish knowledge and giving meaning to his or her life. The ideal Jew is always striving, in individual and even idiosyncratic ways, to move from the periphery to the center of Jewish experience. This is the person who sees Judaism as a lifelong quest to understand the religious experiences that inspired our ancestors and can touch us deeply as well.

Other modern thinkers saw the distinctiveness of Judaism as a spiritual process attuned to the inner life of the individual. Judaism leads the individual to a life lived in deep personal relation to the creator of the world. Jewish spirituality is highly individual and takes place within a people whose spiritual focus is directed toward God. Abraham Joshua Heschel deplored the vacuousness in the American Jewish community and a Jewishness that did not deepen the spiritual and religious life of the individual Jew. He criticized the excessive preoccupation with the communal aspects of Jewish life at the expense of our spiritual lives. The concern for the welfare of the community and its institutions has dominated Jewish life in America for three generations and has diverted our attention from the individual. Jews attend Jewish meetings, belong to Jewish organizations, contribute to communal and national funds. In seeing the forest, we could not see the trees. In building a strong communal life, we have forgotten the spiritual condition of the individual law. The private life of the Jew has become impoverished and is reflected in the spiritual vacuousness of many Jewish homes and synagogues. The concern of the Jewish community should be reversed: unless the religious spirit of the Jew as an individual is enriched, the life of the community will be a wilderness. If the individual is lost to Judaism in his privacy, the people are in danger of becoming a phantom.[15]

The question of what is special about being Jewish continues to engage modern Jewish thinkers. Today, being Jewish is more a matter of choice than of fate and requires a clear answer to the question of what is distinctive about Jews and Judaism. A compelling rationale for Jewish distinctiveness must reside in a value so absolute that nothing else could ever replace it. The distinct Jewish element must be something so unique to Judaism that no other culture or civilization could claim that it can offer a better way. It must provide so persuasive a reason to remain Jewish that it can continue to hold and attract the hearts of Jews. It must provide a raison d'être so enduring as to make the continued existence of the Jewish people an urgent necessity for all Jews. The distinctive element in Judaism must be a sacred myth that is powerful and compelling as a system of meaning. It must reach out to each Jew on a very personal level and address him or her directly.

What does the sacred myth of the chosen people mean? Does it mean that Jews are inherently superior to other people or that the Jewish message is superior? What is it about this belief in chosenness that gives meaning to Jewish existence? The answer to these questions is that the sacred myth of chosenness conveys a belief in a special destiny for the Jewish people that transcends the survival of the people itself. It is not enough for the people to survive, they must fulfill the purpose for which they exist. The destiny of the Jewish people serves a purpose higher than mere survival. That purpose is to represent God's ways by living by His teachings in the world. Therefore, chosenness is a spiritual concept affirming that the higher purpose of Jewish existence is to experience and perpetuate the transcendent dimensions of life.

What is special about the Jewish people is that they are "a kingdom of priests and a holy nation." Unlike other kingdoms, our king is the transcendent God of the universe whose laws are moral and universal. In this kingdom, there is no elite class of priests with exclusive access to the king; every citizen is a priest. We are a kingdom made up entirely of priests of the divine in which all people have the same status and access to God. While we are a nation, it is not a nation just by land, language, or ancestry.

The Jewish people are rooted in a dedication to a higher purpose, that of serving God. The chosen people acquire our special character by representing God's ways in the world and by serving as God's spiritual agents in society. The chosen people must fortify God's image by acting to find God's presence in the world. A midrash explains that God first revealed Himself to Moses in a burning bush in order to teach that there is no place empty of the divine Presence, not even a thornbush.[16] The Kabbalists believed that God's Presence was scattered throughout the universe as "holy sparks within shattered vessels." They described the purpose of the Jew as "uplifting the sparks" by seeking holiness wherever it might be found. In this way, the mission for each Jew is to "repair the world" by penetrating beneath the surface of things and finding the divine kernel, the image of God, which lies everywhere in the world, even in unlikely places. The chosen people are the ones who are called to experience the transcendent dimensions of life in the everyday world and to reveal the hidden sparks of holiness. The mission of the Jewish people is to serve as "priests of the ideal," in the words of one twentieth-century American rabbi: "If by that we mean that Israel should consciously set itself up as a people that is to function as priests of the ideal, if we mean that in a world constituted like that of today, materialist, deterministic, and mechanistic, some group should stand for the idea of the world, not as it is, but as it might be."[17]

The chosen people are a spiritual nation with a unique mission and purpose. Jewish spirituality is the experience of the transcendent dimension of life as an individual and as a member of a people. This spirituality, however, is not otherworldly but rather emphasizes the belief that the truest path to God does not involve leaving the concerns of this world. Jewish spirituality can be achieved only by focusing on strengthening the image of God, the divine spark, wherever it might be found within our world. All human actions, habits, and attitudes are directed toward achieving this transcendence. Jewish teachings emphasize that a human being is a ladder placed on earth whose top touches heaven. This does not mean that we are to transcend this world or view it as inferior to the heavenly world. God created this world in order to give heaven a resting place. God gave this world to Adam and Eve in order that they and their descendants might make of it something heavenly. The sacred Jewish myth does not draw the Jew up to heaven; it draws heaven down to the Jew. Not even the Torah is in heaven; it is here on earth. It is not enough to learn Torah—one must *be* Torah by living in such a way that others can learn from his example.

As spiritual agents of God, the chosen people are called to live according to spiritual values. The Jewish people are called to live in the mundane world of home, family, work, and society but also to recognize that every moment becomes an opportunity to find a deeper meaning, a higher purpose, and a heightened awareness that we are created in God's image. As difficult as it is to seek a higher rung of holiness in the midst of every day, the challenge to the Jew is to find moments of transcendence in the everyday world. Martin Buber wrote that "there is no rung of being on which we cannot find the holiness of God everywhere and at all times."[18] There is nothing unholy—only that which is not yet holy. The chosen people believe that it is possible to achieve holiness, perfection, the messianic era, the kingdom of God—all within the ordinary world of daily life.

The chosen people are iconoclasts, fighters against idolatry in all forms. In Judaism, idolatry is considered one of three cardinal sins for which a person should be willing to sacrifice his life rather than succumb. The rejection of idolatry is such an essential element of Judaism that a non-Jew who repudiates idolatry may be called a Jew.[19] Idolatry does not only mean worshiping idols but can include elevating something human or material to the status of a sacred object. Belief in materialism—the idea that all reality is material and no transcendent realm exists—is idolatry. Belief that there are forces such as the stars and constellations that control our destiny and prevent us from assuming responsibility for our fate is idolatry. It can also refer to anything contrary to human morality, because anything that diminishes the stature of a human being who is created in the image of God ultimately diminishes

God. For example, idolatry can mean fearing another person more than we fear God. Idolatry includes elevating a political cause over the basic exercise of morality and respect for human rights: for example, it is idolatrous to believe that the Land of Israel is more holy than the life of human beings. All idolatry arises out of the hubris of creating God in our image rather than in recognizing that it is we who are created in the image of God. The concept of the chosen people may today have meaning with or without implying divine election, chauvinism, or superiority.

THE JEWISH ATTITUDE TOWARD CONVERTS

Does the belief in the chosen people concept imply that non-Jews have a lower status than Jews? In the eyes of rabbinic law, non-Jews do not have the same status as Jews unless they renounce idolatry and observe the "seven commandments of the sons of Noah." This idea comes from the Torah's reference to the sons of Noah. Shem, Ham, and Yafet were the fathers of the various nations in the biblical period. They were expected to abide by a universal moral law which is incumbent upon all civilized peoples and which guarantees them a similar degree of divine favor as if they themselves observed the Torah. The sons of Noah are held to a lower standard of behavior than Israel but are accountable nevertheless.

The seven universal commandments were developed by the rabbis of the talmudic era. They are: (1) recognition of the rule of law in society; (2) the prohibitions against idolatry, (3) against blaspheming God, (4) against murder, (5) against sexual impropriety, (6) against theft, and (7) against cannibalizing animals, that is, ripping a limb from a living animal for food. Jewish tradition maintains that a Gentile who observes the seven Noahide commandments is equal in God's eyes to a Jew who observes the entire Torah.

The Jewish attitude to converts is an important dimension of the chosen-people concept. Can one choose to become a member of the chosen people? If chosenness is extrinsic—namely, the result of freely entering into a contractual responsibility with mutual and reciprocal obligations—then one can "convert" in or out. If chosenness is essential—that is, biologically inherent to someone who is born Jewish—one cannot easily "convert."

Judaism is clearly and unequivocally opposed to intermarriage between a Jew and non-Jew but welcomes converts. The Bible relates that conversion to Judaism was natural and beneficial. Ruth, the Moabite heroine and daughter-in-law of Naomi, declares that the Jewish people are her people, and their God her God. She is a prototypical convert whose grandson is King David, the preeminent leader of the Jewish people. Some of the greatest sages of Judaism were the children of converts. Joseph, the father of the great sage Rabbi Akiva, was a convert to Judaism.[20]

During the Second Temple period, especially in the first century of the Common Era, Gentiles in the Roman Empire converted to Judaism in large numbers. Josephus, the Jewish historian, reports that prior to the destruction of the Second Temple, many non-Jews converted because of Judaism's appealing rituals, ceremonies, monotheistic belief, and moral teachings. Many more Gentiles, called "God-fearing men," adopted some Jewish practices but did not become full-fledged Jews. Converts were treated as full-fledged Jews as long as they fully embraced Judaism and cut off their ties with their native culture.

This was the period during which the Jewish Diaspora grew and the roots of European Jewry took hold. Some of the growth was due to the influx of large numbers of converts to Judaism from other faiths. Many Jewish communities in the Mediterranean grew by significant numbers of converts during the early Middle Ages. Population increases among Syrian Jewry, the Jewries of Asia Minor (Turkey), Italy, Carthage, and Armenia and the Balkans must have been due to converts and their descendants.[21] By all accounts, Judaism was a successful missionary religion in the first few centuries of the Common Era.

Jewish law accommodated to the realities of conversion. As far back as the first century, converts were accepted as full-fledged Jews regardless of their motivation. A convert whose motivation is religious conviction is on the same par with one who converts for the sake of marriage or under the pressures of living in a Jewish community. The Halakhah accepts converts who become Jews out of conviction or in order to marry, to advance themselves, or even out of necessity under duress.[22] A convert must accept all of the precepts that govern other Jews.[23] But converts are full-fledged Jews. A midrash says that "converts are beloved: in every place, God considers them as part of Israel."[24]

The midrash offers an explanation for why Jews have been dispersed among the nations. Whereas other sources explain the dispersion as punishment, one midrash says, "The Holy One, blessed be He, exiled Israel among the nations only in order to increase their numbers with converts."[25] Another tradition sees converts as a natural outgrowth of the desire to extend God's providence to all humanity. "When a proselyte comes to be converted, one receives him with an open hand so as to bring him under the wings of the divine Presence."[26] The acceptance of converts has even found its way into the prayer book. Three times daily, the weekday *Amidah* includes a blessing for "faithful converts" along with the righteous, the pious, and the scholars of Israel.

Maimonides ruled that there is absolutely no difference between a born Jew and a convert to Judaism.[27] He did not accept the notion that Judaism is a fact of birth alone. A convert has no different legal status from a born Jew. Furthermore, "we are commanded to have great love in our hearts toward converts; God, in His glory, loves converts."[28] Maimonides ruled that converts have the identical religious obligations as other Jews. This includes the obligation to recite such blessings as "Blessed are You, O Lord, our God and God of our fathers," even though the convert's forefathers were not Jews.[29]

There was, however, another tendency in Judaism that viewed converts with suspicion and, at times, as second-class Jews. This development occurred as a result of several factors. First, the experience of converts to Judaism in the early Middle Ages who relapsed to their former religions cast suspicion on the allegiance of converts. Second, there was a tendency to see Jewishness as a biological fact rather than a legal definition. Although this was a minority opinion among Jewish legal authorities, it was a popular view among Jewish people. And third, as Judaism felt itself persecuted from without, it developed an antagonistic attitude toward the non-Jewish world.

The experience with insincere conversion haunted Jewish sages. For example, the famous Rabbi Eliezer ben Hyrcanus changed his position from accepting converts[30] to opposing converts and conversion.[31] This may have been due to the fact that some heathen converts to Judaism later defected to Christianity. The historian Josephus recounts how some converts to Judaism reverted to their earlier ways and persecuted Jews.[32] This led one midrash to warn: "Do not have any faith in a convert until twenty-four generations have passed."[33] The harshest statement comes from the sometimes cantankerous Rabbi Helbo in the third century: "Converts are as hard for Israel to endure as a sore."[34] This opinion reflects his own disappointment with insincere converts and came to be the slogan of those who opposed conversion for whatever reasons.

Judah Halevi, on the other hand, believed that while a convert may be a good Jew, he can never achieve the status of a born Jew. Halevi represents the nativist tendency in Judaism which sees the biological element of generational continuity as the transmission line of Judaism. In fact, he goes against the historical truth that the Jewish population had swelled with the influx of converts whose offspring were by then indistinguishable from born Jews.

Throughout the Middle Ages, Jews were often encouraged to convert to Christianity through threats, persecution, persuasion, enticements, and encouragement. When Jews were forcibly converted to Christianity, they and their descendants were generally considered to be Jews as long as it remained dangerous to return to Judaism. Jews who voluntarily converted to Christianity were often regarded as renegade Jews but Jews nevertheless. Their children, however, were not regarded as Jews.

In Eastern Europe, xenophobia—Jewish fear of non-Jews—grew as the result of continued persecution and anti-Semitism which translated into an iron wall dividing Jew from non-Jew. During the last two centuries, Jewish attitudes changed and opposition to conversion to Judaism grew. Conversely, in many European countries, conversion to Judaism was a crime punishable by death, and Jews no longer solicited or accepted converts.

Despite the fact that trends of both acceptance of and opposition to converts developed in Judaism, the general policy that emerged was one of accepting but not actively recruiting converts. This is formulated by the Talmud: "In our days, when a prospective convert comes to be converted, we say to him: 'What is your objective? Is it not known to you that the people of Israel are wretched, driven about, exiled, and in constant suffering?' If he says: 'I know of this and I am not worthy to be a Jew,' we accept him immediately."[35] Another statement summarizes the policy: "In general, the left hand should repel and the right should draw near."[36]

Jewish policy was originally missionary and openly solicited converts. But as Judaism became more and more an oppressed religion, it turned from proselytizing to isolation and self-protection. One of the casualties of persecution of the Jews was the Jewish attitude to converts. When Judaism was secure, it welcomed converts. When Judaism was in retreat, the tendency was to oppose conversion. The more Judaism was under siege, the less welcoming it was to outsiders. Today, Judaism encourages conversion as a practical response to the growing rate of intermarriage and as one of the means of preserving Jewishness in a family where one spouse was not born Jewish.

What does it mean to believe today that the people Israel is God's chosen people? The sacred myth of the distinctiveness of the Jewish people has taken many forms. For centuries, Jews have believed that the Jewish people are God's chosen and treasured people, "a kingdom of priests and a holy nation," and partners in an eternal covenant with God which is mutual and reciprocal: if we observe the Torah and perform the commandments, God will continue to treasure us from among all nations. For some, the chosen people are distinct and different from all other people because of this covenant. For others, it is hard to believe that God favors one people over another. Still others believe that Jews are chosen to live by a covenant that demands that they live by a higher moral standard than others and serve as representatives of morality to the world. We must be a "light unto the nations" by leading efforts to bring about a better world and to stand for the idea of the world not as it is, but as it can be.

There are many Jews today who have abandoned the idea of chosenness in favor of the idea that the Jewish people have a mutual responsibility to one another to insure our own survival and the survival of the State of Israel as a safe haven for Jews throughout the world. They believe that this can be achieved through *tzedakah* (righteousness), which they define as philanthropy and social justice for all people. A growing number of Jews believe that the Jewish people have a common responsibility to one another to insure the continuity of Judaism as a source of meaning in the modern world through personal spiritual growth and Jewish learning.

The belief in the destiny and distinctiveness of the Jewish people has survived from antiquity to the present because Jews have been animated by a transcendent purpose throughout history. Although there have been various interpretations of the higher purpose of Jewish existence— whether it is the belief in Judaism as a constant striving for realization of an ideal or the belief that Judaism is a spiritual process—Jews can all agree that the search for such meaning is at the very heart of the Jewish people.

The idea of the destiny of the Jewish people distinguishes Judaism from other religions and cultures. The sacred myths of Judaism offer different answers to the fundamental questions concerning the individual and his or her place in the world than do other cultures or religions. Indeed, it may be the very fact that Judaism places the quest for finding a transcendent purpose of life at the center of the Jewish enterprise that most distinguishes Judaism. Although every religion has its own set of answers, the sacred myths of Judaism are constantly posing new approaches. Since this process is perpetual, ours will not be the last generation to struggle with the issue of Jewish destiny and distinctiveness. Still, when we wrestle with these issues, we place ourselves in the long tradition of the Jewish people and its search to understand our special destiny.

5

The Meaning of Torah

A popular Jewish adage asserts that "Israel, God, and the Torah are one."[1]
This saying recognizes the central role of Torah within the Jewish understanding of the relationship between God and the Jewish people.
Torah, which literally means "teaching" and refers to the first five books
of the Hebrew Bible, is the holy text of Judaism and the source of all its
sacred myths. But what are the sacred myths concerning Torah itself?
What do we mean by Torah and how do we understand it to be God's
word?

According to Jewish tradition, the Torah is the written expression of
God's message to the people Israel. The Torah includes the Five Books of
Moses: Genesis, Exodus, Leviticus, Numbers, and Deuteronomy. The
Hebrew Bible is a more extensive collection comprising the Torah, the
prophetic books (*Neviim*), and additional books called the Writings (*Ketuvim*). Jews have traditionally believed in the sacred myth of the divine
origin of the Torah—that "the Torah is from heaven" (*Torah min ha-
shamayim*). By this we mean that God himself announced the Ten Commandments to Moses and the 600,000 Israelites who stood at Mount
Sinai. After Sinai, God communicated the rest of the Torah to Moses as

Israel traveled through the Sinai wilderness, and Moses wrote it down for all Israel to hear. Only the Torah, the first five books, is regarded as divine in origin. The Prophets and Writings are all attributed to human authors even though the texts themselves are regarded as part of a sacred canon.

Jews revere Torah as the word of God and read it publicly three days each week, including the Sabbath, and on special religious occasions. The testimony of Jewish faith, *Shema Yisrael,* commands us to study Torah as the very core of Jewish practice: "And these words which I command you this day shall be upon your heart. Teach them diligently to your children." For two thousand years the primary ritual of Jewish life has been the study of Torah. It is the one activity that unites Jews of all backgrounds and persuasions. Jews have often died defending the right to study Torah. For these reasons, Jews have been called the People of the Book.

Contemporary Jewish polemics leave many with the impression that belief in the divine authorship of Torah divides Orthodox from non-Orthodox Jews. One modern Orthodox writer articulates this view: "The Torah must be seen as a record *not* of man's spiritual genius, but of God's will communicated to mortal and finite man. . . . No interpretation of Judaism is Jewishly valid if it does not posit God as the source of Torah."[2] The question remains, however, how was God's word communicated? Is the concept of divine authorship intrinsic to the belief in Torah as a sacred text? The traditional notion of the divine authorship of Torah is not as fundamentalist or literalist as it appears and represents a far more complex phenomenon.

Concerning the divine origin of Torah, the Jewish tradition itself is far more diverse and accepting of other approaches. The Torah never made a claim for itself that it was entirely of divine origin. Although the rabbis later attempted to turn the divinity of the Torah into dogma, not all rabbinic authorities accepted that view. Many sages suggest that Moses had a hand in writing parts of the Torah as a human author. Medieval authorities maintain that the Torah text as we have it is only one of several possible versions. Some authorities believe the Torah we possess is an abridged version of the divine message, which could not be communicated in a form we could fathom. Others hold that we each hear a different Torah and that there is an infinite number of possible versions of Torah. In this view, all of Torah is relative to the eyes and ears of the beholder rather than a fixed document with one meaning. The Torah is, according to many Jewish thinkers, one exceptional manifestation of an eternal process of hearing God's commanding presence.

THE DIVINE ORIGIN OF TORAH

The sacred myth of the divine origin of Torah explains how God communicated His message to the Jewish people. The myth begins with the Exodus from Egypt around 1200 B.C.E. and culminates in the settlement of the Land of Israel. After leaving Egypt, the Israelites camped through the Sinai desert for six to seven weeks before arriving at Mount Sinai. The actual historical site of Mount Sinai is uncertain, although popular Christian and Muslim legends have identified the supposed location. The Torah describes the setting as the people waited at the foot of the mountain while Moses ascended. God then told Moses: "Now then, if you will obey Me faithfully and keep My covenant, you shall be My treasured possession [*segulah*] among all the peoples. Indeed, all the earth is Mine, but you shall be to Me a kingdom of priests and a holy nation" (Exodus 19:5–6). When Moses repeated this to the people, they responded in one voice: "All that the Lord has spoken, we will do."

The Torah's version of these events continues by recounting that two days later Moses ascended the mountain again. This time, God addressed the Ten Commandments to him, while the assembled people heard only the accompanying thunder and trumpetlike sounds. Moses reported the words of God to the people as God had instructed him. God also commanded Moses to convey the following message to the people: "You yourselves saw that I spoke to you from the very heavens [*min ha-shamayim*]" (Exodus 20:19). The biblical account identifies the heavens as the location from which God spoke and Moses as the conveyor of the message to the people. The passage itself suggests that God uttered only the Ten Commandments and not the entire Torah at Sinai.

Following these events, Moses continued to write down the many other detailed laws God revealed to him at Sinai (Exodus 24:4). God then recalled Moses to the mountain, where He inscribed the Ten Commandments on stone tablets (24:12). Throughout the period of wandering in the Sinai wilderness, God continued to communicate additional rules and regulations to Moses, which Moses then announced to the people. God often delivered these instructions in the Tent of Meeting, a portable meeting place that served as a secure and sacred setting for Moses' encounters with God. Nowhere in these events does it say that God spoke directly to the people. These subsequent pronouncements, together with the narrative describing the events from the creation of the world, the history of the patriarchs and matriarchs, through Moses' death before the Israelites entered the Promised Land, were written down at some unknown point, and the Torah says nothing about who transcribed them. All these written documents became known as the Written Torah or the Five Books of Moses.

Who wrote all this down as the Torah? The Torah itself testifies repeatedly that Moses wrote down all that God had instructed him, but this refers to the original sections about the events at Mount Sinai. Modern biblical scholars claim that the Torah was probably originally an oral tradition which might even have existed in different versions. These versions were woven together by an unknown final editor or editors sometime during the early Second Temple period, possibly in the fifth century B.C.E. The rabbis of the talmudic era concluded that God gave the entire Torah, not only the portions He uttered at Sinai. The rabbis became advocates for the sacred myth of the divine origin of the entire Torah, not just the Ten Commandments. They transformed the biblical narrative about God speaking from heaven from a descriptive to a prescriptive statement. The Mishnah condemns anyone who does not believe in the divine authorship of Torah and excludes him from the world-to-come: "These have no portion in the world-to-come: Those who say that there is no resurrection of the dead, that the Torah is not from heaven, and Epicureans."[3]

The rabbinic anathema includes in its warning that denying certain tenets of rabbinic Judaism or involvement with certain cults will result in exclusion from the world-to-come. This statement implies that there must have been significant disagreement over the question of divine authorship of the entire Torah. It is difficult to identify whom the rabbis were accusing of this heresy. Their other criticisms refer respectively to the first-century Sadducees, who denied the idea of resurrection, and the Epicurean sect, a non-Jewish Greek sect that did not believe in the existence of a divine being who dispenses reward and punishment, which had some influence on the assimilated Jews of the time. This Mishnah formula elevates three principles—belief in the divine author- ship of Torah, belief in reward and punishment, and belief in the ultimate resurrection of the dead—to the status of Jewish dogmas.

The Torah itself places the emphasis on sacred practice, not sacred be- lief. There is no suggestion in the biblical description of Sinai that be- lieving in God as the author of the Torah is important in itself. The sacred practices were crucial because they were God's commandments. The rabbinic expansion of the concept of the divine origin of Torah from the Ten Commandments to the whole of the Five Books intro- duced a new notion that the Torah itself does not imply.

The issue of whether God was the author of the Torah provoked con- siderable debate among the rabbis of the talmudic era. The rabbis gener- ally agreed that God dictated and Moses wrote down the entire Torah, but there were some disagreements over whether Moses wrote certain passages of his own accord. The dispute between two formidable adver- saries, Rabbis Akiva and Ishmael, centered on the extent to which Ju- daism was to be justified as having entirely a divine origin or whether the human contribution could be acknowledged as well. Rabbi Akiva's fundamentalist and Rabbi Ishmael's nonliteralist view held equal stature. Rabbinic Judaism demanded loyalty to the dogma of the divine origin of Torah even though there was no unanimity on whether that meant completely or just mostly divine.

Rabbi Akiva in the second century took a very literalist position and maintained that every word of the Torah is divine. He pointed to a verse that states that a defiant person who reviles the Lord should be put to death (Numbers 15:31). Akiva explained that the definition of one who "has despised the word of the Lord" is "one who maintains that the Torah is not from heaven." Akiva found the principle of the divine ori- gin of Torah so comprehensive that even if one asserted that the whole Torah is from heaven, except a particular verse that was uttered not by God but by Moses, he is included as one who maintains that the Torah is not from heaven.[4]

On the other hand, Rabbi Akiva's contemporary, Rabbi Ishmael, accepted only the general principle of divine authorship that had become known as *Torah min ha-shamayim*. Contrary to Akiva, he did not believe that the verse regarding one who "has despised the word of the Lord" refers to one who denies the divine origin of Torah. Moreover, he credited this verse to Moses himself.[5] Thus, Ishmael adopted a more flexible position and acknowledged a certain degree of human authorship of Torah. He explained that God offered a set of general rules at Sinai—the Ten Commandments—and provided a series of subsequent instructions to Moses in the portable wilderness tabernacle. Rabbi Akiva maintained that God spoke the entire Torah at Sinai and then later repeated large portions of it to Moses.[6]

Rabbi Akiva believed that every word of the Torah had some mysterious meaning that could be deciphered and from which new laws could be discovered. This idea is based on the divinity of the entire Torah, and it gives divine sanction to the rabbinic system. Ishmael's approach relied considerably on the divine origin of the oral tradition but it admitted a greater role for human contributions. In doing so, it forfeited some of the divine justification for rabbinic tradition. If the Torah is entirely divine, Akiva's position is justified. If even one sentence of the Torah is of human authorship, Akiva's position becomes indefensible. What is at stake is that Akiva's position supports the inviolability of rabbinic law while Ishmael's position exposes the rabbinic tradition to challenges of human fallibility.

Among the popular views that God dictated to Moses most, but not all, portions of the Torah, one statement held that Moses contributed substantial portions of the Torah and other biblical books under his own authorship. This tradition maintains that Moses composed the Book of Deuteronomy and chapters 22–24 of Numbers.[7] God dictated and Moses wrote the Torah in most instances, except in these cases where he added his own words. The passage describes Deuteronomy as "Moses' own book," an epithet stemming from the biblical account of God's blessing Moses in the last days of his life. The passage concludes: "Moses wrote down this teaching [*Torah*]" (Deuteronomy 31:9). The ambiguous term "Torah" can refer both to the specific teaching God conveyed and to the Written Torah itself. The ambiguity might have contributed to the idea that Moses wrote the entire Book of Deuteronomy, which finds historical support in the report that Deuteronomy was generally unknown or not considered divine until it was discovered hidden in the Temple in the seventh century B.C.E. during the reign of King Josiah (2 Kings 22:8).

Why did some rabbis exempt the Balaam narrative in Numbers 22–24 from divine authorship and attribute it to Moses? Balaam is the Moabite prophet whom King Balak sent to curse Israel as they passed through Moab across from Jericho before entering the Promised Land. Instead of cursing Israel, Balaam was overcome by an involuntary urge to praise Israel, which he did three times. On the third occasion, he uttered the famous words "How fair are your tents, O Jacob, Your dwellings, O Israel" (Numbers 24:5). Both the literary composition of the Balaam narrative, which is sufficiently different from other parts of the Torah, and the idea of a non-Israelite prophet who had as direct a relationship with God make this biblical passage unique. This led the rabbis to attribute it and Deuteronomy to Mosaic authorship. Moses was regarded as the independent author of both exceptions to the principle of the divine origin of Torah.

Another rabbinic passage credits God with having dictated to Moses all the Torah with the exception of the depiction of Moses' own death. To forestall the charge that God could not have dictated to Moses narratives about events still to come or events after his own death, the Talmud explains that God dictated the words of Torah to Moses up to Deuteronomy 34:5, which describes the moment of Moses' death: "Moses the servant of the Lord died there." From that point on until the end of the Torah, states this rabbinic passage, God dictated and Moses wrote with tears.[8]

THE ORAL TRADITION

The rabbis who wrote the passage in the Mishnah on the three tenets of Jewish faith believed that the author of the commandments wrote the entire Torah and that this belief was sacred. Not only did the rabbis of the Mishnah expand the concept of divine authorship from the Ten Commandments to the entire Torah; they also believed that there were other divine communications to Moses that had not been written down in the Torah. The rabbis called this the Oral Torah (*Torah she-be-al peh*). They maintained that this oral tradition dates back to Sinai and has as much authority and antiquity as the written text. According to the rabbinic tradition, the revelation of God at Sinai was not the final word. Revelation of God's teaching continues in the process of deliberation throughout history by competent and learned Jews who meditate upon God's word and law. This interpretive tradition invests the continuous unfolding of the divine revelation not in God but in the wisdom of the rabbis and the rabbinic tradition. The basis for this is the belief that everything that was, is, and can be known from God was revealed at Sinai but that much of the content of the revelation was implicit, rather than explicit, within Torah. Jews can derive new insights, laws, and interpretations after Sinai, *all* of which are implicit within the Torah text or are part of an oral tradition that supposedly dates back to Sinai. This conveys the idea that Torah is a living document rather than a static code. The rabbis who believed that the Torah is a comprehensive guide to every aspect of life said, "Turn it and delve into it for it contains everything."[9]

The Sadducees, many of whom were priests, were contemporaries of the early rabbis. They agreed to the divine origin of the Written Torah but denied the existence of the oral tradition. The Sadducees believed only in what the Torah stated explicitly. They maintained that the Torah was vouchsafed by Moses to Aaron and the priests, and they therefore regarded the Torah as their sacred priestly preserve rather than the possession of all Israel. The rabbis, however, asserted that they—not the Sadducees—were the true heirs of the Torah because they themselves inherited the oral tradition which their ancestors had conveyed through the generations. The Torah, in their view, was open to interpretation and amenable to uncovering new applications to life. The earliest rabbinic manifesto, known popularly as the *Sayings of the Fathers* (*Pirkei Avot*), identified this chain of oral authority: "Moses received the Torah at Sinai. He transmitted it to Joshua, Joshua to the elders, the elders to the prophets, and the prophets to the men of the Great Assembly."[10]

This passage is remarkable in several respects. First, it affirms that the entire Torah, which includes the Written Torah and the oral tradition, not just the Ten Commandments, was delivered by God to Moses in one event. Second, it defines a chain of transmission over the course of twelve hundred years from Moses to the rabbis by way of Moses' successor Joshua, the elders, the prophets, and the men of the Great Assembly (a relatively unknown group of Torah sages from the early Second Temple period)—one that completely ignores Moses' other successor, Aaron, the first priest, whose descendants preserved the Torah scrolls themselves. Thus, the passage bypasses the priestly line of authority and claims that it is the rabbis who are the true heirs of Moses; the priests, including the first-century Sadducees, have no claim to the mantle. Finally, the rabbis imply that the oral tradition—the rabbinic system of interpretation of Torah—has as much legitimacy as the Torah itself.

The rabbis' belief that the Oral Torah could also be traced back through a chain of tradition to Sinai stems from their deep conviction about divine sanction for the *mitzvot*. The commandments in the Torah, reflecting a different society from the one in which the rabbis lived, often required interpretation, refinement, elaboration, and change in order to render them applicable to new situations. Every legal code generates an evolving system of continuing legislation and legal authorities who can authorize the application of the original laws to new circumstances. This is what the rabbis provided in the tradition of Oral Torah and in the institution of the rabbinate. Human beings must apply the word of God to life, but only divine authority could make the new laws inviolate.

The rabbis knew that many of the laws, rituals, and practices they developed were innovations. They believed, however, that these were logical extensions following from the biblical laws. They were aware that they were innovating but at the same time denied that they were introducing anything new. Their legal justification for innovation was the principle of "vested originality" (*asmakhta*). This is the practice that permits originality and innovation as long as it is vested in or subsumed under an earlier precedent, practice, or text. An innovation that is justified by being related to or derived from an earlier law, ritual, or practice is halakhically legitimate. The innovation can go no further than what the precedent, practice, or text can sustain. The rabbis limited this legal concept by another that prohibited introducing anything that was pure innovation.

The rabbis rationalized their appropriation of Torah by claiming that they alone were the true inheritors of Torah and that their innovations were implicit in the oral tradition. The rabbinic honorific for Moses was "Moses, our teacher" (*Moshe Rabbeinu*), which implied that he was essentially one of them. Even though they clearly distinguished between laws derived from Torah and laws deduced by rabbis, they believed that all were part of one seamless tradition. In the end, Moses' Torah and the rabbinic laws have equal stature in rabbinic Judaism. Nevertheless, the rabbis were aware that such a claim would have astonished Moses:

> Rav Judah said in the name of Rav: At the moment when Moses ascended to heaven, he found the Holy One, Blessed be He, sitting and binding crowns on the letters. He said to Him: "Master of the world, who is delaying your hand?" He said to him: "There is one man who will come at the end of several generations by the name of Akiva ben Yosef who will search [*darash*] every jot and tittle of the letters for mounds and mounds of laws [*halakhot*]."
>
> Moses said to God: "Master of the World, show him to me." He said to him: "Turn around!" Moses went and sat in the eight rows [of Akiva's academy] and could not understand what was being said. His strength waned. When they arrived at a certain matter, his students said to him: "Rabbi, how do you know this?" He said to them: "It is a law of Moses from Sinai." This calmed his mind.
>
> Moses went and returned to the Holy One, Blessed be He, and said to Him: "There is a man like him and you choose to give the Torah through me!" He said: "Silence! This is how it arose in my thought."[11]

God appears to be engaged in a continuous process of weaving calligraphic flourishes onto the Hebrew letters of the Torah scroll in heaven. This suggests that God's Torah is still unfinished and that God continues to embellish it. Also implied is that God's continuing work is the basis of the development of the Jewish oral tradition. When Moses questions God as to why He is still working on His Torah, God answers that Rabbi Akiva, the second-century leader of the Oral Torah tradition, will decipher these flourishes and uncover new laws and interpretations in them. Moses becomes curious and is transported forward twelve centuries to Akiva's classroom.

Moses is dumbfounded at his unfamiliarity with the rabbinic laws—or with the rabbinic interpretation of the Mosaic laws—and his uneasiness makes him feel a stranger to the very Judaism of which he is the founder. His mind is put at ease when he learns that the rabbis attribute to him the very origins of their laws. Although this reassures him, he does not appear to quite understand how it works.

This legend is a masterpiece of rabbinic explanation of how they could innovate new laws and traditions without violating the strictures of the Torah. The rabbis made the belief in the divine origin of Torah sufficiently elastic for innovation yet rigid enough to prohibit radical departures from the text. They asserted, paradoxically, that they were not introducing anything new because their laws were inherent within the Oral Torah while, at the same time, they acknowledged that their system would be unrecognizable to Moses.

THE MEDIEVAL DEBATES

In the Middle Ages, philosophers and mystics agreed on the belief in the divine origin of Torah but attributed new and different meanings to the concept. Moses Maimonides reaffirmed the rabbinic belief but suggested that Torah did not originate through the process of speech as we know it. It involved a form of prophecy whereby Moses was able to fathom God's intention. In his codification of thirteen principles of Jewish belief, he defined it this way: "The eighth principle: that the Torah is from heaven. We believe that this entire Torah which was given by Moses, of blessed memory, was uttered entirely by the mouth of the Power, that is, was conveyed to Moses entirely from God in the manner called metaphorically 'speech.' It is not known how it was conveyed other than it was conveyed to Moses. He acted like a scribe to whom one dictates and he writes it down."[12]

Maimonides believed that Moses was a morally and intellectually gifted prophet who possessed unusual abilities. Foremost among them was the ability to absorb God's thoughts at Sinai, to let God think through him, and to communicate God's thoughts in a manner that would be accessible to ordinary human beings. Moses' gift was his ability to communicate a sublime message in human terms. His imaginative mind was the prism through which the divine message was refracted and communicated to the 600,000 Israelites.

What Moses conveyed, however, was not exactly what God communicated. According to Maimonides, God communicated a profound philosophic message about divine existence, knowledge of God, human nature, the relationship between individuals and God, and human destiny. The content of that revelation was so sublime that no one but Moses could grasp it in all its subtlety. Therefore, Moses communicated the message through narratives, parables, and stories which conveyed these truths in somewhat simplified form. Moses, when faced with transmitting an abstract philosophic revelation, resorted to a strategy of dilution that would make divine truths more comprehensible to mere mortals. Thus, as Maimonides said, quoting a rabbinic aphorism: "Torah speaks in the language of the sons of man."[13] It is up to the perceptive reader of Torah to seek to understand the more subtle meaning, which unsophisticated readers do not generally grasp

Maimonides viewed the Oral Torah as the tradition that elaborates, explains, and continues Jewish practice and beliefs. While he believed that Jewish practice was fundamental, Maimonides believed that proper beliefs were even more important. He respected the text of the Torah as the revelation of God but understood that to mean that Torah is not God's word directly but rather God's message filtered through Moses.

THE KABBALISTS

Kabbalah offered a different sacred myth of the divine nature of Torah. The leading Kabbalist of the thirteenth century, Nahmanides, agreed with his rabbinic predecessors that "Moses, our teacher, wrote down this book [Genesis] with the whole Torah from the mouth of God *probably* at Mount Sinai."[14] His qualification that it was "probably" written at Sinai also follows the view of Rabbi Ishmael, which comprehends the divine origin of Torah in a more limited sense.

To the Kabbalists, what God revealed at Sinai was not just a text but rather His very being through the medium of language. The Torah is not a book with a message so much as it is the manifestation of God's essence. According to the Jewish mystical tradition, God did not simply dictate the Torah nor did Moses simply transcribe. Torah was, however, the product of God's thinking and the offshoot of the *Sefirot*. The second *Sefirah—hokhmah,* or divine wisdom—is the first stage of divine thought. Within the *Sefirot,* divine thought is an archetype of the Written Torah. The Kabbalists called it "preexistent Torah." This preexistent Torah is identical with God's very being. Later on, at Sinai, divine thought was given its earthly concretization. Kabbalists believed in the divine origin of Torah but they understood it in a new sense: not as the Torah *from* God but as the Torah that *is* God. Since the Written Torah is the elaboration of the preexistent Torah, the Written Torah is ultimately the extension of God's essence in the form of letters, words, and names. Nahmanides had this in mind when he declared that "the entire Torah is composed of the names of God." This means that the Torah is the manifestation of the *Sefirot,* which are God's own names.

The Torah, according to Kabbalah, has two natures. It is the medium of divine expression and the vehicle through which the mystic can retrace the steps of the process leading back to God. The words of the Torah are not merely combinations of letters that constitute narratives. They are vessels that point to hidden essences, the *Sefirot.* The relation of the *Sefirot* to the words of the Torah is analogous to the relation of the soul to the body. The words of the Torah are "bodies" that contain the "soul" of God's being. The names, or words, of the Torah are ultimately expressions of divine power, not mere words referring to earthly things. One who knows how the divine power is infused in the words is able to harness and utilize the power contained in them. In other words, the mystic who understands the proper connection between the language of the Torah and the *Sefirot* is able to manipulate the power in the names and establish a connection to God.

Jewish mysticism, therefore, is a system of creating connections to God across the abyss through the medium of the Torah. One who can perceive the divine essence hidden in the Torah is able to cleave directly to the *Sefirot* and transcend the world in which he or she lives. The study of Torah is, therefore, the highest form of knowledge. The Torah is the vehicle by which the mystic knows God. This sacred myth of the divine nature of Torah is very different from the contemporary belief that the Torah is a book to be read like any other. One does not, according to

Kabbalah, read the Torah; one searches out the hidden or secret meanings. These meanings are the *Sefirot,* their dynamics, and the hidden codes showing how the realm of God is related to our world. It is against the background of a mystical understanding of the Torah that Kabbalists present their ideas in the form of biblical commentaries and homilies.

A passage from the Zohar illustrates this idea:

> Rabbi Shimon said: Woe to the human being who says that Torah presents mere stories and ordinary words! If so, we could compose a Torah right now with ordinary words. And better than all of them! To present matters of the world? Even rulers of the world possess words more sublime. If so, let us follow them and make a Torah out of them! Ah, but all the words of Torah are sublime words, sublime secrets! Come and see: The world above and the world below are perfectly balanced: Israel below, the angels above. Of the angels, it is written: "He makes His angels spirits" (Psalm 104:4). But when they descend, they put on the garment of this world. If they did not put on a garment befitting this world they could not endure in this world and the world could not endure them. If this is so with the angels, how much more so with Torah who created them and all the worlds and for whose sake they all exist! In descending to this world, if she did not put on the garments of this world, the world could not endure. So this story of Torah is the garment of Torah. Whoever thinks that the garment is the real Torah and not something else—may his spirit deflate! He will have no portion in the world that is coming. That is why David said, "Open my eyes so I can see the wonders *out of* Your Torah!" What is under the garment of Torah? Come and see: There is a garment visible to all. When those fools see someone in a good-looking garment they look no further. But the essence of the garment is the body; the essence of the body is the soul!
> So it is with Torah. She has a body: the commandments of Torah. Called "the embodiment of Torah." This body is clothed in garments: the stories of this world. Fools of the world look only at that garment, the story of Torah; they know nothing more. They do not look at what is under the garment. Those who know more do not look at the garment but rather at the body under that garment. The wise ones, servants of the King on high, those who stood at Mt. Sinai, look only at the soul, root of all, Real Torah! In the time to come they are destined to look at the soul of the soul of Torah![15]

The study of the Torah is the loftiest purpose of human life because it is the pursuit of the transcendent through its own self-expression. The sacred myth of Kabbalah explains that the Torah is a kind of road map to God. The entire world is Torah because all of existence is a garment for God. The mystic unpeels the layers of the garment to reach the essence at its very core.

DECIPHERING THE TEXT

The Kabbalists explained that each one of us has our own internal Torah, that is, our own understanding of Torah. They believed that the 600,000 Israelites who heard God utter the commandments at Sinai each heard the Torah in his own way. Therefore, each word of the Torah has 600,000 faces or different legitimate interpretations. There is not one fixed Torah but rather a plethora of meanings and a multitude of approaches to the text. Without giving up the fundamentalist thesis of the divine character of the Scriptures, this theory loosens and personalizes the concept of revelation. In principle, every one of us has our own access to revelation, which is open only to us and which we must discover.[16] Only participation in the ongoing process of interpretation will yield the layers of meaning inherent in the Torah.[17] This position validates the interpretive tradition of Judaism while radically opening the limits of that tradition to new possibilities. The issue is which of the 600,000 faces of Torah we cultivate as our own.

The Jewish tradition developed four categories or approaches to the study of the Torah. The Zohar coined the acronym *PaRDeS* ("garden" or "paradise") as a mnemonic device referring to the four methods of approaching Torah. *PaRDeS* refers to (1) *peshat,* the plain or literal meaning of the test, (2) *remez,* the veiled meaning that the text hints at but does not make explicit, (3) *derash,* the midrashic or homiletic interpretation, which is derived from reading between the lines of Torah, and (4) *sod,* the esoteric or mystical meaning.

The approach of *peshat* is to define the plain sense or literal meaning of the text. The *peshat* meaning is the goal of the Jewish interpretive tradition and its major contributors, such as Rashi and Nahmanides. Today, *peshat* includes the techniques of biblical grammar, which help us to develop a clear linguistic analysis of each passage. It utilizes the findings of archaeology which provide data from the ancient Near Eastern cultures that corroborate and refute some of the common assumptions of biblical interpretation. For example, the comparative studies of ancient Near Eastern creation myths show that several of the Genesis narratives are retellings of common myths from a monotheistic perspective. These studies highlight the uniqueness of Israelite religion, with its borrowings and differences from contemporaneous civilizations.

Derash, the midrashic method, which means to "search out," is the product of Jewish literary analysis of texts. This technique employs rules of interpretation called hermeneutics, which pay close attention to comparison of similar expressions in different passages and draw on other logical techniques such as inference, induction, deduction, and contradiction. *Derash* seeks to develop extended meanings of individual words or phrases based on these rules of interpretation in order to derive moral teachings or halakhic rulings. *Derash* also employs literary analysis in order to supply meaning to cryptic biblical passages. When a biblical passage puzzles the reader or raises questions without apparent answers, the reader can enlist the technique of *derash* to find an answer.

Frequently, *derash* or midrash became the basis for elaborate and fanciful excursions into folklore, legend, and anecdote. For example, the biblical account of the patriarch Abraham leaving his father's house did not supply any detail about the conditions of his upbringing. The midrash filled in the missing pieces by supplying a fanciful story of how Abraham was the son of an idol maker. One day he was moved to destroy the idols in his father's workshop but panicked when his father was about to catch him in the act. He placed the hammer in the hand of the one remaining idol as his father walked in. He told his father that the surviving idol destroyed the others. When his father scoffed at the absurd notion that the idol could act, Abraham pointed out that the very absurdity of the answer proved the folly of idolatry.

Remez employs "hints" and allegory to derive new and extended meanings from unlikely Torah passages. This technique was especially useful to those biblical interpreters who wanted to reconcile secular knowledge with Jewish tradition. For example, Jewish philosophers who favored this technique interpreted the narratives of the biblical patriarchs allegorically as representing the destiny of the soul in this world and in the afterlife. This made it possible for them to preserve the Torah as a source of higher truth while introducing new theories beyond the plain meaning of the text.

Another technique employed by practitioners of *remez* is the use of *gematria,* an analogy between two words based on the numerical equivalence of the Hebrew letters of each. If two words have equal numerical significance, practitioners of *remez* can discover an analogy between them and derive the deeper significance. For example, the rules for the Sabbath that appear in Exodus are introduced by the phrase "These are the things [*elleh ha-devarim*] that the Lord has commanded you to do" (35:1). Practitioners of *gematria* note that the numerical value of "these are" (*elleh*) is thirty-six. To this they add the following values: "the" (*ha*) counts as one word and "things" (*devarim*) as two since it is plural. The sum equals thirty-nine. In their view, the verse hints at the thirty-nine classes of labor prohibited on the Sabbath.

Sod was employed primarily by the Kabbalists, who believed that each word or combination of words of Torah corresponds to the *Sefirot* or to processes within the world of the *Sefirot.* It is the symbolic technique of uncovering the hidden allusions in the words of Torah through mystical insight. The Kabbalists studied Torah—or decoded it—because it is a window to divinity. They were concerned not with the plain meaning of the text (although they still adopted the normative practices and rituals derived from it) but with the metatext of the Torah. This metatext is the version that exists within God and represents a reality higher than the apparently mundane events recorded in the Torah we see.

MODERN RELIGIOUS THINKERS

For twentieth-century philosopher Martin Buber, the Torah is not a text to be read but a voice to be heard. Following the idea that Torah is the expression of Moses' encounter with the Eternal Thou, he concludes that the Torah is best heard as a living voice rather than as a written text. The "immediacy of the spokenness" of Torah will bring the listener back to the moment at Sinai.[18] The listener will be brought into the very experience in such a way that he will be moved to a life of dialogue between himself and the Eternal Thou. The listener will become a hearer. Buber and Franz Rosenzweig, who shared his view, collaborated on a German rendering of the Bible that sought to convey this approach of the spoken word. The power of the spoken word is transformative and reorients the listener wholly toward God.

Buber's approach to revelation is based on the idea that God is not a being about whom one speaks in the third person but a being to whom one speaks directly. Buber's God is a distinctly other being who can only be experienced personally and who has always been experienced by humans since ancient times. Revelation is therefore a dialogue between two distinct beings. It is not a humanistic impulse but a real encounter. The difference between Buber's belief and the sacred myth of the divine nature of Torah is that while Buber's God enters into a relationship with the people Israel at Sinai, there was no message, law, or book transmitted—only a profound relationship established. Buber challenges the traditional notion of revelation as a one-sided concept that misses the fundamental equality of each partner in the I–Thou encounter. The Torah from heaven, for Buber, is the interpretation that Israel gave to the I–Thou encounter. Torah is not God's revelation but rather the creative elaboration by the Israelite people of the I–Thou encounter. Torah, therefore, is the revelation that is possible at any moment of the I–Thou encounter between the human I and the Eternal Thou.

Franz Rosenzweig goes further than Buber, who never accepted the validity of the *mitzvot*. Buber did not accept an inherited law, only what he himself felt was the imperative in his own personal relationship with the Eternal Thou. Rosenzweig concludes that the revelation at Sinai did not end with the establishment of a relationship. Moses, in his I–Thou encounter with God, experienced the presence of God and felt himself to be commanded by God. What God revealed at Sinai was only the first commandment or maybe only the sound of the first letter of the first commandment. The rest of the revelation was recorded as the human experience of God's word. It was not God's word that was recorded at Sinai. Rather, it was the human account of that experience that was preserved. Rosenzweig's position preserves the reality of revelation and the subjectivity of the human experience of that reality. Judaism for Rosenzweig is the process of seeking continuous experience of the commanding presence of God. Torah for Rosenzweig is a continuing human experience. The only command that Rosenzweig would follow was the one that he himself genuinely experienced as God's command. He also felt that the *mitzvot* were valid for him as earlier records of encounters with the Eternal Thou.

Mordecai Kaplan rejected belief in the supernatural view that the Torah is divine in favor of a new definition of Torah that includes "whatever knowledge would enable us Jews to retain our individuality as a people, discern our true identity and know the means and methods of achieving it." Torah thus includes all human knowledge drawn from Jewish and other traditions. Kaplan believed that there is a natural religious impulse that expresses itself in community. This means that religion is not superimposed from without by God. It is instead the system of meaning that arises naturally out of humanity. God did not create the Jewish people, the Jewish people created Judaism.[19] The virtue of Torah for Kaplan was that it expresses the historical religious experience of the Jewish people and embodies their creative approaches to the ultimate questions of human existence. Revelation is a metaphor for discovery and creativity arising out of the natural religious impulse. In Kaplan's view, God does not reveal Himself in a supernatural manner. Rather, humanity discovers God and creates meaning out of that experience.

Gershom Scholem, one of the most daring Jewish intellectuals of the twentieth century, reflected on the nature of Torah from the perspectives of the Jewish mystics. He argued that the communication of revelation at Sinai is essentially unintelligible and so had to be replaced by Moses with other meanings. Torah is then a transparent text that acquires meanings rather than a common text conveying fixed meanings. The "sign of true Revelation is no longer the weight of the statements that contain communication in it, but the infinite number of interpretations to which it is open."[20] Torah is a personal encounter which becomes whatever we make of it. This is reminiscent of the hasidic belief that we must become nothing but an ear that hears what God is constantly saying within ourselves. We should not study Torah but become a living Torah by listening to the transcendent voice within us.

MODERN BIBLICAL SCHOLARSHIP

The sacred myth of the divine nature of Torah was first challenged by the Jewish philosopher Baruch (Benedict) Spinoza in seventeenth-century Holland. Although he believed that Moses composed important segments of Torah, he held that the primary author was the scribe Ezra in the fifth century B.C.E.

In the nineteenth century, German Protestant biblical scholars, notably Julius Wellhausen, first opened the door to serious evaluation of the question of divine or Mosaic authorship. The identification of different styles and repetitions, which they attributed to multiple authors, was the basis of their challenge to the divine nature of Torah. This theory, which became known as the Documentary Hypothesis or Form Criticism, set out to identify the texts of at least four different authors: (1) the Jahwist or J author, who calls God YHVH, (2) the Elohist, who used the divine name *Elohim*; (3) the Deuteronomist, the author of the book known by that name; and (4) the Priestly author who composed Leviticus, the priestly document.[21]

In summarizing the state of biblical scholarship, one contemporary writer explained:

> Ninety per cent of biblical scholars agree on this—that the Penta-teuch, or Torah, was compiled from different sources. These are clearly distinguishable by style and content. The two earliest, known as J and E, date from as early as the time of David and Solomon, in the tenth century B.C.E. and the following century. These two sources . . . make up much of Genesis, Exodus and Numbers. The third source, D, comprises all of Deuteronomy except the last two chapters, and is generally connected with the scroll found in the Temple by the High Priest towards the end of the seventh century B.C.E. in the reign of King Josiah. . . . The fourth source, the P or Priestly source, is clearly distinguishable by its dry, legalistic style and its focus on cultic practice.[22]

Although this theory has been challenged, it had a profound impact upon biblical scholarship. It was the first of many new critical approaches to subject the biblical text to literary, historical, and archaeological analysis. The analysis had the effect of challenging the prevailing notions of *Torah min ha-shamayim*.

The American-Jewish biblical scholar Nahum Sarna sums up the implications of modern biblical scholarship: "Above all, biblical scholarship was touched decisively by the development and application of critical, historical and analytical methods used in the identification and isolation of literary sources and the determination of their dating. No longer could the Pentateuch be regarded as a unitary work divinely dictated, word for word, to Moses."[23]

Modern literary critic Robert Alter's literary approach to the Bible differs from that of many modern Bible scholars. He sees the biblical text not as a carefully edited "patchwork of frequently disparate documents,"[24] as did the modern critical scholars, but as a complex artistic whole. He is closer to the midrashic tradition which sees the text as an "intricately interconnected unity."[25] He differs from the midrashic approach by looking at each narrative as part of a continuum which unfolds and reflects back on earlier narratives, rather than as words, phrases, and verses which each require isolation and elaboration. The Bible allows the reader to be a knowing spectator who does not derive a specific didactic lesson from the text. The Bible conceives meaning through a process that never reaches closure but rather requires "continual revision, suspension of judgment, weighing of multiple possibilities, [and] brooding over gaps in the information provided."[26] Alter views the final author of the Bible as a literary genius who employs the literary techniques of prose fiction, including the "artful use of language, the shifting play of ideas, conventions, tone, sound, imagery, syntax, narrative viewpoint, compositional units, and much else."[27] His approach to the conscious artistry of the Bible emphasizes its humanistic dimensions, particularly the disparity between the divine promise of Israel's destiny and the "wayward paths of human freedom, the quirks and contradictions of men and women seen as moral agents and complex centers of motive and feeling."[28]

Modern Bible scholars such as Sarna and Alter have been able to put the text back together again, after the dissections of the Form Critical method, and appreciate the text that has come down to us as a unity despite multiple authors and a skillful final editor. The artistry and inspiration of the text transcends the problem of identifying its authors; it continues to speak to us as it has to each preceding generation.

Modern critical scholarship, however, continues to pose a serious dilemma for traditional Judaism. If the entire edifice of Judaism is built upon the foundation of the divine nature of Torah, a challenge to the foundation could lead to the collapse of the entire structure. Indeed, for many people the conclusion that Judaism is the product of human religious understanding renders it as having no greater value than any other culture or philosophy. The modern Orthodox are well aware of the challenge to Jewish practice that the historical approach represents. As Hayim Donin writes, "If it [Jewish law based on Torah] is only a set of man-made tribal laws, anyone is indeed justified in eliminating what no longer suits him."[29] Understanding Torah in its broadest sense as the Written and Oral Torah together, each of the Jewish religious denominations has had to face squarely the challenge of what they mean by divine revelation.

The approach of Conservative Judaism to Torah has evolved over the course of this century. In its early history, the Jewish Theological Seminary, the academic institution of the Conservative movement, avoided confronting the question of divine authorship directly. The movement wavered between its Orthodox roots and its understanding that saw Judaism as a religion of ongoing historical development. The Conservative practice through the first half of the twentieth century was "to teach the Bible critically, with the exception of the Torah, the Five Books of Moses. To us the Pentateuch is a *'noli me tangere'!* Hands off! We disclaim all honor of handling the sharp knife which cuts the Bible into a thousand pieces."[30]

After World War II, Conservative Judaism relativized the idea of the divine nature of Torah so that it was to be understood not as literally divine, but rather "divinely inspired." That is, revelation is relative and depends on the way in which it is perceived by each individual. This changed the concept fundamentally but kept the principle intact:

> We regard the Law, both written and oral, as the revelation of God. What Moses, the prophets, sages and rabbis taught, from Sinai to our day, is divinely inspired. . . . Hence, we accept as fundamental to vital Jewish religion, the principle of *Torah min ha-shamayim,* "the Torah as a revelation of God. . . ." This conception does not mean, for us, that the process

of revelation consisted of the dictation of the Torah by God, and its passive acceptance by men. . . . Not only does Revelation differ in content and depth, varying with the individual, but it is not limited in time. In other words, it is not an event but a process.[31]

In its 1988 manifesto, the Conservative movement tries to find a middle ground between relativism—the view that all "truth" is relative rather than absolute—and fundamentalism: "Conservative Judaism affirms its belief in revelation, the uncovering of an external source of truth emanating from God. This affirmation emphasizes that although truths are transmitted by humans, they are not a human invention.. . . As such, we reject relativism, which denies any objective source of authoritative truth. We also reject fundamentalism and literalism, which do not admit a human component in revelation. . . ."[32]

ENCOUNTERING THE TORAH

The dilemma for many modern Jews is how to relate to a tradition as old as Judaism. To many, being Jewish suggests compromising one's freedom of thinking and autonomy of action and accepting archaic ideas and restrictive forms of behavior. Is it possible to be fully Jewish without somehow retreating from today's world into another way of thinking and acting? The challenge is acute when it comes to identifying the role of Torah learning in Judaism. Many people have been alienated from Torah study by their experience with Bible classes and Sunday school during childhood. They have to overcome their negative experiences with Torah before they can appreciate it as adults. Torah is the foundation of Jewish thought and the source of Jewish behavior. The study of the Torah is the single most common Jewish ritual. It is also the most challenging task confronting a modern Jew because this most ancient of Jewish texts is, on the surface, the most foreign of all Jewish texts.

The adult who returns to the study of Bible with a fresh eye and insights drawn from *peshat, derash, remez, sod,* classical midrash, modern biblical scholarship, or contemporary literary approaches will find a different appreciation of the text. The text can be approached in an infinite variety of ways, depending on our own perspective. One does not need to believe literally in the sacred myth of the divine origin of Torah in order to be one of the 600,000 legitimate faces of Torah. As is the case on other issues, the Jewish tradition promotes a surprisingly open and pluralistic notion of biblical truth.

What is the value of Torah for our lives? Can an inherited ancient tradition such as the Torah speak to us today? The Torah is the one continuous element in all of Jewish civilization that has united Jews of different beliefs and perspectives. It is the meeting ground where Jews of all persuasions can find their common history, ancestry, beliefs, and sacred myths. As the story of the Jewish people—its heroes and villains, their strengths and weaknesses—it records the epic of the chosen people as a people seeking to create a sacred life in the world. The Torah defines the role models for Jewish living from Abraham, God's devoted servant, to Moses, the great leader whose own impatience and anger limit his effectiveness. The Torah presents the problems of a community struggling to define itself while dealing with internal conflicts and threats from without. It defines the meaning of right and wrong and establishes universal criteria for a just society and the proper treatment of society's less fortunate members. The Torah establishes the ties to land and language that persist despite the passage of three thousand years.

The Torah is not a static icon but a dynamic and malleable text which reveals different insights each time we look into it. It is there to meet us at whatever level we reach it. It can be read as a book of ancient law and lore or as a timeless expression of the human condition. The stories it narrates demonstrate that character determines destiny and that we are ultimately responsible for the direction of our lives. The Torah's insights into human character and family relationships provide a mirror in which we see our own lives reflected. The narrative shows that the effort to be human requires us to examine the connection between our character and our actions. Our heroes appear as imperfect human beings driven by the same drives and impulses we wrestle with. We take courage in the fact that Abraham, Isaac, Jacob, Joseph, and Moses struggled with the same issues in their lives as we do in ours.

The Torah is also a partner that was there for our ancestors and offered them a course and a direction in their lives. How does one construct a set of principles and guidelines by which to live? The Torah offers the same message to every generation: We were once a slave people living in the land of Egypt. God chose us and we accepted His call to live as moral people and as a holy nation. Each generation is called to observe the Sabbath in remembrance of creation, to commemorate Passover and the Exodus from slavery, to seek righteousness by creating a just society that extends equal protection to men, women, and children, whatever their religion and station in life.

There is no one right interpretation but only the interpretation that is right for each one of us. There are many traditional and nontraditional explanations to help us understand Torah. Judaism encourages us to see ourselves as if we actually stood at Sinai and heard the commanding message of God. There is a tradition that encourages each Jew to write his own copy of the Torah scroll during his lifetime. This can be interpreted to mean that we must each make the Torah our own through finding our own connection with it. It is not the possession of heaven, the rabbis, or scholars. Torah is the inheritance of each and every Israelite and each one of us must relate to it in our own way. We can go further, as the Hasidim did, and say that we must each become Torah by listening to the inner voice, the voice of God, which continues to reveal itself to us just as it did to our ancestors at Sinai.

6

The Mitzvot

The revelation of Torah, regardless of how we understand it, comes from God. This extraordinary encounter of the Israelites in the Sinai wilderness with the presence of God provides an important clue about the unknowable and invisible God: the way that we live matters to God.

Mitzvot are laws in a wider sense than most secular legislation. The *mitzvot* are laws based on God's commandments and the practices developed by our sages specifically in order to implement God's will. Some of the *mitzvot* are based on rational explanations, some are based on spiritual considerations, and some seem completely incomprehensible to us. Nevertheless, *mitzvot* characterize the Jewish way of life in which actions and behavior are prescribed.

The covenantal relationship between the individual, the community, and God is predicated on the performance of the *mitzvot*. Each *mitzvah* also affords us the opportunity to immerse ourselves in the transcendent experience in which it originated. Whereas Christianity sometimes teaches that salvation is achieved through faith, Judaism believes that everything depends on our actions—the performance of the *mitzvot*. The observance of the *mitzvot* also gives expression to the sacred myths and beliefs of Judaism. The notion of being commanded by God is at the very heart and soul of those sacred myths and beliefs of Judaism. The idea that Jews have special obligations means that Jews express their sacred myths in concrete actions.

A *mitzvah* means a "command," not a good deed, even though all *mitzvot* are considered good deeds. The *mitzvot* are highly specific actions that are seen as a distinctively Jewish form of behavior. The *mitzvot* affirm the belief that God created the world and everything within it. We are, therefore, commanded to remember God as creator of the universe. Jews have composed blessings that can be said when we see a rainbow, a flash of lightning, the beauty of nature, and the first blossoms of spring. There are blessings we say when we break bread, eat, or drink—all of which remind us of the underlying miracle of creation.

When creation was complete, God rested. In commemoration of the creation, a Jew observes the Sabbath each week. It is not a day of rest for the sake of relaxation but a weekly reminder that we are commanded to imitate God in all our actions. Therefore, we are expected to avoid all those actions that were part of creation, including igniting fire, creating something new, or building.

The *mitzvot* express the belief that God chose the Jewish people from among all the nations of the earth and led them from slavery to the Promised Land. In remembrance of the Exodus from Egypt, we are commanded to respect others and treat them with the dignity and rights that God accorded us. We are reminded that because we were once slaves in Egypt, we have moral responsibilities to others that demand a commitment to the ideals of freedom and justice. In recognition of the Torah as the embodiment of God's teachings, Judaism developed laws governing the proper treatment of society's vulnerable classes, such as women, workers, and the poor.

There is only one, true God, and to attribute ultimate value to anything else is regarded as idolatry. The rituals of Judaism draw our attention to the supremacy of God. Thus, we celebrate God as the sole ruler of the world on Rosh Hashanah and Yom Kippur, and commemorate the Exodus from Egypt on Passover, the giving of the Torah on Shavuot, and God's care during the wandering in the Sinai wilderness on Sukkot.

HALAKHAH: THE JEWISH PATH

Jewish law is called Halakhah, which means the "path" or the "way." Halakhah is the system of Jewish behavior codified as religious law. It has its origins in the Torah but is the product of rabbinic Judaism. It covers religious behavior, such as the observance of the Sabbath and festivals, and directs the normative practices for daily prayer—what to say, when to pray, and the proper ways to pray. It prescribes the moral conduct we are required to follow in relation to other people. It establishes the laws pertaining to family and community life, including business, political conflict, and war, down to the smallest details. It is the comprehensive system of regulated Jewish behavior.

The word "Halakhah" is Aramaic, the language spoken by Jews in the first centuries of the Common Era, and is derived from the use of the Hebrew verb "to go" (*lalekhet*). The rabbis of the Talmud explained that Moses was told by God to "make known to the people *the way they are to go* (Exodus 18:20).[1] One Jewish legal scholar defined Halakhah as "something which came from ancient days and will last to the end of time, something according to which Israel goes."[2] The method for deciding what exactly is the Halakhah is based on the Torah. The Book of Deuteronomy imposes upon Israel the duty to establish a court of seventy jurists—made up of priests, Levites, and a chief judge—to create new laws not expressly given in Torah for applications that were not anticipated. In ancient times, Jewish courts in Israel decided matters of law for the entire Jewish community. The local courts in each major town were called *bet din* (house of judgment) and the supreme or district courts were called Sanhedrin. The Sanhedrin, which met during the First and Second Jerusalem Temples, were composed of seventy-one judges.

Only rarely in ancient Jewish history did sects appear that did not accept the central authority of the Jerusalem court. The two most important were the Samaritans, who accepted only the authority of Torah but not the Oral Torah, and the Dead Sea community sectarians. The Samaritans were probably descendants of the ancient tribe of Joseph's sons, Ephraim and Menasseh, who continued a biblical Israelite religion independent of rabbinic Judaism within northern Israel. In the eighth century C.E., the Karaite sect appeared in Babylonia (Iraq) and spread throughout the Mediterranean, Ukraine, Russia, and the Baltics. Karaites followed the biblical religion of Israel and were scrupulously devoted to the study of the Hebrew Bible but did not accept most of the rabbinic tradition.

Throughout the Middle Ages, Jewish communities created their own semiautonomous self-governments while living under Christian and Muslim rule. They followed the regulations of the ruling powers but created their own political structures within their separate society. The Halakhah served as the instrument of self-government, and legal matters were decided by the rabbis, who served as judges. The Halakhah provided much more than religious guidance because it reached into every aspect of Jewish communal life, including commerce, taxation, and relations with non-Jews.

THE 613 *MITZVOT*

The individual practices, customs, and rituals that constitute Halakhah are made up of 613 individual *mitzvot*. These specific *mitzvot* are explained in the great collections of Jewish law. The first collection of Jewish law was the Mishnah, compiled in Israel at the end of the second century C.E. by Judah Ha-Nasi. The Mishnah was studied by later rabbis, who added their own interpretations, called the Gemara, which together with the Mishnah made up the multivolume work called the Babylonian Talmud, completed around 500 C.E. In the twelfth century, Maimonides organized all of talmudic and subsequent law into a fourteen-volume encyclopedia of Jewish law called *Mishneh Torah*. In the sixteenth century, Joseph Karo further explained the *mitzvot* in his code of Jewish law, the *Shulhan Arukh,* which, along with the commentary of Rabbi Moses Isserles of Cracow, has since become the accepted guide to Jewish practice.

Where did the number 613 come from? It is an ideal number which conveys the idea that the *mitzvot* are comprehensive rather than strictly limited in number. Tradition maintains that the 613 commandments consist of 365 prohibitions and 248 positive commandments.[3] The Talmud explains that the number 365 corresponds to the days of the year and 248 corresponds to the parts of the human anatomy. This embellishment is meant to convey the idea that the *mitzvot* include every area of human behavior (i.e., 248) that can occur within time (i.e., 365).

The categories of Halakhah are complex and varied. Biblical law distinguishes between *hukkim* (statutes) and *mishpatim* (ordinances). *Hukkim* are laws or rituals that appear to be inexplicable, such as the prohibition against eating pork, whose intention is not self-evident. *Mishpatim* are laws—such as the prohibition against murder, robbery, incest, and idolatry—that are self-evident and essential for the proper conduct of individual and social life.

The rabbis of the talmudic era distinguished between laws deriving directly from Torah (*de-orayta*) and those deriving from rabbinic legislation based on interpreting Torah (*de-rabbanan*).[4] An example of a *mitzvah mi-de-orayta* is the set of rituals governing the observance of the Sabbath, which comes from the Torah. Examples of a *mitzvah mi-de-rabbanan* include the use of candles on the Sabbath and festivals and the celebration of Hanukkah, neither of which is mentioned in the Torah. The rabbinic sages also differentiated between positive commandments (*mitzvot aseh*) and prohibitions (*mitzvot lo taaseh*)—do's and don'ts—and between laws governing relations between man and God (*mitzvot bein adam la-makom*) and laws governing relations between human beings (*mitzvot bein adam le-chavero*). Another medieval tradition distinguishes between obligations of the limbs (*chovot ha-aivarim*) and obligations of the heart (*chovot ha-levavot*). The obligations of the limbs are those *mitzvot* that require specific action and physical deeds, while obligations of the heart are those spiritual and intellectual attitudes and beliefs that are not related to physical expression.

Custom (*minhag*) also played a significant role in Halakhah. Local or regional customs or folk practices were often followed at particular times and places, and achieved the status of law. One of the earliest examples is the custom of bundling the lulav (palm branch) and etrog (citron) on the holiday of Sukkot in commemoration of the fall harvest.

Classical rabbinic literature also distinguishes between *mitzvot* that are obligatory for both men and women and those obligatory for men only. According to traditional Halakhah, men become liable for religious obligations at the age of thirteen and women, in a limited sense, at the age of twelve. Both men and women are required to observe the negative commandments beginning at legal age. Men are obligated to perform all the positive commandments. Women are obligated to follow the positive commandments but are exempt from observing those that are time-limited or related to specific seasons, such as building a *sukkah* (booth) on Sukkot.[5] They are, however, obligated to follow certain time- or seasonally defined commandments, such as observing the Sabbath, Passover, Hanukkah, and Purim. Women are traditionally exempt from studying Torah.

Halakhah represents the culmination of oral traditions and legal practices of Jews living in the Land of Israel and Babylonia. The *mitzvot* were generally agreed-upon practices that did not require written codification until after the destruction of the Second Temple in 70 C.E. The destruction of the primary center of Jewish activity shifted the emphasis on practice from the Temple, which included sacrifices and tithes, to new centers of religious activity, including the home, prayer house, and study house. The domestication of Jewish observance after the destruction of the Temple turned every head of household into a priest, every table into an altar, and every meal into a ritual sacrifice.[6] The focus shifted from the priesthood to the rabbinate, which stressed public teaching, learning, and communal worship in institutions that came to be known as the prayer house (*bet kenesset*) and study house (*bet midrash*).

The destruction of the Temple in 70 C.E. resulted in the dispersion of Jews from the Land of Israel to other parts of the Roman Empire. The rabbis of the time perceived that the destruction and dispersion threatened the integrity and unity of Jewish life. It was no longer sufficient to rely on oral traditions and generally accepted practice. There were also deep divisions within the Jewish community about how to proceed following the great catastrophe. Some groups had determined to resist the Roman occupation by any means necessary, including armed revolt. Others sought to escape occupied Jerusalem and establish alternative communities in the Judean Desert. Still others were drawn to the sects of Jewish Christians who believed that salvation came from within rather than through worldly activity.

In the wake of the destruction, the followers of the rabbinic leader Yohanan ben Zakkai emphasized the need to establish a set of Jewish norms that would preserve the fragile traditions of the past and provide a foundation for future generations. Yohanan ben Zakkai founded a community in Yavneh, a town on the Mediterranean seacoast, where his followers could continue to teach their traditions. He was afraid that the upheavals of the war with Rome would continue and that it would someday be impossible for Jews to know what practices to follow. He and his followers began to codify their practices, going back to the rulings of their predecessors Shammai and Hillel, the leading sages of the early rabbinic period:

> When the sages entered the vineyard at Yavneh, they said: "A time will come when a man will seek a Torah teaching and will not find it, a ruling of the scribes and will not find it. . . so that one precept of the Torah will not be like another." Hence, they declared: "Let us begin with Shammai and Hillel."[7]

Their efforts eventually resulted in the editing of the Mishnah around 200 C.E. by Judah Ha-Nasi, who addressed the need to preserve and transmit the traditions of Yavneh. Throughout the previous two centuries, the Halakhah had been memorized and recited by teachers and students. The ability to recite halakhot according to the name of the sage whose ruling it was, was considered a great skill. Judah Ha-Nasi, however, decided that the time had come to commit the halakhic traditions to writing. This compilation was organized into six broad thematic categories and known as the Mishnah.

The process of Halakhah evolved beyond recitation to the creative exploration of the application of Halakhah to new situations. As the Jewish community living in the Babylonian Diaspora grew, Jewish legal scholars established academies (yeshivot) in which they explored the traditions of the Mishnah, debated matters of law, and engaged in the process of searching out the meanings of the Torah text and their application to real-life problems. The discussions based on Mishnah ranged far afield. These discussions took place in many different yeshivot in Israel and the Babylonian Diaspora from 200 through 500 C.E. Beginning in the sixth century, different groups of sages in Israel and Babylonia began to transcribe and edit the accounts of the halakhic discussions in the various rabbinic academies. The commentaries on each section of

Mishnah were called Gemara. The Mishnah and Gemara when edited together were called the Talmud, the twenty-volume compilation of rabbinic discussions that took place in the yeshivot. Each of the two major centers of Jewish life produced its own Talmud, reflecting the unique contributions and preoccupations of its milieu. The Babylonian Talmud, however, is regarded as the authoritative compendium of Jewish law and lore over the Jerusalem Talmud.

In addition, separate collections of rabbinic interpretations and homilies on selected books of the Bible began to appear in the first century. These collections, known as Midrash, were primarily biblical commentaries but also included halakhot derived specifically from biblical passages. Midrash became a valuable medium for expressing Jewish law and belief, and was directed primarily at educating the Jewish public. Midrash is a genre of literature as well as the name of many collections of interpretations of particular books of the Bible.

There was a healthy difference of belief among the rabbinic sages concerning the very purpose of Halakhah. One approach maintained that the law was a gift from God which provided humanity with the opportunity to fulfill God's expectation. More than God needed obedience, Israel needed the law to achieve merit and find favor with God. Rather than seeing Halakhah as a burden, the rabbis of the Mishnah saw it as an opportunity to fulfill their convenantal responsibilities: "Rabbi Hananyah ben Aqashya said: The Holy One, Blessed be He, wished to give merit to Israel, therefore He multiplied for them law and commandments."[8]

The followers of Rabbi Akiva saw the *mitzvot* as the unfathomable expression of God's will. The *mitzvot* cannot be understood rationally but only as a mystery whose true reason is known to God. In the legend of Moses appearing in Rabbi Akiva's yeshivah cited earlier (p. 143), Moses appears dumbfounded at the difference between the practices as he knew them directly from God's instructions and those of Akiva's time thirteen centuries later. It also portrays Moses as being reassured when Akiva announces that all the new, unfamiliar halakhot are actually from Moses' time. Why then is Moses confounded? The passage implies that while Moses transmitted God's law at Sinai, many detailed laws had since been communicated through the generations and were equally valid. "It is a law of Moses from Sinai" means that the *mitzvah* was implicit in the Torah and later generations made it explicit.

Another view saw the *mitzvot* as a test of human submission to God's will. Although Halakhah consists of innumerable detailed practices, it is not the details that matter. The important thing is that the myriad of laws, arbitrary as they might be, inculcate a spirit of obedience and connectedness with God in the individual: "Rav said: The precepts were given only for the purpose of trying[9] people thereby. For what difference does it make to the Holy One, Blessed be He, whether one slaughters [an animal] at the neck or the nape? This proves that the purpose is to try mankind."[10]

The rabbis believed that while the *mitzvot* were incumbent upon the Jews, non-Jews were obliged to follow certain laws as well. Rabbinic legend held that these laws were transmitted to the descendants of biblical Noah and that their fulfillment would result in non-Jews qualifying to achieve immortality in the afterlife.[11]

MAIMONIDES' VIEWS ON LAW AND SPIRITUALITY

Moses Maimonides is recognized as one of the supreme halakhic authorities of all time. His *Mishneh Torah* serves as the definitive code of Jewish law. He was scrupulous in his own personal religious observance and was respected as the rabbinic leader of the Egyptian Jewish community in the twelfth century. He held that the observance of all the *mitzvot* was indispensable as the outward expression of what Jews believe and necessary as the means of preserving the moral fiber of the Jewish community. He considered the Halakhah equally valid for the Jewish philosopher and the ordinary Jewish individual. He did believe, however, that Halakhah was not the only way in which a Jew was obligated to serve God. In fact, he maintained that personal spirituality in addition to faithful practice of the law constituted the proper life for a Jew. Maimonides' understanding of spirituality was highly intellectual, and he saw Jewish belief as the rational, scientific knowledge of philosophy. Although we understand spirituality today differently from Maimonides, his view that observance without spirituality is empty is central to understanding Judaism.

Maimonides presented a model of the ideal Jew that presupposed living according to traditional Jewish law but suggested that the intellectual life of an observant Jew should be equally demanding. He composed a parable in which he illustrated his own view of the ideal among various types of Jews:

> The ruler is in his palace and all his subjects are partly within the city and partly outside the city. Of those who are within the city, some have turned their backs upon the ruler's habitation, their faces being turned another way. Others seeks to reach the ruler's habitation, turn toward it, and desire to enter it and to stand before him but up to now they have not yet seen the wall of the habitation. Some of those who seek to reach it have come up to the habitation and walk around it searching for its gate. Some of them have entered the gate and walk about in the ante-chambers. Some of them have entered the inner court of the habitation and have come to be with the king, in one and the same place with him, namely, in the ruler's habitation. But their having come into the inner part of the habitation does not mean that they see the ruler or speak to him. For after their coming into the inner part of the habitation, it is indispensable that they should make another effort; then they will be in the presence of the ruler, see him from afar or from nearby, or hear the ruler's speech or speak to him.[12]

Maimonides' parable identified seven categories of people: (1) those outside the city, (2) those who are within the city but facing away from the king, (3) those who are within the city but do not see the palace, (4) those who are near the palace searching for its gate, (5) those who have entered the gate and are walking within the outer rooms, (6) those who are with the king in his inner chamber but who do not see him or speak with him, (7) and those who make another effort in his presence to establish contact with him. Of those who make the additional effort, there are those who see the king and those who hear or speak with him.

Clearly the king of the parable is God and the categories of subjects represent various types of people. Maimonides explained that those who are outside the city are non-Jews who have no religion or cogent system of belief. In his view, they can hardly be considered human. Those who are within the city but are facing away from the king are followers of various false religions and philosophic systems. They are even worse than the first, since the more they persist in believing in their false views, the further from the truth they stray.

Those who are within the city but do not see the palace are, according to Maimonides, "the multitude of the adherents of Torah," whom he identifies as "the ignoramuses [*ammei ha-aretz*] who observe the commandments." This refers to the simple Jew who follows the commandments blindly without seeking to understand why. Such an identification disparages the simple, traditional observant Jew as someone who is included within the kingdom but who does not see the king at all. This is all the more striking because Maimonides was himself the author of the *Mishneh Torah,* the magisterial code of Jewish law—the very law they were at least observing. This portrait of the simple Jew led to considerable opposition to Maimonides and his teaching. Nevertheless, although Maimonides did not place a high value on this type of Jew, he did not dismiss the importance of basic Jewish observance of the *mitzvot.*

Maimonides identified those who are walking around the palace searching for its gate with the halakhic authorities who support traditional Jewish belief and are concerned with determining the proper laws but who do not think philosophically about religious belief. They are the Talmudists, who determine Jewish behavior but do not analyze Jewish beliefs. They also include those who have studied mathematics and logic, which Maimonides regarded as elementary fields of knowledge preliminary to the study of philosophy.

There are also those who are with the king in his inner chamber but do not see him or speak with him. These are the natural scientists, who study the physical world and have come to understand that God is the cause of the world but who do not know God on any deeper level. It is striking that Maimonides placed scientists on a higher level than the talmudic authorities by saying that they were closer to God. This aroused further opposition to him.

Those who make another effort in his presence to establish contact with the king are the philosophers, who have achieved knowledge of God through proofs for existence and understanding of God's essence. This is the rank, he says, of the philosopher-scientists. These philosophers include those who devote their entire life to understanding the true nature of God. Even greater than the rank of the philosopher is the rank of the prophet. A prophet, according to Maimonides, is an individual whose good moral habits cultivate and strengthen his intellectual capabilities and lead him to develop a sophisticated intellectual understanding of Jewish belief. But, unlike the philosopher—whose progress ends with an intellectual system of belief—the prophet goes further. The prophet receives an illumination from God, who reveals the truth to him not in the systematic language of philosophy but in the deeper, intuitive certainty of heart-knowledge. The philosopher reaches truth through thinking, while the prophet reaches beyond this and thinks the same thoughts God is thinking. The prophet does not become God, but his mind thinks God's thoughts. Prophets are philosophers who have an even deeper relationship with God through hearing, seeing, or speaking with Him.

Maimonides thus ranks Jewish virtue in ascending order: the observant Jew, the Talmudist, the philosopher, and, ultimately, the prophet. The philosopher follows philosophy as far as it can take him. Beyond that point, God takes over and communicates the truth directly to the prophet/philosopher. While Maimonides viewed Halakhah as fundamental, he believed that philosophy was a more certain path to knowledge of God. He also promoted the pursuit of wisdom through a dual curriculum of Jewish and secular knowledge in which truth was sought wherever it might be found. This medieval ideal of the humanistic Jewish intellectual was a person open to the currents of many ideas. The typical image of the medieval rabbinic Jew as a cloistered scholar devoted to the study of Torah and Talmud and the practice of Judaism was not the only reality.

JEWISH LAW AND THE CHALLENGE
OF MODERNITY

A debate over the value of law and ritual has divided modern Jewry since the beginning of the nineteenth century. Many nineteenth-century Jews were influenced by the German philosopher Immanuel Kant, who taught that human reason could free enlightened people from the shackles of external authority. Humans possess an autonomous sense of morality, which they arrive at through reason rather than through externally imposed laws. The exercise of this autonomous human sense through ethical action leads to true happiness. God, for Kant, is what humanity has called the force behind the moral imperative. God, he says, has nothing to do with the moral sense because it is innate within human reason rather than imposed from without.

Kant saw the laws of formal religious movements as externally imposed rather than autonomous and self-evident. Religious ritual and law are regarded as irrelevant human inventions and outward obedience to authority. Contemporary Jewish followers of Kant argued that the essence of Judaism is ethics, not ritual or law. Many Jewish thinkers were troubled and even embarrassed by the notion that God would reveal a law containing mere prescriptions for ritual. They were more accepting of the idea that God revealed a law consisting of ethical truths. This left many Jewish intellectuals in the position of believing in the ethical portions of Torah but ignoring the ritual elements. Ever since Kant, religious law has been seen as inferior to the rules by which we choose to lead our own lives. This has been a modern challenge to the Halakhah and to the idea that Jewish law is worthwhile.

The challenge was not only philosophical but also an outgrowth of the changing political situation Jews faced in western Europe. Beginning in France after the Revolution, Jews were given their political and civil rights within the emerging states of Europe. The Emancipation of the Jews, as this empowerment was known, proceeded sporadically and often followed bitter public debates about the civic worthiness of the Jews. The opponents of Emancipation argued that Halakhah—especially the dietary laws and the prohibition against intermarriage—the sense of Jewish peoplehood, the belief in the Messiah, and the devotion to the Land of Israel were indications that the Jews formed a "state within a state" and could not be trusted to be loyal citizens. The price of admission into modern European societies was the willingness on the part of the Jewish people to abandon their distinctive forms of separateness, to surrender their form of communal self-government, and to restrict Judaism to what could be practiced at home and in the synagogue. The rabbis who were once communal leaders and jurists became preachers and ministers to the specifically religious needs of their congregants. Halakhah was restricted to a private matter, not the comprehensive system of Jewish self-government. This posed a new challenge to the individual and the community: how to reconcile a Jewish way of life with the opportunities of living fully within the secular society.

How was this challenged addressed? In the nineteenth and twentieth centuries, as Jews created new forms of religious expression, the desire to preserve the autonomy of human reason continued to undermine the authority of Halakhah. Early Reform Jews rejected the Halakhah as a body of law, abolishing the dietary laws and many other rituals and observances. They emphasized instead the prophetic ideals of biblical Judaism—justice, equality, ethics—as the essence of Judaism. The prophetic ideals were, to them, the unadulterated heart of Judaism and, freed from the overlay of rabbinic legalism, precisely what established common ground between Jews and non-Jews. They were also the values they invoked in their claims to equal rights as Jews within modern societies.

In the last two decades the pendulum has begun to swing in the direction of incorporating *mitzvot* into Reform practice on a selective basis. This has occurred because of two factors. First, Reform Judaism has recognized the importance of ritual as an expression of personal values and meaning. Second, Reform has concluded that Judaism without specific Jewish ritual cannot easily be conveyed from one generation to the next as a living force in people's lives.

Modern Orthodoxy also came into being in the modern period. Prior to the modern era, there was no term for Orthodoxy: Jews throughout the world were bound by a common dedication to Halakhah despite ethnic differences in practice, such as between the Sephardim and Ashkenazim. Samson Raphael Hirsch, the German leader of the modern Orthodox movement, stressed the compatibility between Judaism and modernity. One could be a halakhic Jew and still participate in modern society through business, commerce, culture, and social interaction. This came to be known as *Torah im derech eretz* (Torah and the way of the land), which means Orthodox practice alongside participation in modern non-Jewish society. In reality, this often meant that Jewish observance was restricted to the privacy of the home and synagogue, while in public one showed no traces of Jewish practice.

Conservative Judaism emerged as another response to the challenge of modernity, one that sought to find a middle ground between Orthodoxy and Reform. It saw the Halakhah as evolving rather than as a static, unchanging entity. It also saw Judaism as having experienced profound historical changes in the past in response to changing circumstances. Conservative Jews believed, however, that tradition and continuity were important values which tempered and limited the extent of permissible change. They promoted the notion that Judaism and the Halakhah should be modernized but that only rabbinic authorities committed to the Halakhah could determine those changes.

Conservative Judaism distinguishes its version of Judaism as a separate and distinct way that differs from any other formulation. The ideal human being, according to Conservative Judaism, is characterized by three attributes. First, he embraces all human and Jewish concerns as if they are part of the same all-encompassing identity. The Conservative ideal is equally predisposed to Judaism and to the wider sphere of human concerns; it does not perceive any contradiction between them. In a modification of Franz Rosenzweig's dictum, this is expressed in the credo "Nothing human or Jewish is alien to me." That human concerns should be refracted through the prism of one's own Jewishness is offered by Conservative Judaism as another variation on this approach. Within a scheme of an all-emcompassing Jewishness, human concerns are Jewish concerns. The ideal person is a traditionally observant Jew whose values are shaped by Jewish faith, one who follows the dietary laws of *kashrut* and observes the Sabbath and holidays. He maintains a Jewish ambiance in the home with Jewish books, art, music, and ritual objects. He creates a Jewish family whose behavior is governed by the ethical insights of Judaism.[13] Second, the ideal Conservative Jew is a learning Jew who studies Hebrew, delves into the classics of Jewish literature, and is engaged in thoughtful approaches to contemporary Jewish ideas and events. Jewish learning should be a lifelong pursuit, part of an effort to integrate Jewish and general knowledge. Third, the ideal Conservative Jew is always striving to be a more knowledgeable and observant Jew and to be open to deepening his Jewish experience.[14]

Conservatism upholds Halakhah as the binding force of Judaism even as Halakhah is subject to change. The criterion for change, however, is not human autonomy but religious authority: "*Halakhah* is the historical expression of what the Jewish people believe is God's will. *Halakhah* is also a means of preserving the Jewish people, a moral code, and the vehicle by which man and God show their love for each other. *Halakhah,* when taken together with *aggadah,* history, language and culture, make up Jewish identity. . . . *Halakhah* can change with changes in sensibility but only rabbinic leaders can authorize changes in law."[15] For example, the movement now permits driving to synagogue on the Sabbath as a measure to accommodate the suburbanization of the Jewish community and out of a desire not to disenfranchise the vast majority of its membership. Most Conservative congregations have supported the participation of women in the ritual life of the synagogue as a necessary consequence of changes in the values of society. These changes have not all been implemented harmoniously, and a small but vocal segment of the leadership of the Conservative movement has dissented from what it sees as excessive liberalization in Conservative practice.

Reconstructionism, the only new Jewish denomination to originate in America, emerged as the vision of Mordecai Kaplan. Judaism, according to Kaplan, is more than religion, although religion plays an important role in Judaism. Judaism is a civilization that encompasses religion, history, social organization, standards of conduct, nationhood, ethics, spiritual ideals, language, literature, and the arts. Kaplan stressed the importance of participating in the life of the Jewish community, apart from religious practice and celebration, as a distinctive feature of Judaism. He contributed to the beginning of the Jewish center movement in North America which he hoped would encompass a synagogue, community center, and school. He believed that the Jewish people, not God or Torah, were the creators of Judaism. He taught that loyalty to Judaism should be measured by participation in Jewish life, not by the extent of traditional practice.

Kaplan saw the *mitzvot* as Jewish "folkways." Revelation was the way in which the biblical community understood its own experience. But the Jewish folkways of that community—the *mitzvot*—have no inherent validity for another generation. Since God's revelation is, for Kaplan, a metaphor for discovery and creativity arising out of the natural religious impulse, modern creativity has equal weight and authority. The freely chosen consensus of the community determines the folkways of contemporary Jews.

Is it possible to preserve the Jewish people without practicing traditional Jewish observances today? According to Kaplan, God is not the transcendent being of earlier Jewish theology. Kaplan's God is real insofar as He is immanent and present within humanity and society. He is not a supernatural being but rather the apotheosis of human creativity. Therefore, God's commanding law is not God's revelation but rather the human perception since antiquity of what is right action. However, within Kaplan's nonsupernatural Judaism, there is no need for *mitzvot* unless they serve the purpose of maintaining Jewish survival today: "Rejecting the assumption that the Jewish people must be maintained so that their religion may live, Reconstructionism declares—The Jewish religion must be maintained so that the Jewish people may live."[16]

While there is general agreement among the various denominations within contemporary Judaism that there are specific required religious actions, Jews disagree on what they are and whether the Halakhah itself is binding or voluntary. It is difficult to generalize, but Orthodox Jews generally agree that the totality of the Halakhah is obligatory, while non-Orthodox Jews believe that selective observance is a matter of personal choice. Orthodox Jews accept Halakhah—both the Written and Oral Torah—as a binding requirement for them. Moreover, they regard Orthodox rabbis as the only legitimate authorities for deciding matters of Halakhah and turn to them for halakhic guidance on a wide range of issues in their personal, professional, and communal lives.

There are, nevertheless, a number of subdivisions within the Orthodox community. At its most extreme, there are the fundamentalist ultra-Orthodox groups of Hasidim (pietists and mystics) and Haredim (fundamentalists), which share a rejection of the secular world in favor of Jewish insularity and life within the "four walls of Halakhah." There are many differences between the Hasidim and Haredim, including deep divisions on religious and political issues. For example, Haredim tend not to recognize the existence of the secular State of Israel, while the largest groups of Hasidim do. Hasidim follow the mystical teachings of their masters even though they differ little in formal practice from the Haredim. Modern Orthodoxy, of which Yeshiva University in New York City serves as the institutional center, subscribes to the notion that "Torah-true Judaism" and a modern scientific outlook are compatible.

This group believes both in the inviolability of Halakhah and in the idea that Halakhah need not be an obstacle to full participation and integration into the mainstream of society, particularly in the workplace. While it does not recognize the validity of non-Orthodox Judaism, Orthodoxy is concerned primarily with promoting the values of learning and observance among its own followers.

A CASE STUDY: THE JEWISH DIETARY LAWS

The Jewish belief in spirituality through Halakhah can best be seen in a concrete example rather than through abstract formulations. The dietary practices are one of the best known and least understood areas of Jewish law. The basic details of the laws that came to be known as *kashrut* are explained in many passages in the Bible.

In the early sections of Genesis, God establishes vegetarianism as the norm for human dietary consumption (1:29). Yet in the account of Noah and the Flood, He distinguishes between clean and unclean animals, and indicates that the clean animals are permitted for human consumption (7:2 and 9:3). Genesis 32:33 contains the prohibition against eating the sciatic nerve as a result of Jacob's wrestling with the angel. The actual detailed dietary laws are found in Leviticus 11:2–47 and 7:23–27 and Deuteronomy 14:4–21. The only explicit reasons given there for the specific list of permitted and prohibited foods are that they lead to holiness: "For I the Lord am your God: you shall sanctify yourselves and be holy, for I am holy. You shall not make yourselves unclean through any swarming thing that moves upon the earth" (Leviticus 11:44). This enigmatic statement has engendered many attempts to provide better explanations in order to identify the spiritual component in Halakhah.

Based on this biblical passage, the Jewish dietary laws—a series of halakhic practices known as *kashrut* (prepared)—have developed. They encompass an elaborate list of prohibited foods including, but not limited to, pork products (ham, bacon), rabbits, insects, reptiles, rodents, some seafood (clams, shrimp, lobster, scallops), and predator birds (eagles, vultures, hawks). The laws identify the permitted foods: animals, such as cows, with split hoofs that chew the cud; fowl (chicken, turkey); and fish with fins and scales. Animals selected for food must be in good health and have to be slaughtered with a knife at the neck in a particular way that avoids pain to the animal. The blood has to be drained and the meat soaked and salted to remove the blood. The meat can be purchased only in a kosher butcher store. Meat products and dairy products cannot be eaten at the same meal, and there is a required waiting period between eating the two. Separate dishes, cooking and eating utensils, and often separate sinks are maintained for preparation and consumption of meat and dairy food.

Food has to be inspected at every stage of the process by a *mashgiach* (kosher supervisor) to assure that everything is being done according to Halakhah. Packaged goods, which often contain many ingredients, are inspected and certified as kosher by several local and national Orthodox rabbinic organizations. Many kosher-observant Jews will purchase only certified products. Vegetables are the only exception to the restriction on purchasing certified kosher foods. Many Orthodox Jews will only eat out in kosher restaurants, while other kosher-observant Jews will eat in regular restaurants but order only dairy, fish, or uncooked items. There are many other kosher rules that go into great detail about Jewish food rituals.

According to the Talmud, "Eating swine is [one of the laws] about which you are not permitted to speculate."[17] *Kashrut* was regarded as one of the *hukkim,* that is, one of the biblical laws that are not rationally explicable. God decreed them to be, and that is all. Throughout history, however, Jewish thinkers have sought reasons for these commandments. The first-century Egyptian-Jewish *Letter of Aristeas* shows an early attempt to explain the dietary laws as permitting only "gentle" animals and prohibiting predatory ones, such as vultures, in order to promote human righteousness: "Through these creatures then, by calling them unclean, He set up a symbol that those for whom the legislation was drawn up must practice righteousness in spirit and oppress no one, trusting in their own strength, nor rob anyone of anything, but must guide their lives according to justice, just as the gentle creatures among the birds."[18]

The rabbinic tradition also sees the dietary laws as a means of reinforcing the distinctiveness of Israel and their separation from other peoples: " 'I have set you apart from the peoples, that you should be mine' (Leviticus 20:26). Let not a man say:'I do not like the flesh of swine.' On the contrary, he should say: 'I like it but must abstain as the Torah has forbidden it.' "[19]

Maimonides, however, insisted on the rational basis for all *mitzvot.* The reason for the dietary laws, he explained, is self-discipline and regulation of human appetites. The subjugation of desires by the mind is what distinguishes humans from animals. Therefore, the purpose of the dietary laws is to train people in regulating their appetites and cultivating their reason:"These ordinances seek to train us in the mastery of our appetites. They accustom us to restrain both the growth of desire and disposition to consider the pleasure of eating as the goal of man's existence."[20]

Maimonides believed that certain foods used in pagan sacrifices were prohibited to distinguish Judaism from paganism. He added that the dietary laws are medically sound in that they prohibit specific unhealthy foods:

> All the food which the Torah has forbidden us to eat has some bad and damaging effect upon the body. . . . The principal reason why the Torah forbids swine's flesh is to be found in the circumstances that its habits and its food are very dirty and loathsome. . . . Meat boiled in milk is undoubtedly gross food and makes a person feel overfull. I think that most probably it is also prohibited because it is connected with idolatry. Perhaps it was part of the ritual of certain pagan festivals.[21]

Another medieval author, Isaac Arama, believed that there is a spiritual dimension to diet. Certain foods have a detrimental effect on the soul, body, and mind. The Jewish dietary laws are synonymous with correct eating: "The reason behind the dietary prohibitions is not that any harm might be caused to the body, but that these foods defile and pollute the soul and blunt the intellectual powers, thus leading to confused opinions and a lust for perverse and brutish appetites that lead men to destruction."[22]

Samson Raphael Hirsch, the leading Orthodox thinker of the nineteenth century, explained that the connection between the human body and the mind is mediated by food. The fact that the Jewish dietary laws permit vegetarianism without any restrictions suggests that

> just as the human spirit is the instrument which God uses to make Himself known in the world, so the human body is the medium which connects the outside world with the mind of man. . . . Anything which gives the body too much independence or makes it too active in a carnal direction brings it nearer to the animal sphere, thereby robbing it of its primary function, to be the intermediary between the soul of man and the world outside. Bearing in mind this function of the body and also the fact that the physical structure of man is largely influenced by the food he consumes, one might come to the conclusion that vegetable food is the most preferable, as plants are the most passive substance. Indeed we find in Jewish law all vegetables are permitted for food without discrimination.[23]

The religious, intellectual, and spiritual explanations of the dietary laws were rejected by early Reform Judaism. According to the Pittsburgh Platform of 1885, they no longer serve a useful purpose because their observance seems to have no moral, aesthetic, or rational basis other than to segregate the Jews from non-Jews: "We hold that all such Mosaic rabbinical laws as regarding diet. . . originated in ages and under the influence of ideas entirely foreign to our present mental and spiritual state. They fail to impress the modern Jew with a spirit of priestly holiness: Their observance in our days is apt rather to obstruct than to further modern spiritual elevation."[24]

The Conservative approach preserves the traditional observance of the dietary laws but emphasizes a spiritual reason. The dietary laws are valid because they elevate the common act of eating from an animal activity to a transcendent event. They also serve to maintain Jews as a people distinct from all others. Whereas Reform Judaism sees the distinction between Jews and non-Jews to be a reason for eliminating the dietary laws, Conservative Judaism seeks to preserve Jewish distinctiveness as a positive value: "It is a part of Judaism's attempt to hallow the common act of eating which is an aspect of our animal nature. It likewise sets us apart from the nations. Thus it achieves its objective, holiness, in these two ways, both of which are implied in the Hebrew word *kadosh*; inner hallowing and outer separateness."[25]

It is ironic that this explanation, which is largely hortatory and sermonic, should resonate in the variety of food fetishes common today. Many people believe that "you are what you eat," and eating today has become a form of self-expression and, in some cases, self-definition. Different cuisines and individual diets distinguish people and mark their individual styles. Perhaps *kashrut* can best be explained in our times as a form of spirituality through everyday behavior among Jews. The Jewish dietary laws draw our attention to eating as a conscious act and remind us of our relationship to the environment, animals, and the food chain.

The explanations of the dietary laws demonstrate that there is a considerable range of opinion within Judaism about the reasons for these specific practices. The answer often given in the past when people asked the reason for Jewish laws was "*Geschribben*" (It is written), that is to say, laws derive from biblical prescriptions. The actual answers offered within the tradition, however, are far more nuanced and reflective of the changing spiritual concerns of Jews over time. Precisely because the reasons for the dietary laws were not set out, Jews have been able to offer explanations that reflect the spiritual concerns of their own times.

THE SPIRITUAL DIMENSION OF JEWISH LAW

Why is it necessary for a Jew to follow Halakhah or individual *mitzvot* if one is sensitive to the spiritual dimensions in his or her heart? The discussion of the Jewish dietary laws shows that there have been a variety of spiritual explanations for a set of rituals that are, at bottom, inexplicable. Why not choose other actions to express one's spiritual values? Why should one observe practices that may not have the same meaning to us as to previous generations? Spirituality is seen today as an essentially private matter, where the individual is the only one to decide what makes sense. Although every religion concerned with spirituality has its own fixed disciplines, in the West we tend to regard conformity to unvarying regimens as the enemy of individual spirituality. Does this mean that Judaism is contrary to our basic feelings about spirituality?

One answer to this question asserts that spirituality is to be found not in what you feel but in what you do. According to Rabbi Joseph Soloveitchik, the leading contemporary spokesman for Halakhah and modern Orthodoxy, the only real expression of one's deepest convictions is how one acts in the world on a consistent basis. Halakhah is not about enforced conformity, which stifles the individual's autonomy and creativity. Rather, it is within the very realm of Jewish law that the fullest expression of human autonomy and creativity is to be found. Halakhah deals with real-life issues of economics, work, social and family relations, sexual behavior, and personal ethics—every area of life. Halakhic man lives in the real world, facing real existential dilemmas and confronting them through the Halakhah, which strives to make sense out of and apply values to mundane reality. He does not succumb to mystical escapism or retreat into the spiritual refuge of the synagogue for answers to his problems. His Halakhah brings him face to face with realities of life—"the marketplace, the street, the factory, the house, the meeting place, the banquet hall."[26] This reality constitutes the religious life more than does the synagogue. Halakhic man lives his beliefs, convictions, and religion in all his actions.

Soloveitchik identified "halakhic man" as the ideal type of modern religious hero in ways that shaped the very character of American Orthodoxy. Soloveitchik was heir to a tradition of Lithuanian Jewish Talmudism that believed that the raison d'être for Jewish existence was to uncover the will of God—what God expects of us—through Torah learning. Practically, this meant that the life of a Jew should be devoted to Talmud study, for "the world would collapse if, at a given moment, it would be deprived totally of the support provided by Torah learning."[27]

Reform Judaism, at the other extreme, sees the individual as a free agent to decide what obligations in life are worthy of pursuit. These decisions are informed by one's ethical duties and responsibility to maintain the Jewish people. Reform Judaism suggests that the Jewish ideal is to find a balance between "duty and obligation," on the one hand, and "human autonomy," on the other. A Jew is primarily guided by ethical obligations toward Jews and non-Jews, but also by the duties of creating a Jewish home, lifelong Jewish learning, religious observance, and participating in the life of the synagogue and community.[28] Reform Judaism, however, encourages the individual to weigh all claims of duty against the autonomous judgment of human reason and conscience. "Within each area of Jewish observance, Reform Jews are called upon to confront the claims of Jewish tradition, however differently perceived, and to exercise their individual autonomy, choosing and creating on the basis of commitment and knowledge."[29] Reform Judaism believes that each individual has the authority and the ability to make the appropriate choices.

A different view of the *mitzvot* is presented by Franz Rosenzweig, for whom Jewish law is not an externally imposed invention that limits the exercise of human autonomy. Instead, Jewish laws are commandments arising from the relationship between God and human beings which we must personalize if they are to have any meaning for us. The deep experience of the human relationship with God and God's call to humanity lead us to respond by freely accepting God's command.

Rosenzweig represents the generation of young German Jews in the 1920's who sought an authentic spirituality and rediscovered a home in traditional Judaism. He is remembered as a major modern religious philosopher, a Bible translator, and cofounder of the Frankfurt Lehrhaus, a unique institute for adult Jewish learning. Yet Rosenzweig is best known for an episode in his personal biography that has become a modern paradigm for the spiritual return to Judaism. As a young man, he decided that Judaism was a useless and dispensable tradition. This was not a surprising conclusion, given the vacuous modern German Jewish culture with which he was acquainted. In 1913, he decided to convert to Christianity, which he believed offered a more vital spiritual home. He was a genuine seeker who decided to approach conversion to Christianity like the first Christians, moving from Judaism to a new faith. His intention was to attend Orthodox Jewish services on Yom Kippur and then, immediately afterward, to be baptized. However, he was so moved by the intensity and religiosity of the unfamiliar Orthodox service that he experienced a spiritual conversion to Judaism and abandoned his plans for baptism.

From that point on, Rosenzweig devoted his life to understanding Judaism from within. He did not easily fit into any of the traditional denominations or expressions of Jewish life. Although he became increasingly observant and accepted Halakhah, he refused to ally himself with Orthodoxy, which he saw as setting Jews apart from the rest of the world and reducing Judaism to the routine performance of *mitzvot*. To him, Judaism was a spiritual process which one must approach one step at a time with respect and anticipation. Observance of the *mitzvot* was a process of understanding the experience that led to the *mitzvah* before undertaking the regular performance of that act. When someone asked him if he observed a particular *mitzvah,* he answered, "Not yet," indicating that coming to Judaism is a lifelong dynamic process of growth and understanding rather than a static identity. All that is required is the affirmation "Nothing Jewish is alien to me."

Rosenzweig was eager to embrace the experience of Jews from earlier times, who felt themselves commanded by the presence of God to accept the *mitzvot.* The rituals of Judaism are the results of ancestral experiences and encounters with God which are then recorded as laws. They can be best understood by both mementos and opportunities for us to experience our relatedness to God. In other words, *mitzvot* are records of earlier experiences to which Jews aspire.

This position puts a great deal of confidence in the experience of others and a willingness to use *mitzvot* as a stepping stone to place ourselves in the commanding presence of God, as they had. While Rosenzweig believed that he as an individual could in the end accept only those *mitzvot* that gave him a sense of being in personal relationship with the commanding God of Sinai, his close friend and colleague Martin Buber was not willing to rely on the experience of others. For Buber, only the direct experience of the individual counted. Buber sought the same existential relationship with the Eternal Thou as Rosenzweig, but he adopted a more radically personal position.

Buber accepted only his own experience of God, not the authority of tradition and Halakhah. The Halakhah was indeed the result of the sacred experiences of earlier generations, but this did not mean it was binding upon him. Jewish spirituality is not based on past experiences. Each individual must be his own Moses, seeking a direct and unmediated dialogue with God. As we saw in chapter 5, Buber believed that God was not a transcendent being in the heavens but the name given to the deep but real experience of the human self relating to the fullness of another human being. It is not surprising that Buber remained a nonpracticing Jew from a halakhic point of view. For him, it was sufficient to be spiritual in one's own heart.

Abraham Joshua Heschel understood the *mitzvot* in another sense entirely. The deep religious experience of God within the world requires not just an inwardness and spiritual expression but also a concrete manifestation in deeds. For Heschel, the *mitzvot* are the deeds that give outward expression to the inner religious experience. The inner religious experience of Judaism is the "sanctification of time" and the *mitzvot* are the "architecture of time." It is not enough to be spiritual in your own heart, we must be spiritual in the world. The Sabbath, for example, is a "sanctuary in time" in which a Jew turns all his actions, speech, and thought away from the mundane and toward eternity. The *mitzvot* that define the activities permitted and prohibited on the Sabbath do not constitute the essence of the day but are ways that lead us toward holiness. Jewish spirituality is expressed in specific actions that make the Sabbath "a profound conscious harmony of man and the world, a sympathy for all things and a participation in the spirit that unites what is below and what is above."[30] Even more, the Jewish ritual actions lead to genuine spirituality. The difference between Buber and Heschel is that the former seeks a holiness of immanence while the latter seeks a holiness of transcendence. For Buber, true spirituality is reached through personal experience within the world. For Heschel, true spirituality is reached through the *mitzvot* that elevate us above the mundane.

The *mitzvot* are also symbols that are intrinsic to every Jewish community, are part of its distinctiveness and serve to include those who belong to the community and exclude those who do not. Ritual confers identity by articulating the shared values of particular social groups among themselves and from one generation to the next. Some *mitzvot* are behavioral expressions of deeply rooted Jewish myth. For example, the *mitzvah* of circumcision is a symbolic ritual that establishes the connection of a newborn male child to God's covenant with Israel. It reinforces and is reinforced by the sacred myth of Jewish peoplehood, its history and destiny.

Every Jewish religious denomination recognizes that *mitzvot* are the embodiment of Jewish spirituality. They are the concrete actions that express the sacred myths of the Jewish people. The sacred myths have evolved to reflect changing beliefs. A nontraditional Jew might ask: Should not the *mitzvot*, which express the sacred myths, change as well?

Why should we observe practices that may not have the same meaning to us as they did to our ancestors? Why not choose other actions to express our spiritual values?

The best answer to this spiritual challenge was provided by Franz Rosenzweig. Before we can assume that the traditional *mitzvah* is empty of spiritual significance, he held, we should immerse ourselves in it in order to search for the experience that was the living force behind the action in the first place. The spiritual experience of others has value that might not be immediately apparent. Only the actual experience of a *mitzvah* might allow that fundamental spiritual power to emerge. This position suggests that a Jew who seeks the spiritual path within Judaism might begin with an act of immersion in ritual experience: becoming involved in the experience of the Sabbath, Torah learning, the dietary laws, or some other *mitzvah*. The path to Jewish spirituality does not require us to take more than one step at a time.

At the same time, the example of the Jewish dietary laws shows us that traditional *mitzvot* can continually be invested with new spiritual significance. Someone interested in pursuing Jewish spirituality might find it useful to adopt a specific ritual but invest it with his or her own personal meaning. This act of identifying with the traditional behavior of the Jewish people but for different reasons is important for the sake of communal cohesion. If everyone were to pursue his or her own spiritual practices, there would be little left that could be experienced with others. Individual spirituality leaves a legacy only when it finds a home within a community. Private spirituality lived outside of a community leaves few heirs.

Spirituality is both individual and communal. While the sacred myths of Judaism provide meaning to individuals, the *mitzvot* are the way we signify our beliefs within a community. Jewish spirituality is very concrete and emphasizes that our actions must reflect our beliefs. The sacred myth of Judaism expresses the Jewish belief that through observance of the *mitzvot* we can reach beyond ourselves to experience the transcendent or we can bring the transcendent into the everyday, and that we do so individually as well as communally. For this reason, Halakhah, the Jewish path, is the way of the Jewish people.

7

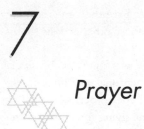

Prayer

What does it mean to reach out to a hidden, invisible God through prayer? If the goal of spiritual life is to achieve and maintain a relationship with the transcendent, prayer is the most spiritual of all human activities. The motivation for prayer lies in our human need to reach beyond ourself. What allows us to actually pray is the conviction that we are able to communicate beyond ourself. Prayer is predicated on the sacred myth that God hears us and cares about us. Prayer is the service of our heart, expressing our deepest aspirations and the hope that we will be heard.

Prayer is a universal and deeply personal impulse which is expressed in many spontaneous ways. In Judaism, prayer is also a *mitzvah* that requires that a Jew pray three times daily according to a fixed liturgy from the Siddur, the Hebrew prayer book, and offer specific blessings at various moments throughout the day. Jews often express their most deeply personal feelings in silent prayer, while public prayers meet the halakhic requirements of Judaism. Judaism strikes a balance between personal spontaneity and public formality in prayer.

Jewish prayer expresses and articulates the sacred myths of Judaism in words that can be understood by all. The reinforcement of what Jews should believe occurs through the regular repetition of the words of the prayers in their original Hebrew or in English translation. If the performance of the *mitzvot* is the spiritual means of achieving transcendence through our behavior, prayer is the means of expressing our spiritual beliefs about transcendence through words.

Jews believe that prayer is one of the *mitzvot* but also that it transcends the other *mitzvot*. Prayer in Judaism is seen as more than an expression of belief. It provides a sense of belonging to a community and affirms one's Jewishness in a social context. Being together in a synagogue with others who share our beliefs is often more important than the meaning of the words themselves. The synagogue is more than a house of prayer—it is the place where we affirm our values within a social context. Each congregation represents a slightly different social context, and so we tend to affiliate with the congregation that best reflects our values. Synagogues also communicate Jewish values across generations. Congregations provide a valuable social message because the synagogue is the only institution in Jewish life where entire families are brought together with other families. Although many secular contexts for expressing one's Jewishness are available through social-welfare and voluntary associations, the nature of the religious community is unique.

Religious rituals such as prayer not only express but actually shape our beliefs. Traditional Jewish prayer involves a surrender to a mode of consciousness quite different from routine consciousness. To the involved worshiper, attention to the service itself necessitates a receptivity to stimuli not encountered anywhere else. The physical sensation of singing, the presence of unusual ritual objects, the use of the Hebrew language, the codes, signals, and rituals of the service, and the invocation of religious concepts all contribute to the transformation of routine consciousness. If this involvement is sustained over time, it can produce a sense of connectedness to the other worshipers and spiritual fulfillment. Eventually, participation in regular prayer can shape our beliefs through repetition, routine, and reinforcement of the spiritual message.

Jews traditionally believe that prayer is meaningful not only because it expresses what we believe but also because it works. Some believe that prayer works because God listens, while others think that it primarily has a profound effect on us. Many people pray spontaneously at different moments in their lives or when they experience inner feelings on a deep level. This has been called variously praying, wishing, pouring out one's heart, conducting an interior conversation, or meditation. Spontaneous prayer is one of the deepest and most personal forms of human expression because it takes place privately and often unconsciously. It has always been an important part of Jewish spirituality.

The proper Hebrew term for what is called, incorrectly, "prayer" in English is *tefillah*. The word is derived from the Hebrew root *pll,* which means "to judge," "to intercede on behalf of someone," or "to hope." *Tefillah* therefore implies an act of self-judgment or intercession on one's own behalf before God, or the expression of hopeful sentiments. *Tefillah* is the standard Jewish term referring both to the liturgical dimension of Judaism and to the spontaneous outpouring of the human heart. There is no good English equivalent for the word. The act of praying is also called *davening* in Yiddish.

Jewish liturgy is largely based on three types of prayers: thanksgiving (*hodayah*), praise (*tehillah*), and request (*bakashah*). Although each genre has a different purpose, the content of many of the prayers is similar, and they express a consistent system of Jewish beliefs. Many of the prayers reflect the rabbinic understanding of Judaism. What Jews believe today is often different from what the rabbis of earlier times believed. Since Jewish belief is continually evolving and not static, there is considerable room for doubt about, disagreement with, and even reformulation of rabbinic beliefs expressed in traditional Jewish prayers found in the Siddur. Before we look at how more recent Jewish beliefs are expressed in prayer, we will begin with how the sacred myths of rabbinic Judaism make praying possible and are expressed in the words we utter.

Traditional Jewish prayer expresses the belief that God existed alone before He created the world and will exist long after the world might cease to exist. God is the creator, sustainer, and ruler of the world. He established the rhythms of nature and set the regular patterns of night and day, the four seasons, birth and death. At any moment, God could withdraw His support from the world and allow it to collapse. Because of His love for the world, He constantly regenerates and renews life. In comparison to God, all human artifice and invention are inferior; all human rulers and earthly kings are flawed and insignificant. No other being is worthy of our recognition or praise. In our very existence we are the proof of God's perfection. We have been created with a pure soul and body, making us the pinnacle of creation. We testify to God's majesty in what we say and do. We are created in the image of God—but He is the potter and we are the clay.

The rabbis believed that even though we were created in the image of God, we often lose our way. Jewish prayer reiterates the belief that God will nevertheless have mercy on us and forgive our sins because He is a compassionate being who remembers His covenant with our ancestors. We frequently recall the covenant, the gift of Torah, and the historical events that remind us of God's love. In prayer, we recommit ourselves to do God's will and live a life of righteousness and goodness. Although our moral fate is in our hands, we turn to God and ask Him to protect us from illness, oppression, and catastrophe. We may not understand why we suffer, but we still have confidence in God's goodness. We ask for strength as we work to overcome our human faults, for forgiveness for our failures, and for the courage to continue. Our task will never be complete, since we can never reach moral perfection, but when we call out to God, He is there and provides us comfort and assurance.

Jewish prayer reflects the faith that God loves the Jewish people despite our failings and is with us no matter where we may be. God gave us the Torah as a sign of the covenant between us and Him. If we follow it, we will be assured of health, safety, happiness, and eternal life. God will fulfill our aspirations and the hopes of the Jewish people. Many of our prayers express the hope that God will redeem us and lead us back to the Land of Israel, that He will renew the glory of Israel and allow it to live free in its land, true to God and at peace with its neighbors. We pray for the rebuilding of Jerusalem, the city of our people, as a model of perfect life on earth and the place where God's Presence once dwelt.

Our prayer acknowledges moments of joy and seasons in which we celebrate the life of the Jewish people. God created for us a rich emotional life of joy and gladness, love and relationships, peace and friendship. We take part in all that the world has to offer us and recognize God as the author of the world. When we age, we thank God for the gift of years. When we have children, we thank God for the miracle of birth.

When we die, we hope for rest for our souls, freedom from our troubles, reward for our good deeds in life, and comfort for our survivors. We ask God's help in making our hearts open to Him, to Torah, and to other people.

As a sign of His love, God has given us the Sabbath as a special day for rest and spiritual renewal. The Sabbath shows us what a perfect existence might be like and orients us toward a day that is all Sabbath. It is the blueprint for sacred living, when we live focused on the transcendent dimensions of life. It teaches us that redemption is not always in the future but can be had within our own life. It reminds us that the rest of our life is not yet holy and asks us to aspire to reach holiness throughout our life. The greatest gift God can give us, however, is peace within our own heart and within the world. Our prayers recall our striving to view other people kindly, to be modest and fair in all our dealings. We look to a world free of bloodshed and greed. Our thoughts are concentrated on improving ourselves and making the world a better place.

THE DEVELOPMENT OF THE SIDDUR

There are many examples of spontaneous personal prayer in the Bible. They include the prayer of Hannah, a childless woman who pleaded with God for a son and was assured by the priest Eli that her prayer would be answered. People around her recognized that she was deeply engaged in a personal and silent prayer. The Bible explains that "as she kept on praying [*titpallel*] before the Lord, Eli watched her mouth. Now Hannah was praying in her heart; only her lips moved, but her voice could not be heard" (1 Samuel 1:12–13). When she gave birth, she dedicated her son Samuel to a life of service as a priest. At that moment, her heart was filled with a prayer expressing her thanks and praise to God (1 Samuel 2). Her prayer is a model of spontaneous prayer in the Bible.

The earliest form of Jewish worship of God, according to the Torah, is the sacrifice (*korban*). Sacrifices were instituted while Israel still wandered in the Sinai Desert and were continued in the First and Second Temples. They were ritual acts where animals were slaughtered, wine and oil were poured on an altar, and grains were offered in order to thank, mollify, and please God. Sin offerings (*hattat*), in which animals were slaughtered and burned on the altar, were conducted on the festivals, holidays, and certain special occasions. Similar guilt offerings (*asham*) were made to atone for certain religious and legal infractions. Bulls, sheep, goats, and birds were burned on the altar as offerings of personal repentance (*olah*) and as twice-daily and regular holiday sacrifices (*olat tamid*). Liquids (*nesekh*) were poured on the altar during most burnt offerings.

A mixture of grain offerings (*minhah*) accompanied most burnt offerings but was intended mostly for the personal consumption of the priests, whose responsibility was to conduct the sacrifices. Peace offerings (*shelamim*), which marked family and national events, were voluntary sacrifices of animals; part were burned and part eaten in a communal meal of thanksgiving. A portion (*tenufah*) of the thanksgiving offering was waved in the air, signifying that it belonged to God. The sacrifice was often placed on an altar by the priests and ignited. Its smoke rose and ascended until the odor supposedly reached and satisfied God. Sometimes the leftovers or the consumable itself were eaten or used by the priests who conducted the rituals. Israelites were instructed to make pilgrimages to Jerusalem three times each year—on Passover, Shavuot, and Sukkot—and to bring sacrificial offerings with them.

Following the destruction of Solomon's Temple in 586 B.C.E. and the exile of many Jews to Babylonia, nearly seventy years passed before the Israelites were allowed to return to Jerusalem and rebuild the Temple. Many Jews who chose not to return developed ritual alternatives to the sacrifices. Within the Babylonian Diaspora, the practice of studying the Torah text itself emerged as the main alternative to sacrifice. The Torah was seen as belonging not only to the priests but to the populace as well. It was first read publicly to the Jewish community, which assembled on special occasions for this purpose. The recitation, interpretation, and translation of the Hebrew text into Aramaic, the vernacular language, emerged as an educational ritual within the Jewish community, both during the exile and afterward. Memorizing and transmitting the Hebrew passages of the Torah became an accepted tradition among a new professional class known as scribes. Fathers were obligated to teach the text to their sons, adult males were expected to devote one month of the year around Passover to intensive Torah study, and adult learning became an accepted norm in the Babylonian Diaspora. Meanwhile, in the Land of Israel, when the Second Temple was built and sacrifices were reinstated, the tradition of popular Torah learning did not disappear. The public reading of Torah within the service was common in the mishnaic period, although the readings were not standardized into set weekly portions (*parashiyot*), as we know them today, until centuries later.

The practice of reciting formal written prayers was probably introduced into Jewish practice during the Babylonian exile. Synagogues, which emerged during the period as places where Torah study was conducted, gradually assumed prayer functions as well. Many of the earliest synagogue prayers were composed and set to music, such as the psalms, hymns, and poetry taken from the Bible. The first prayer to be written specifically for the liturgy was the *Amidah,* also known as the Eighteen Benedictions or Silent Devotion. This was followed by the inclusion of the *Shema* ("Hear, O Israel, the Lord is our God, the Lord is one"), the *Birkat ha-Mazon* (Grace after Meals), and the Rosh Hashanah Additional Service (*Musaf*), which includes the blowing of the of Shofar (ram's horn). Prayers were recited in the synagogues by the community to coincide with the morning and afternoon sacrifices in the Temple. The term for these prayers is *avodah* (service), the same word used for sacrificial offerings.

The rabbinic tradition has its own mythology about the origin of written prayers. In legislating the times for daily prayers, they attributed their origins to the patriarchs. According to one midrash, Abraham instituted the morning prayer (*Shaharit*); Jacob, the evening prayer (*Arvit*); and Isaac, the afternoon prayers (*Minhah*).[1] They claimed that later generations of pious men ordained that Israel pray three times daily[2] and that 120 elders instituted the *Amidah* and arranged its blessings in their proper order.[3]

When the Second Temple was destroyed, it was no longer possible to offer sacrifices. Observance of the central rituals of Judaism and the pilgrimage festivals became impossible. The very continuity of Judaism could have been jeopardized had it not been for the fact that Judaism had already begun to develop alternatives to sacrifice. Not only did written prayers become part of the synagogue service, but Torah study emerged as a ritual as important as the prayer services. Torah learning, prayer, and moral goodness became the central rituals of Judaism. With the replacement of priestly sacrifices by written prayers, praying became the obligation of each individual Jew, not only of the priest. Even though the rabbinic sages of this period made formal prayer an alternative to the sacrifices, they ultimately regarded Torah learning as more important than prayer.

According to Halakhah, certain prayers can be said only when a prayer quorum (*minyan*) is assembled. The minimum number that defines a congregation is ten adult males. This is based upon Moses' designation of the ten scouts who explored the Land of Israel at his command as a "congregation." Rabbinic legend maintains that the divine Presence dwells in the midst of a congregation of ten men who pray together.

Jewish prayer generally consists of the public recitation of written prayers in the synagogue. All Jewish prayers are written in the first person plural ("we") to emphasize the collective longings of the Jewish people. Despite its public nature, prayer is a solitary act during which each individual prays to God. Written prayers are not spontaneous creations; they are often drawn from biblical sources. But many prayers began as expressions in people's own words or as common and popular versions of particular beliefs. The general framework for prayers existed in the talmudic period but was not fixed as word-for-word formulations until later. Prayers in the talmudic period were recited from memory.

The order of the prayers was not fixed until the ninth century, when recognized services were bound together in prayer books called the Siddur, which means "order." The first Siddur was the Seder of Rav Amram Gaon (ca. 850), based on the traditions of Jews living in Babylonia. Subsequent Siddurim (plural) reflecting Babylonian practice were modified in light of other traditions and circulated as the prayer books of Germany Jewry (*Mahzor Vitry*) and later of Sephardic Kabbalistic Jewry (*Nusah ha-Ari*). The first printed prayer books appeared in Europe in 1485, shortly after the printing press was developed.

American Jews utilize prayer books that are published by each modern denomination. Each book includes many of the most common written prayers but adds, removes, or modifies other prayers to express the denomination's own set of beliefs. There are traditional Orthodox

prayer books such as Philip Birnbaum's *Daily Prayer Book* (1949) and the
Art Scroll Siddur; Conservative prayer books such as *The Sabbath and
Festival Prayer Book* (1946) and *Siddur Sim Shalom* (1985); Reconstructionist prayer books such as *Kol Haneshamah* (1989); and Reform versions that include *The Union Prayer Book* (1894–95, 1922, 1940) and the
more recent *Gates of Prayer* (1984).

The prayer book contains prayers composed in every era of Jewish
history. The prayer book is an anthology of Jewish literary creativity and
includes selections from the Bible, Mishnah, Talmud, the genres of
midrash and poetry, and the writings of Maimonides and the Kabbalah.
Every prayer book is a tour through Jewish literary and spiritual history.
Some prayers, such as the *Shema* and the psalms, reflect ideas of the biblical era. Most prayers, including the *Shemoneh Esreh,* were composed
during the rabbinic period and express the religious ideology of the rabbis. Medieval prayers included in the prayer book were often composed
to express personal variations on the sacred myths of Judaism. The
Midrash of the Ten Martyrs, for example, recited on Yom Kippur, is a
medieval chronicle about the Roman persecutions in the second century. It expresses the belief that when Jews were forced to choose between denying Judaism and death, death was preferable. This belief in
martyrdom was called "sanctification of God's name" (*kiddush ha-Shem*)
and became a central tenet of Judaism during the period of the Crusades, when many Jewish communities in central Europe were deci-
mated. The *U'Netaneh Tokef* prayer for Rosh Hashanah and Yom Kippur,
according to legend, was composed as a hymn by the dying martyr
Rabbi Amnon of Mainz, a victim of the First Crusade in 1096. Modern
prayers have been composed and added to the prayer book, such as
prayers for the welfare of the United States and the State of Israel.

The prayer book is a treasury and compendium of Jewish beliefs that
is constantly evolving to better represent those beliefs. Because Jewish
belief develops over time, the prayer book reflects a range from the
Torah, Talmud, and Midrash to Maimonides, Kabbalah, and Hasidism.
For example, the *Yigdal* prayer, which is often recited at the conclusion
of evening services, is a poetic summary of Maimonides' *Thirteen Articles
of Faith*. It is a poem about God, stressing His unity, eternity, incompara-
bility, infinity, and unknowability. On the other hand, *Lechah Dodi*

(Come, My Beloved) is a kabbalistic hymn sung at the Friday evening service which describes the Sabbath as the time during which the masculine and feminine aspects of God are in harmony and produce auspicious benefits for the world. The two prayers are the literary products of two different beliefs about God. They both have their place in the same prayer book. This does not mean that the prayer book is a chaotic, inconsistent collection of random views. Rather, it illustrates that the prayer book is a developing treasury of written records of Jews who have sought to understand God and the transcendent dimensions of life.

There is a wide range of ideas in Judaism, and many different ideas can legitimately be considered under the umbrella of Judaism. At the same time, the recitation of the prayer book was generally regarded as a required duty for all Jews at specified occasions. While prayers express the pluralistic ideas of Judaism, the time and place for their expression is dictated by Halakhah. To some extent, Judaism can be seen as a system of common practice rather than dogmatically correct belief. This process of reformulation and retelling of Jewish belief has always been part of Judaism. Our ability to adapt in this way is one of the secrets of Jewish survival.

THE PURPOSES OF PRAYER

For the rabbis of the talmudic era, the primary purpose of prayer was to educate us in the sacred beliefs of Judaism through regular repetition and reinforcement.[4] This kind of prayer discipline was a Jewish innovation in the ancient world and was adopted by Christianity and Islam later on.[5] Prayers of thanksgiving and praise express the view that there is a divine dimension in all aspects of reality: "The righteous pronounce a blessing over every single matter that they eat, drink, see, or hear."[6] A rabbinic passage indicates: "An evil person is thought of as dead because he sees the sun shine and does not bless God . . . or because he sees the sun set and does not bless God. . . . But the righteous recite blessings upon everything they eat, drink, see, or hear."[7]

Prayers of request convey the idea that we can inspire God to intervene in the course of events. According to rabbinic thinking, God is moved by the prayers of Israel. When Israelites pray, God symbolically "hugs them in His arms, kisses them, remembers their exile, and hastens their redemption."[8] The midrash explains that the more a person turns to God to answer his needs and wants, the more God loves him.[9]

Prayer was seen as the spiritual dimension of Jewish ritual behavior. The Talmud explains that prayer is "service of the heart," based on the verse "to love the Lord your God and to serve Him with all your heart" (Deuteronomy 11:13). Other passages stress the importance of heartfelt prayer: "A man's prayer is not heard until he makes his heart [soft] like flesh."[10] Prayer was regarded as requiring great mental concentration and effort. One's thoughts should be directed to God: "When you pray, know before Whom you stand."[11] All distractions should be avoided: "Even if a man is greeted by a king while praying, he may not return the greeting. And even if a snake is wound around his heel, he may not interrupt his prayer."[12]

The critical ingredients in rabbinic prayer are intention (*kavanah*) and attentiveness. The personal element of intention is what gives the words of prayer the power to be heard. The most important factor is the concentration on and conviction in the meaning of the words of prayer. There is a report from the early rabbinic period of Jewish pietists who would devote at least one hour before the morning liturgical services to establish the proper *kavanah*. Later followers of rabbinic Judaism reaffirmed this idea in different ways. Maimonides stressed that prayer offered without concentration on the meaning of the words is worthless. The Safed Kabbalists of the sixteenth century developed a comprehensive theory of meditations known as *kavanot,* by which they meant specific preparations and thoughts to precede prayer.

MAIMONIDES ON PRAYER

Even though the spiritual dimensions of prayer were a central concern to the rabbis of the Talmud, medieval philosophers thought that they had not gone far enough. The eleventh-century Bahya ibn Pakuda argued that the *mitzvah* of prayer is not fulfilled by the physical act of praying according to Halakhah. Equally important are the "duties of the heart"—the spiritual beliefs and attitudes we bring to prayer. It is not just what we do but how we do it that matters. Prayer is a duty of the

heart that requires humility, suspension of worldly thoughts, and attention to the meaning of the words: "For you must know that words are a
matter of the tongue, but meaning is a matter of the heart."[13] More important than the ritual expressions of prayer are the spiritual love of God
and the soul's submission to Him. The fixed formulae of prayer are
meant to serve as guideposts so that one does not forget to express
thanksgiving and praise.

Maimonides affirmed the validity of traditional prayer from a religious standpoint. In the *Mishneh Torah,* he described in detail the laws,
regulations, and purposes of prayer. But from a philosophic standpoint,
which he expressed in *The Guide of the Perplexed,* he believed that traditional prayer may be meaningless. He explained that God is wise and
cunning and understood that the ancient Israelites, prior to the revelation of Torah at Mount Sinai, were steeped in idolatrous and pagan conceptions. Their common experience of worship was based on the idea
that the gods were appeased by sacrifices and offerings of animals, food,
and wine. At Sinai, God intended for them to break with idolatry and to
worship Him as the sole God of the world, who led Israel out of Egypt
and gave them the Torah. But God recognized that a sudden departure
from common practice is psychologically difficult. So He conceded that
sacrifices and burnt offerings would continue as the form of worship
even as He demanded that He alone be recognized as the true God and
the sole object of that worship. This implies that, over time, God would
use His wisdom and cunning to lead Israel to a more appropriate form
of worship, one that was preferable in both form and content.

When the Second Temple was destroyed in 70 C.E., sacrifices were
permanently abolished and liturgical prayer was accepted as the sole
form of divine worship in Judaism. Maimonides, however, implied that
even liturgical prayer is a compromise with the truth and that only
"meditation without any works" is appropriate as divine worship. By
this, he suggested that pure philosophic thinking about God is the only
true prayer because it is free of anthropomorphism (descriptions of God
in physical terms) and anthropopathism (descriptions of God as having
human emotions), both of which corrupt the true conception of God.
Philosophic thinking about God consists in the negation of all positive
statements about God because the latter are too limiting. Thus, the only

acceptable form of thinking about God is in negatives, of what He is not. For example, we cannot say that God is living; we can only say that He is not not-living. Since negation is an intellectual process, verbal prayers are meaningless.

True prayer for Maimonides is silent meditation. With just a hint of his own radical position, he implied that were it possible to legislate Jewish religious behavior in his day without regard to human nature, which is unaccustomed to drastic change, he would abandon traditional prayer in favor of philosophic meditation on the ineffable nature of God. But he recognized that this would be impossible without creating havoc within the Jewish community and destroying the simple and direct expressions of faith that many people embraced. The permissibility of traditional prayer was a compromise between truth and the human need for fixed customs.

THE MYSTICS' BELIEF IN PRAYER

Spanish Kabbalists believed that the two primary purposes of religious observance were to connect the soul to its source in the *Sefirot* and to restore the intrinsic unity within the *Sefirot* through ritual actions. These two functions, the unitive and restorative, permeate every aspect of Jewish mysticism's approach to religious life.

Since, according to mystic belief, the soul comes in a sense from the realm of the *Sefirot,* it naturally yearns to return there. All forms of religious experience are vehicles that transport the human soul upward through the heavens and palaces of the upper world to the gate of the realm of the *Sefirot.* Jewish mystics are extremely cautious on the question of how high the soul can ascend on the chain of divine being. Most agree that the rituals are not directed at, nor does the soul ascend to, the infinite God.

Because of the prohibition against violating the differences between God and human beings, Jewish mysticism does not say that the self is absorbed into God at the moment of mystical union. Most Jewish mystics do not believe that the separate existence of the soul is annihilated or that the soul is absorbed into the *Sefirot* at the moment of unity with God. The soul may come to stand in the highest domains of the *Sefirot,* but it never becomes a *Sefirah.* Its separate identity remains, and the human never merges into the divine. Mystical union is called "communion" (*devekut*). It does not convey the same degree of oneness as does the Latin base "union." It is a communion of two separate and distinct entities that retain their separateness.

The mystics place special emphasis on attentiveness to each specific prayer. They stress that prayer must be directed to the appropriate *Sefirah.* Knowledge of the specific effects of each prayer is an indispensable feature of mystical consciousness. The Kabbalists instruct their followers on which *Sefirot* each prayer should be directed to. *Kavanah* involves the concentrated effort of the heart and body in the performance of the ritual.

Mystics also believe that the words of the prayers take on a life of their own. The words, once uttered, become entities unto themselves and ascend upward to the *Sefirot,* with which they unite: "All that which man thinks and every meditation of his heart is ineffective until his lips utter them out loud. . . . That very word which he utters splits the air, going, rising and flying through the world, until it becomes a voice. That voice is borne by the winged creatures who raise it up to the King who then hears it."[14]

For the Kabbalists, daily prayer reunites the feminine aspect of God, which they called the divine Presence (*Shekhinah*), with the other *Sefirot.* The rabbinic prayer quorum of ten is a precondition for the completion of the *Shekhinah* because it symbolizes the ten *Sefirot.* The *minyan* invites the *Shekhinah* into its midst and symbolically joins with her. Just as there are ten *Sefirot,* there must be a quorum of ten men assembled for each regularly scheduled prayer service:

> Blessed is the man who is among the first ten to arrive at the synagogue. Among them is completed that which ought to be completed [i.e., the quorum and the reenactment of joining the ten *Sefirot* together]. These are sanctified by the *Shekhinah* before any others, as has been explained. Ten should arrive at the synagogue simultaneously rather than separately so as not to delay the completion of the limbs [of the ten *Sefirot*], just as man was created by God all at once and all his limbs were perfected together.[15]

The notion that there is a correspondence between human religious actions and divine processes is axiomatic in Jewish mysticism. This is evident in the mystical approach to the synagogue itself. As the synagogue, called the "minor sanctuary" (*mikdash me'at*), replaced the Temple, so formal prayers replace Temple sacrifices as the authorized form of worship. In mystical symbolism, the destroyed Temple still exists within the *Sefirot* as the divine prototype of the earthly Temple. The synagogue, therefore, corresponds to one of the *Sefirot*:

> It is commanded to build a sanctuary below corresponding to the [heavenly] sanctuary above.... One should build a synagogue and should pray within it daily and worship the Holy One, Blessed be He, for prayer is called worship.[16] The synagogue should be constructed with great beauty and adorned with all manner of refinements because the synagogue below corresponds to the heavenly synagogue.[17]

Because of the correspondence between the earthly synagogue and the *Sefirot,* the Zohar preferred conventional prayer said in a synagogue to prayer offered anywhere else. In fact, the Zohar introduced into the body of Jewish customs several new practices and rites based on mystical principles. For example, the preference for synagogue prayer over prayers said elsewhere is based on the idea that since the *Shekhinah* can only be reached by a narrow path, earthly prayers must be concentrated into a narrow channel in order to ascend. The very structure of a synagogue is preferable to an open field because the former would concentrate and the latter diffuse the ascending channel of prayer. The Zohar also introduced to Halakhah the notion that a synagogue must have windows so that the prayers could ascend through the narrow passage of the window and exit the synagogue. The Zohar further held that congregational prayer is preferable to individual prayer because God scrutinizes critically the worthiness and actions of an individual who prays alone. His prayer can ascend only as far as his *kavanah* warrants. Congregational prayer, however, ascends easily because of the aggregate merit of those assembled. If, however, one cannot pray with a congregation, one should at least pray at the same times as the congregation.

HASIDIC PRAYER

The Baal Shem Tov, the founder of the eighteenth-century hasidic movement, viewed prayer as the most important of the *mitzvot*. Prayer, rather than study, was the path to union with God. Moreover, personal prayer rather than written prayer was given new importance. For example, the following fable is recounted in many collections of hasidic lore:

> There was once a simple herdsman who did not know how to pray. But it was his custom to say every day: "Lord of the world! You know that if You had cattle and gave them to me to tend, though I take wages from everyone else, from You I would take nothing." Once, a rabbi was passing and heard the man pray in this way. He said to him: "Fool, do not pray in this way." The herdsman asked: "How should I pray?" Then the rabbi taught him the *Shema* and other prayers so that he would no longer say what he was accustomed to. After the rabbi left, the herdsman forgot all the prayers and did not pray. And since the rabbi told him not to pray as he once had, he said nothing. And this was a great catastrophe.

The hasidic virtue of simplicity, in keeping with its populist origins, seems to contradict the rabbinic view, which sees prayer within the framework of Halakhah. Hasidism emphasizes the spiritual power of Jewish prayer. For example, the hasidic attitude to communal prayer is that it is based upon a powerful and indispensable spiritual interdependence within the group:

> Once in a tropical country, a certain splendid bird, more colorful than any that had ever been seen, was sighted at the top of the tallest tree. The bird's plumage contained within it all the colors in the world. But the bird was perched so high that no single person could ever hope to reach it. When news of the bird reached the ears of the king, he ordered that a number of men try to bring the bird to him. They were to stand on one another's shoulders until the highest man could reach the bird and bring it to the king. The men assembled near the tree, but while they were standing balanced on one another's shoulders, some of those near the bottom decided to wander off. As soon as the first man moved, the entire chain collapsed, injuring several of the men. Still the bird remained un-

captured. The men had doubly failed the king. For even greater than his desire to see the bird was his wish to see his people so closely joined to one another.[18]

Hasidism also introduced a revolutionary new approach to the goals of prayer. Hasidism understood prayer as a purely spiritual act whose goal was the spiritual breakthrough of the soul toward the divine. The Hasid could transcend his own sense of separate identity during prayer until he achieved a state of nothingness in which he and God became one. Hasidism saw the ultimate spiritual value in prayer as the result of divesting himself of corporeality, detaching himself from this world, and rising above nature and time in order to attain complete union with the divine "Nothing"[19] or *Eyn Sof.* This meant that the Hasid sought an oceanic feeling, a disintegration of the boundaries of individuality, and a state of undifferentiatedness from God.

For the Baal Shem Tov and the Maggid of Mezritch, the leaders of early Hasidism, contemplative prayer begins with concentration on the words of the fixed liturgy. The individual concentrates not only on the meaning of the words themselves but on the shape of the letters that make up the words. This allows him to disassociate his thoughts from himself and replace his sense of individuality with a sense of being filled with God. When he loses himself, he is filled with divinity. He attempts to empty his mind of all concrete thoughts, personal desires, and self-awareness. True prayer is not possible unless the person praying annihilates his sense of self as a separate being. All thoughts that relate to one-self are obstacles to contemplative prayer.

Rabbi Nachman of Bratslav (1772–1810), the great-grandson of the Baal Shem Tov, is a unique figure in the development of Jewish prayer. Nachman saw prayer as a battleground in which the Hasid wages war against the obstacles that conspire to prevent his nearness to God. These include depression, despair, loneliness, sexual thoughts, distractions, and a sense of alienation from God. He concluded that prayers written in Hebrew were inferior to personal prayers offered in Yiddish, his vernacular. He is reported to have spent many hours in his adolescence secluded in the attic of his parents' home, struggling against melancholy and a sense that God did not notice or care about him at all. He would pray for hours on end for God to bring him near. He fought throughout his life against dark thoughts about God being unreachable across the abyss.

Ideal prayer, according to Nachman, occurs when the individual goes into isolation and pours out his heart to God with all the sadness, pain, and doubt that is in it. This is prayer "with a broken heart," in which one overcomes the obstacle of sadness and empties one's heart sufficiently for it to become filled with God. Such prayer allows one to overcome the doubts that result from futile intellectual arguments about God and faith. Prayer with a broken heart helps achieve simple faith in God, free of doubts and heretical thoughts. Nachman allowed himself to enter the dangerous forest of doubts about God, but he encouraged his followers to pray to God in simplicity and purity of heart.

For the Hasid, prayer requires great preparation and should be undertaken with a sense of earnestness. He should not approach God with a sense of unworthiness but rather should fortify himself with the courage of knowing that he too contains the divine Presence. Prayer should be offered in joy because joy ascends and sadness drags us down. But the ideal is an intensity so great that the Hasid stands ready to die in the moment of prayer.

The Hasid should begin slowly by concentrating on each word in order to conserve strength and warm up gradually. He needs to invest intense emotional energy in prayer because prayer is direct communication with God. The Maggid of Mezritch counseled his followers: "You must cry to God and call Him father until He becomes your father."[20] When the Hasid reaches that level of intensity, the divinity within him is reunited with God. It is not so much his words that ascend to God as the burning desire of his heart to be reunited with its creator. The greatest obstacle to this kind of prayer is self-absorption, which diverts our thoughts away from God and back to ourself. The Hasid must forget himself in prayer and think only of God, so that it is not he who is reciting the words; the words are recited through him.

WOMEN AND PRAYER

The traditional relationship between women and prayer has undergone profound change in recent years. Orthodox Judaism has created new opportunities for women to conduct prayer rituals within the limits of Halakhah. Conservative Judaism has ordained women rabbis and removed most halakhic barriers to the full participation of women in religious rituals. Reform Judaism has accepted women as possessing full and equal rights in all areas of religious practice.

Women have always attended synagogue and been present during sermons and Torah study, but from at least the twelfth century they were assigned to a special, separate gallery called "the benefit of women" (*ezrat nashim*). From rabbinic times, women were not allowed to lead services, read the Torah publicly, or receive honors; nor were they counted in the *minyan*. Women's chanting and singing in the synagogue was regarded as indecent because a female voice was thought to be sexually distracting to men.[21] Since medieval times, however, some women have served as prayer leaders for other women.[22] Women who were able to follow the prayer service had their own prayer leader, called a *firzogerin* (frontsayer). Some women would attend religious services to pray, while others would pray in the home. According to Halakhah, women are exempt from *mitzvot* that must be performed at specific times, such as reciting the *Shema,* sitting in a *sukkah,* and wearing *tefillin,* but they are obligated to pray, to affix a mezuzah to a doorpost, and to recite the Grace after Meals.[23]

Although there are few literary records of women's involvement in prayer, this is a reflection of the fact that Jewish literature has been a predominantly male preserve. The best evidence of women's spirituality comes from the genre of Yiddish literature known as *techines* (supplications), which include the personal prayers of Eastern European women since the sixteenth century. While these were not included in the formal synagogue liturgy, many *techines* were recited by women in synagogue as well as in women's prayer groups.

Many *techines* mentioned the biblical matriarchs—Sarah, Rebecca, Rachel, and Leah—in a manner parallel to the way the official prayers invoke the merits of Abraham, Isaac, and Jacob. They were often prayers that spoke directly to God in deeply familiar terms. Some *techines* were meant to be recited in synagogue. Others were recited at the time of ritual obligations that were specific to women, such as the resumption of marital relations after menstruation, preparing hallah bread for Sabbath, and lighting Sabbath candles. Some were personal prayers offered in the kitchen, the home, the *mikveh* (ritual bath), or the cemetery, and some accompanied special moments in a mother's life, such as childbirth and the circumcision of a son.[24] They were often written in the first-person voice rather than in the plural common to most traditional prayers.

Jewish women today, inspired by feminism, have sought to reclaim these traditions and expand on them to create a women's contemporary Jewish spirituality. In addition to reviving older rituals and creating new practices, such as women's study and prayer groups, Jewish women have raised concerns about the language of the traditional liturgy. Some prayer books have added more inclusive language. For example, the opening blessing of the *Amidah* invokes the God of Abraham, Isaac, and Jacob. A revised version adds an additional reference to the God of Sarah, Rebecca, Leah, and Rachel. These changes follow in the long tradition of an evolving Siddur that adapts to meet new understandings of what Jews believe.

THE ONGOING EVOLUTION OF THE SIDDUR

At this point, we have to consider what is involved in revising the liturgy of the Siddur to reflect contemporary Jewish beliefs. The sacred myths do not always reflect the changing categories of meaning of modern men and women. This has led to attempts to reformulate the sacred myths so that they do convey meaning today. Conservative, Reconstructionist, and Reform prayer books narrate new versions of the traditional sacred myths. As a result, Jews of these denominations have changed the traditional prayers and created new ones to reflect their interpretations of Jewish belief.

In the last two centuries, some Jews have been embarrassed by the notion of chosenness as superiority. Conservative, Reconstructionist, and Reform Judaism have attempted to remove from Judaism those elements that suggest that Jews are inherently better than others. This has been most evident in the arena of prayer-book reform. While the original Hebrew of the festival *kiddush,* the blessing over wine, stresses Jewish distinctiveness, various attempts have been made to remove this idea. Most efforts involve preserving the original Hebrew, which is chauvinistic, while modifying the English to remove the idea of chosenness. The original Hebrew version reads:

> Blessed are You, Lord our God, King of the universe, who has chosen us from among every nation, exalted us above every language, and sanctified us by Your commandments.

The Sabbath and Festival Prayer Book of the Conservative movement (1946) translated it:

> Blessed art Thou, O Lord our God, King of the universe, who didst choose us for Thy service from among all peoples. Thou didst exalt us above all tongues by making us holy through Thy commandments.[25]

This passage differs from the traditional Hebrew in several significant ways. First, the idea of inherent uniqueness which appears in the Hebrew is softened by the idea that Jews are chosen to serve God. This reflects the influence of the Reconstructionist movement, which rejected the notion of Jewish superiority, on Conservative Judaism. Second, the idea of the linguistic uniqueness of the Jewish people is preserved, but it is made subservient to the idea that Jews are exalted by virtue of the commandments. In each case, the traditional emphasis on chosenness is preserved but tempered subtly by a new emphasis on the dependence of Jewish uniqueness on observance of the *mitzvot*.

The more recent Conservative *Siddur Sim Shalom* (1985) eliminates the archaic English but continues to emphasize the idea that chosenness is dependent on the *mitzvot* and is not an independent quality of the Jewish people:

> Praised are You, Lord our God, King of the universe, who has chosen and distinguished us from among all others by adding holiness to our lives with His *mitzvot*.[26]

This translation uses the Hebrew term *mitzvot* rather than "commandments" to show that certain religious concepts are best expressed in Hebrew.

The Union Prayer Book first appeared in 1894 as a radical ideological manifesto of American Reform Judaism, which removed all references to chosenness, messianism, nationhood, and other concepts it had rejected. Subsequent revisions in 1923 and 1945 reflected an unease among Reform Jewish leaders about their dramatic departure from traditional belief and practice and their growing sense of affinity with the idea of the Jewish people as a distinctive ethnic and national unit. *The Union Prayer Book* removed the festival *kiddush,* although in another context it preserved the formula of the *kiddush*:

> We render thanks unto Thee that Thou hast called us from among all nations, and hast consecrated us to Thy service.[27]

The references to chosenness and superiority have been replaced with the notion of "calling," an echo of the "mission-people" idea. Peoplehood has been replaced by the idea of a religious group devoted to serving God.

Gates of Prayer, the 1975 Reform prayer book, restored much of what *The Union Prayer Book* eliminated. This new book, which appeared in both a left-to-right and right-to-left version, made an emphatic statement about the importance of tradition, peoplehood, and Hebrew. It restored the traditional *kiddush* blessing although in abbreviated form:

> Blessed is the Lord our God, Ruler of the universe, who has chosen us from all the peoples, exalting us by hallowing us with His *mitzvot*.[28]

This translation restored chosenness, peoplehood, and *mitzvot* but maintained the earlier Reform idea that the exalted station of the Jewish people is a feature of its religion. The ideological shift reflected the growing centrist tendencies within the Reform movement and its strong ties to Zionism and peoplehood.

The new Reconstructionist prayer book, *Kol Haneshamah,* published in 1989, changes the Hebrew drastically to reflect the movement's flat rejection of the chosen-people concept. The English translation of the blessing faithfully reflects the modified Hebrew. The three-part phrase of the traditional blessing ("chosen, exalted, sanctified") is replaced by a new formula:

Blessed are you, the Holy One, our God, the sovereign of all worlds, who has called us to your service, and made us holy with your *mitzvot*.[29]

This version of the traditional blessing preserves the now-familiar stock phrase "called us to your service," which Reconstructionism introduced to replace chosenness.

The Siddur is a human creation which continues to evolve. Its contents reflect the beliefs we can profess at a moment of ultimate truthfulness and intimacy. Yet, as we have seen in this instance, we keep coming back to our sacred myths even as we reinterpret them and continue to grapple with their implications. The Siddur is the standard against which we measure our Jewish beliefs and the framework in which we define our relationship to God.

THE EXPERIENCE OF PRAYER

Jewish prayer is the discipline of expressing our deepest beliefs about the transcendent dimensions of life and our relation with God. It is our response to the ineffable, to the mystery of God, to the miracles of daily life. Prayer transports us from the mundane to the transcendent. Prayer does not have to be just words. It can also be in silence, in our minds and in our hearts. The greatest prayer, however, is to pray for the ability to pray, to respond to the wonder of God's world.

Prayer, according to Abraham Joshua Heschel, begins in radical amazement, the human sense of wonder at the miracles that are daily with us. Everywhere in the world, Heschel sees God reaching out to us. What meaning is there to the life of a Jew, he asks, if it is not to acquire the ability to feel the taste of heaven?[30] We respond to God's reaching out with our answer—prayer. We reach out in prayer to God, but it is really God reaching out to us. Prayer is the poetic expression of the Jewish sensibility which sees God's hand in creation. It is, ultimately, a deeply private experience:

If the individual is lost to Judaism in his privacy, the people are in danger of becoming a phantom. . . . Unless a person knows how to pray alone, he is incapable of praying within the congregation. The future of congregational prayer depends on whether the Jews will learn how to pray when they are alone.[31]

The leading philosopher of contemporary Orthodoxy, Rabbi Joseph Soloveitchik, views prayer as the opposite of prophecy. The prophet communicates God's message to humanity. But prayer is the human being addressing God. Prayer, in his view, is possible when prophecy has ceased. In the absence of God's communication to us, in the absence of God's presence, we address God. God could only command us to pray if He were ready to enter into a personal relationship with us through prayer. Prayer, therefore, is the highest form of intimacy between humans and God. God is the gift to the lonely man of faith who calls out to Him in prayer.

Why then should we pray in public and not just in private? Jewish prayer satisfies the need for community, which cannot be fulfilled alone. By participation in the group, we are able to transcend our own particular situation. We elevate our own individual predicament by placing it in the context of those of others with whom we share ties of kinship, mutual support, and empathy. Tradition recognizes that there are benefits in the communal act of prayer: "A man upon whom calamity has befallen should make it known to the public, so that many people may entreat [God's] mercy for him."[32] Similarly, the blessing *Birkat ha-Gomel,* recited by one whose life has been saved from mortal danger, is said in the presence of a *minyan* to publicly acknowledge God's saving grace. In this way, we also let others know about the personal miracle that God has performed.[33]

Jacob Petuchowski, the philosopher of Jewish prayer, argues that Jewish prayer satisfies the need for community by creating a participation in the group that transcends time and place. This is a particularly American Jewish phenomenon, where Jewish communality is expressed within the synagogue, whose primary function is prayer. Today, the very act of congregating in a synagogue is an expression of community. The prayers themselves may even be superfluous to the very act of affirming participation in the community.

Communal prayer can also be a vehicle for reflection touched off by a personal association with the fixed words of the prayer.[34] It can trigger thought processes in us that allow us to think about our deepest spiritual concerns. For example, if we have difficulty relating to some concepts within the prayer book, the prayer service itself can provide an occasion for reflection. This detour from group prayer allows us solitary moments of personal prayer and reflection. The regimen of prayer affords the time and space for the meditations that continually change and adjust our perspectives.

8

The Messiah

Messianism is one of the most significant of the ideas that Judaism has bequeathed to the world. To many people today, messianism appears to be an archaic notion based on a supernatural fantasy, a form of escapism from the difficulties of the real world. To others, messianic belief is a matter of faith about the outcome of history that defies rational explanation. Messianism, however, has shaped the outlook of Western religions and contributed in fundamental ways to religious, political, and social developments throughout history.

The idea of the Messiah is central to the beliefs of the major Western religions, especially Judaism and Christianity. Jewish messianism influenced the rise of Christianity and remains one of the major sources of difference between Jews and Christians. Jewish messianism has affected Jewish political and religious activity for centuries and continues to do so even today.

Messianism is the idea that history is movement in time toward a specific outcome—whether a return to a golden age of the past, a march toward a utopian future, or a cataclysmic prelude to a better world. Today many people, including many Jews, are imbued with the secular notion that redemption is brought about not by God or a Messiah but by the political, military, social, economic, and technological forces of humanity. There are some ultra-Orthodox Jews who reject the secular interpretation of history and believe that the Messiah will bring an end to this era of history. The chasm that separates the outlook of different Jewish groups on this issue is wider than any bridge can span.

The idea of the Messiah as the personal redeemer was not a part of the ancient Jewish vision. The biblical prophets were concerned with the future age, not with the figure of the redeemer. For them, the redeemer was simply a king of Israel. Two centuries before the beginning of Christianity, the idea of a personal redeemer appeared among Jewish sects in Israel. The Jews of the first centuries of the Common Era believed the Messiah had not yet come, while the followers of Jesus— strongly influenced by contemporary Jewish messiansim—asserted that he was the Messiah. The belief that the Messiah has arrived and that he is Jesus is the teaching that most acutely divides Judaism from Christianity.

What is the Jewish conception of the Messiah? What is the Jewish view of the messianic age? Where do Judaism and Christianity differ and agree on this question? The answer to these questions can be found by going back to the Bible, where the theories of redemption were first introduced.

THE ORIGINS OF THE MESSIANIC IDEA

The Jewish idea of the redeemer began as the concept of a model king who set the standard for ideal Jewish existence. Centuries later, as the likelihood of Jewish independence faded under the yoke of Roman rule, it evolved into the notion of a spiritual redeemer who would release the Jewish people from the bonds of suffering. The idea of Messiah as redeemer first appeared among spiritual circles in the late Second Temple period. The rabbis were divided between those who thought that the Messiah was a king in the past and those who believed he would be a future redeemer from the line of David. The Messiah as redeemer was finally incorporated into normative Judaism after the destruction of the Second Temple in 70 C.E.

Let us go back to 1000 B.C.E., when King David united the two kingdoms of Israel and Judah and made Jerusalem his capital. Among his accomplishments, he defeated the Philistines and other foreign enemies, expanded the borders of the kingdom from the Nile to the Euphrates, established the religious foundations of ancient Israel, and created an effective monarchy that unified the religious, military, judicial, and political apparatus of the nation. The popular concept at the time was that David's reign established a golden age in which Israel was united under the rule of a model religious, political, and military leader. Although the united kingdom lasted only a short time, the image of David as the ideal leader generated hope in the restoration of the Davidic monarchy by his descendants. It is no surprise that claims to leadership of the Jewish people throughout Jewish history have often been expressed in terms of restoring Davidic rule. From the early Christians, who claimed that Jesus was the descendant of King David, to Theodor Herzl, the founder of modern political Zionism, who was seen as the modern embodiment of King David, to David Ben-Gurion, the first prime minister of the State of Israel, the imagery of King David prevails. The Davidic monarchy and Israel's hopes for redemption are linked throughout Jewish history.

David's united kingdom continued through the reign of his son Solomon. In the next generation, under Rehoboam's rule, the fractious nation split into the separate kingdoms of Israel and Judah. Amos, a prophet in the northern kingdom of Israel (eighth century B.C.E.), denounced the excesses in contemporary Israelite society, including exploitation of the poor, luxury, corrupt judges, and political violence and oppression. He warned that God would someday bring a day of reckoning to exact punishment for these ills. He called this day of reckoning "the day of the Lord" (*yom adonai*), a time of divine punishment. While some thought the day of reckoning was a day of national deliverance, the prophet spoke of doom and despair for the northern kingdom of Israel—"Blackest night without a glimmer" (Amos 5:18–20).

The biblical prophets were charismatic Israelite leaders throughout the period of the monarchy and after the destruction of Solomon's Temple in 586 B.C.E. They were often critical of the moral lapses of the people and the political excesses of the king. When they thought the kings failed to live up to the high ethical standards of Israelite religion, they criticized them publicly and privately. The prophets also defined a reli-

gious outlook which they proffered to the people as an alternative to
the political machinations of the kings.

The future, especially the consequence of corrupt human behavior in
the face of the demands of God, was of great concern to the prophets.
Amos' younger contemporary Hosea believed that, following the punishment of the northern kingdom, God would reinstate an everlasting
covenant, more permanent than the first, and Israel would undergo a
change in character and benefit from a permanent peace. This is a day of
betrothal between Israel and God. God says, "I will espouse you forever:
I will espouse you with righteousness and justice, and with goodness
and mercy, and I will espouse you with faithfulness." It would be a time
of renewal for Israel in its land, when "the earth shall respond with new
grain and wine and oil" (Hosea 2:21–24).

The prophet Micah (late eighth century B.C.E) warned that the social
injustices of the rulers of Judah would be severely punished. The rulers
who had dispossessed the Israelites belonging to other tribes would
themselves be dispossessed. Micah reassured the dispossessed that God
would someday "bring together the remnant of Israel" (Micah 2:12).

The prophetic Book of Isaiah reflects the work of at least two distinct
authors. The first author (chapters 1–39) writes about events that took
place between 740 and 700 B.C.E. The second, Deutero-Isaiah (chapters
40–66), reflects events that occurred at the time of the destruction of
Solomon's Temple. First Isaiah prophesies about Jerusalem, the corruption of its judges, the sins of its inhabitants, and the likely devastation it
will face if it does not repent and change. Like other prophets, he sees a
future resolution to contemporary problems. Isaiah's vision, however, is
benign, beatific, even utopian:

> In the days to come [*acharit ha-yamim*],
> The Mount of the Lord's House
> Shall stand firm above the mountains
> And tower above the hills;
> And all the nations shall gaze on it with joy.
> And the many peoples shall go and shall say:
> "Come, let us go up to the Mount of the Lord,
> To the House of the God of Jacob;
> That He may instruct us in His ways,
> And that we may walk in His paths."

For instruction shall come forth from Zion,
The word of the Lord from Jerusalem.
Thus He will judge among the nations
And arbitrate for the many peoples,
And they shall beat their swords into plowshares
And their spears into pruning hooks.
Nation shall not take up
Sword against nation;
They shall never again know war. (Isaiah 2:2–4)

In the succeeding chapters, Isaiah condemns the Jerusalemites and especially their corrupt judges, but in chapter 11 he returns to his expectation of moral regeneration. The agent of restoration is the son of Jesse, a descendant of King David who restores the moral capital of Jerusalem. This paean to a Davidic restoration king places great hope in the person of the individual king:

But a shoot shall grow out of the stump of Jesse,
A twig shall sprout from his stock.
The spirit of the Lord shall alight upon him:
A spirit of wisdom and insight,
A spirit of counsel and valor,
A spirit of devotion and reverence for the Lord. . . .
Thus he shall judge the poor with equity
And decide with justice for the lowly of the land.
He shall strike down a land with the rod of his mouth
And slay the wicked with the breath of his lips.
Justice shall be the girdle of his loins,
And faithfulness the girdle of his waist.
The wolf shall dwell with the lamb,
The leopard lie down with the kid. (Isaiah 11:1–6)

Isaiah's "days to come" soon develop into the more terrifying and destructive "day of the Lord." His initial vision has become more severe, less optimistic. In his "Babylon Pronouncement" (732–727 B.C.E), he predicts that the day of the Lord will come sometime in the future and bring terrible punishment upon the city of Damascus, while Israel will be restored to its land (Isaiah 13:6–10).[1]

This punishment of Babylon will bring with it divine renewal for Israel and the ingathering of its dispersed people. Isaiah's vision includes, as part of the redemption, the eventual return to Zion of those who had settled in other countries. This passage, like so many others, reflects the trauma of the dispersion and exile from Zion and the hope for national redemption and eventual restoration of independence. "And in that day, a great ram's horn will be sounded; and the strayed who are in the land of Assyria and the expelled who are in the land of Egypt shall come and worship the Lord on the holy mount, in Jerusalem" (Isaiah 27:13). Isaiah promises that a "remnant" of the people will survive the day of the Lord to return to Zion.[2] This theme of survival after the great day of the Lord— a national catastrophe and defeat at the hands of foreign enemies—is picked up in the seventh-century B.C.E. Book of Zephaniah (2:9).

The prophet Ezekiel was deported to Babylonia with many other Jerusalemites in 597 B.C.E., before the final defeat of Jerusalem. He shared Isaiah's sense of impending disaster and hopes for restoration. He described the restoration of Judah as a miraculous event of such proportions that he likened it, in its improbability, to the resurrection of the dead (Ezekiel 37:1–14). He also imagined a mythic battle led by God against Gog and the land of Magog which would prove God's power and his favoritism for Judah (chapters 38–39).

The prophets reiterated hope for a royal redeemer. The most specific reference is Zechariah's hope that Zerubavel, grandson of King Jehoiachin of Judah, would be the redeemer king (Zechariah 4:9). Later prophets, such as Malachi, believed that the restoration would be preceded by God sending a messenger, the prophet Elijah, to prepare the way for the day of reckoning, a day of "burning like an oven." Then, acting as a "relentless accuser," God would judge and punish the sinners (Malachi 3:1–5). The prophet Joel announced that God will "restore the fortunes of Judah and Jerusalem, gather all the nations and bring them down to the Valley of Jehoshaphat" (Joel 4:1–2). There, God will punish the gentile nations for their treatment of Judah and Israel.

While many of these speculations represented the peculiar religious ideology of the individual prophet, they also shaped the views on redemption of later generations. The prophets generally held that Israel and Judah were corrupt and would pay for their sins with defeat, destruction, and exile—"the great day of the Lord." Ultimately, God would preserve a remnant of His people, whom He will gather and restore to Israel. He will judge and punish the wicked, bring back the Davidic kingdom, resurrect the dead, reinstate the covenant, and change the human nature of the people Israel. Redemption meant a change in the moral fiber of the people and a return to the glory of the Davidic era.

To understand Jewish messianism, it is necessary to distinguish between the biblical meaning of the Messiah and the biblical idea of redemption. There is no reference to the Messiah as a spiritual redeemer anywhere in the Bible. The term "Messiah" in the Bible means "the anointed one" and refers to the ideal human king of Israel. The biblical view of redemption, on the other hand, presents the future as an ideal age in a better world. Some of these prophetic visions predict that the renewal of human society will come after a period of catastrophic events. Others present the future as an unknown, unpredictable utopian era whose time and nature cannot be predicted. These diverse passages have animated the spirit and inspired people to pursue light in dark times.

When did the idea of a Messiah develop? The Jewish belief in a Messiah stems from the hope that the golden age of King David will be restored. The prophet Nathan reassured David that his dynasty would endure, that God's people would live safely in the Land of Israel, that their enemies would be defeated, and that God would favor His people Israel forever (2 Samuel 7:8–16). The Davidic legend became the predominant image that shaped the future hopes of ancient Israel. In the period after the collapse of the monarchy, and especially after the destruction of Solomon's Temple in 586 B.C.E., hopes focused on the return of a king, a descendant of David, as the redeemer of Israel.

The term for the "anointed one" who restores the glory of Israel to its ideal state is *mashiach*. The king was identified as the "anointed one" because the ritual of coronation involved pouring olive oil over the king's head (2 Samuel 5:3; 1 Samuel 16:13). David's predecessor, Saul, was called "the Lord's anointed"—*mashiach adonai* (1 Samuel 24:6)—indicating that he was a ruler chosen by God. The term was also used for priests (Leviticus 4:3), non-Israelite kings (Isaiah 45:1, referring to Cyrus of Persia), the patriarchs (Psalm 105:15), and the people of Israel (Psalm 89:39), but it referred primarily to kings in the Davidic line of succession. In later Judaism, *mashiach* also referred to the individual savior or redeemer whose spiritual powers cause a change in the world order and conditions of human existence.

Nearly one thousand years later, shortly before the Maccabean revolt, at the time of Daniel, the idea of the Messiah came to mean an individual redeemer who is also a king. The Book of Daniel was probably completed during the reign of Antiochus IV Epiphanes, the Seleucid (Greco-Syrian) monarch who ruled Palestine from 174 to 164 B.C.E. Antiochus sought to hellenize Jerusalem by replacing the high priest Onais III with Jason and Menelaus, both Hellenistic Jews. He killed thousands of Jews in Jerusalem following rumors of a rebellion, transformed the city into a Greek *polis,* dedicated the Temple as a sanctuary to Zeus, and outlawed the practice of Judaism. His harsh restrictions provoked the Maccabean revolt, whose history has been memorialized in the celebration of Hanukkah. The Book of Daniel offers a vision of redemption that differs from other biblical ideas. Daniel predicted that the future would involve a great day of judgment accompanied by the resurrection of the dead (Daniel 12:1–2). This is the only biblical book that speaks of an individual redeemer, a Davidic prince, as the "anointed prince" (*mashiach nagid*). But the reference is still to a member of the Davidic dynasty, not a superhuman redeemer.

Jewish literature during this period included two genres that had their inspiration in the prophetic writings. The one known as eschatology ("end of days") includes literary speculations on the destiny of mankind, the "end of history," and the ultimate stage of human history. This genre encompasses Jewish works written after the Book of Daniel and before the composition of the New Testament literature. Its themes include the Messiah, judgment day, the messianic era, the time-to-come, retribution, resurrection of the dead, and the afterlife.[3] The second genre, known as apocalyptic literature, is composed of Jewish writings that purport to be revelations or prophecies, including mysterious and secret wisdom about the end of days and other eschatological matters. The Book of Daniel is itself an example of apocalyptic literature and served as a model for other imaginative renderings of Jewish eschatology. Many of the ideas of Jewish apocalyptic writings entered the Talmud and later Jewish literature, and influenced early Christianity.

While the concept of a restoration king is prophetic, the idea that the redemption of Israel will be brought about by a spiritual rather than a royal redeemer first occurs in eschatological and apocalyptic literature. In particular, the Book of Enoch, one of the pseudepigraphies (literary works written under an assumed or fictitious name), which was originally composed in Hebrew around 68 B.C.E,[4] is the earliest known Jewish work in which the figure of an individual called the Messiah appears. The book dates from the late Hasmonean era and reflects Jewish ideas that go beyond that of Messiah as king. Following the Maccabean victory in 164 B.C.E., the Hasmoneans, a priestly family, consolidated their political victories over the Seleucids and, by 140 B.C.E., had established a hereditary dynasty in which their leader, Simeon, was confirmed as high priest by the Greeks who exerted loose control over the Jews. During this period, the Hasmoneans greatly expanded the borders of their kingdom and converted foreign peoples to Judaism. One of Simeon's successors, Aristobulus, assumed the title of king as well. The Romans, however, abolished the Jewish monarchy in 76 B.C.E. The years following this brief era of independence were ones of growing redemptive expectation and increased eschatological and literary activity. It was a time when Jews perceived that the gap between the biblical promises to Israel and the real conditions of Jewish subjugation had become unbridgeable. Many Jews despaired of ever returning to the glorious era of national independence. Some concluded that redemption would occur only on the spiritual and not the historical plane.

This may help explain why the mention of a spiritual redeemer (*mashiach*) appears. The history of the Hasmonean era demonstrated that political independence and the restoration of the monarchy did not guarantee national redemption because the Jewish kings were corrupt and controlled by the Greeks. Despite the victory against the foreign occupiers, the Jews were unable to fulfill the biblical promise of a restored kingdom. Dashed hopes in the wake of the abolition of the monarchy prompted a more spiritual view of redemption. In the wake of this disappointment, Jewish thinkers began to see the Messiah not as king— since the kingship had been corrupted—but as a human spiritual redeemer. This spiritual notion made it possible to imagine the arrival of a new era whose appearance is dependent only upon God and not upon politics. The arena for redemption shifted from the realm of the external world, where Rome occupied Palestine, to the inner world, where God alone directs events. In any event, the prophetic verses on redemption lent themselves to new interpretations that were not far afield from the meaning of the texts themselves.

The Book of Enoch is the earliest surviving Jewish record of belief in a spiritual Messiah. It speaks of God in terms drawn from the books of Daniel and Ezekiel. It presents Jewish ideas about the Messiah that eventually formed the basis of Christian belief. The anonymous writer describes God as a figure whose "head was white like wool" (Daniel 7:9). The term "son of man" comes from the books of Ezekiel and Daniel (7:13), where it is symbolic of the prophet, while in Enoch it takes on a new meaning as the redeemer. The redeemer has an angelic appearance, exudes righteousness, knows the mysteries of God, and is called "God's chosen." He offers support to humanity, serves as a teacher or leader to the world, and is an agent of good fortune.[5] He is chosen to turn humanity back to the true worship of God. He is described as having been designated for this task even before the creation as a hidden redeemer, waiting for the right moment (1 Enoch 48:4–6). This is the first explicit reference in Jewish literature to the spiritual redeemer being called God's "anointed" (1 Enoch 48:10). The hidden redeemer has been known only to a few since the time of creation, but his time has not yet come. When he is revealed, he will be recognized as having greater stature than any king. He will be universally recognized as the redeemer, with the power to dispense forgiveness and mercy.

The idea of Messiah has thus evolved from king to spiritual redeemer. This redeemer has a largely spiritual task of restoring the true worship of God. The notions of Davidic ancestry and national catastrophe are absent from the new approach. Perhaps it was because this was a period in which the likelihood of political redemption was remote that Jewish thinkers turned to a spiritual and otherworldly hope; perhaps the idea of the individual redeemer was implicit in Scripture. In either case, these passages reflect the spiritual, otherworldly outlook of late Second Temple–period Judaism. This new development in the history of messianism set the stage for new Jewish ideas and the rise of Christianity among some Jews. Christian belief in Jesus emerged out of one of the strains of Jewish messianism.

The views expressed in the Book of Enoch represented one authentically Jewish school of thought among the many Jewish groups of the period. For one ascetic group, called the Essenes, the issue of messianism was a burning contemporary concern. As they waited out the "day of the Lord" in the Judean Desert, the Essenes developed a semimonastic way of life. For the Pharisees, the precursors of rabbinic Judaism, messianism was not a central preoccupation until after the destruction of the Second Temple in 70 C.E. The Pharisaic rabbis were more interested in the meaning of Torah and in the challenge of achieving moral goodness and holiness in the present than in some messianic future, although Pharisaic Judaism came to incorporate a messianic outlook that included the notions of both a restoration king and a spiritual redeemer. Those Jews who were deeply imbued with messianic expectations turned either to the early Jewish followers of Christianity or to the Essenes. In the aftermath of the destruction of the Second Temple, the Essenes disappeared while Pharisaic Judaism survived.

The earliest explicit references to an individual redeemer within rabbinic Judaism emerge from the circles of Rabbi Yohanan ben Zakkai and his disciples during the generation of the destruction of the Second Temple. While other groups retreated from society or turned to fight the Romans in the wake of the destruction of the Temple, Yohanan succeeded in developing a religious program for the reconstruction of Judaism. He maintained a strict silence on his own messianic beliefs, which he broke only on his deathbed:

> And when Rabbi Yohanan ben Zakkai took ill, his students came to visit him. When he saw them, he began to cry. They said to him, "Light of Israel, why are you crying?" He said to them, "If I were taken before a king of flesh and blood—who is here today and in the grave tomorrow, whose anger is not eternal, whose power to arrest me cannot hold me forever, who could kill me but not with an everlasting death, or whom I could mollify, even bribe with money—I would still cry. But, now that I am being brought before the King of kings, the Holy One, Blessed be He, who lives forever—whose anger is eternal, whose power over me is eternal, who can blot out my existence forever, who cannot be mollified or bribed, and who leads me on a path to the Garden of Eden or to Gehenna, I know not which—should I not cry?" They said to him: "Bless us, our teacher!" He replied, "May it be His will that the fear of heaven be always upon you like the fear of [a king of] flesh and blood." His stu-

dents then said, "Is that all?" He replied, "This is so that a person who transgresses should not say to himself that no one saw him." And, at the moment of his death, he uttered: "Empty the [water] vessels because of the impurity [of impending death] and prepare a throne for Hezekiah, king of Judah, who comes."[6]

Yohanan's comment about the vessels is explained by the fact that a corpse, in Jewish law, brings impurity. His last statement urges his followers to ready a throne for the Messiah, who, according to Yohanan, is a descendant of the historical figure Hezekiah, king of Judah, who ruled from 719 to 691 B.C.E.

What does he mean by this? There was considerable attraction to the idea that Hezekiah fulfilled Isaiah's prophecy of the restoration of the Davidic line. Assyrian attacks on Jerusalem in 701 B.C.E., led by Sennacherib, were repelled by Hezekiah's ingenious military strategy (2 Kings 18–19). He restored the Israelite cult in the Temple and preserved national independence in the face of these attacks. His status as the restoration king made him a central figure in the messianic teachings of the later rabbis who believed that the prophetic Messiah had come long ago and was a king who lived and died. The coming Messiah, who would be a human king and redeemer of Israel, would be measured against his standard.[7] Yohanan's identification of the Messiah with Hezekiah is not new. The Messiah, according to Yohanan, is the restoration king of the Davidic line.

These rabbis disagreed over whether biblical prophecies about the restoration king referred to Hezekiah's restoration of the Davidic monarchy in the eighth century B.C.E. or to an unidentified future redeemer who had not yet come. These differences of opinion represented real differences in the exegesis of the biblical texts. Rabbi Yohanan asserted that the world was created for the sake of the Messiah[8] who was yet to come. In the third century C.E., an anti-Christian polemicist, Hillel son of Gameliel, rejected Yohanan's belief in a future messianism by asserting that the biblical prophecies had already been fulfilled in Hezekiah. Hillel said, "There is no Messiah for Israel"—meaning no *future* Messiah. Hillel's view was not prevalent, and most sages were concerned with the future arrival of the Messiah.

The rabbis developed an elaborate set of theories about the messianic era that included the following elements: (1) Elijah the Prophet as precursor of the Messiah, (2) the ingathering of the exiles, (3) the arrival of the Messiah, (4) the dying Messiah, (5) the messianic era, and (6) the time-to-come. Centuries later, Maimonides systematized the rabbinic views and codified Jewish messianic belief into dogma.

ELIJAH THE PROPHET AS PRECURSOR OF THE MESSIAH

Elijah, a zealous Israelite prophet of the ninth century B.C.E., is described in the Bible as the fierce opponent of all forms of paganism carried out within the boundaries of Israel. The Bible also depicts an encounter between Elijah and God that takes place at the same spot where God revealed the Torah to Moses. After a tumultuous display of thunder and fire, God's "still, small voice" addresses the prophet. This account concludes with Elijah's disappearance as he is carried off to heaven in a chariot of fire (2 Kings 2:1–11). According to tradition, Elijah lives on in "concealment." He is also viewed as the messianic harbinger (Malachi 3:23–24) who appears to men as the revealer of heavenly secrets.[9]

One of Yohanan ben Zakkai's disciples, Rabbi Joshua, attributes the belief that Elijah is the precursor of the Messiah to several generations of predecessors. The identification is based on the legend that Elijah did not die but merely was "assumed" up to heaven. Elijah's primary function is to resolve the issue of the ritual status of certain families who have been tainted by mixed or forbidden marriages. This work is important because of the belief that the dispersed tribes of the Jewish people will be returned to the Land of Israel in messianic times. Elijah is also said to anoint the Messiah with oil.

THE INGATHERING OF THE EXILES

One of the first acts of the Messiah would be to gather into the Land of Israel the Jewish people dispersed throughout the world. This theory assigns a role to Elijah in the ingathering of the exiles. It also reflects an argument over the significance of the biblical verse in Ezekiel that refers to the ingathering of the exiles: "I will take you from among the nations and gather you from all the countries, and I will bring you back to your own land" (36:24).

Many viewed the fulfillment of the biblical prophecy of gathering in the exiles as a necessary stage in the messianic process. According to some rabbis, including Rabbi Akiva, not all the ten lost tribes will return. Not all people who identify themselves with the people Israel will be included in the return to the Land of Israel. Akiva knew that many Jews in the Diaspora had little interest in returning to Zion. He believed that the Diaspora was a permanent feature of Jewish life.[10] Tradition also held that the ten tribes had settled in Africa and Asia (2 Kings 17:6) and were forever lost to the house of Israel.

Despite the disagreement over the extent of the ingathering, Jewish messianism believed that the end of the Jewish dispersion (*galut*) would occur in the messianic age. The prayer book includes the following blessing in the *Amidah,* the primary Jewish prayer: "Sound the great horn to herald our freedom, raise high the banner to gather all the exiles, and gather the dispersed from the four corners of the earth. Praised are You, *Adonai,* who gather the dispersed of His people Israel."

THE ARRIVAL OF THE MESSIAH

The rabbis speculated on the conditions under which the Messiah was likely to appear. He will not arrive on the Sabbath, since that would require people to violate the Sabbath in welcoming him.[11] Elijah will arrive no later in the week than Thursday, leaving room for the Messiah to arrive by Friday. Elijah will announce the arrival of the Messiah from Mount Carmel in the Land of Israel.[12] Many rabbis believed that the Messiah would arrive suddenly on the eve of Passover, the first redemption, which serves as a model of the final redemption.[13]

One statement from the time of the rabbis describes the era leading up to the Messiah in the darkest terms of societal corruption:

> In the footsteps of the Messiah, arrogance [*chutzpah*] will increase; prices will rise; grapes will be abundant but wine will be costly; the government will turn into heresy; and there will be no reproach. The meeting place [of scholars] will become a bordello; the Galilee will be destroyed; the highland will lie desolate; the border people will wander

from city to city and none will show them compassion; the wisdom of authors will stink; sin-fearing people will be detested; truth will be missing; young men will humiliate the elderly; the elderly will stand while the young sit; sons will revile their fathers; daughters will strike their mothers, brides will strike their mothers-in-law; and a man's enemies will take over his house. The face of the generation is like the face of a dog! Sons have no shame in front of their fathers; and on whom can one depend? Only upon our father in heaven.[14]

This era will be characterized by God's war against Gog and Magog and other catastrophic events. Another statement, which may date from the time of the Hadrianic persecutions (132–35 C.E.), offers the dark assessment that the Messiah will arrive in a period when Jews collaborate with their enemies, Torah learning disappears, poverty increases, and religious despair deepens: "The son of David will not arrive until informers are everywhere. Another view: Until there are few students left. Another view: Until the last coin is gone from the pocket. Another view: Until people despair of redemption . . . as if there is no support or help for Israel."[15]

Some sages predicted that the Messiah would not arrive until Israel observed the commandments more fully:

> Rabbi Judah said in the name of Rav: If all Israel had observed the very first Sabbath, no nation or tongue would have ever ruled over her. . . . Rabbi Yohanan said, following Rabbi Simeon bar Yohai: Were Israel to observe two Sabbaths punctiliously, they would be redeemed immediately.[16]

Some rabbis believed that the arrival of the Messiah had no relation either to political and societal events or to individual actions. They believed that there were a finite number of souls destined to enter the world and reside within human bodies. When the supply of fresh souls was exhausted, the Messiah would arrive.[17]

The rabbis were concerned with the question of how to prepare for the Messiah. Two of Yohanan ben Zakkai's students, Eliezer and Joshua, argued over whether repentance is a precondition for the coming of the Messiah. Rabbi Eliezer believed repentance is necessary, while Rabbi Joshua argued that it is not. Their argument continued as a duel of words

between the two men until Rabbi Eliezer conceded that Jewish suffering will come to an abrupt and sudden end without any precondition.[18]
One later sage, Rav, who opposed all eschatological speculation, cautioned that only moral goodness can hasten the Messiah: "Said Rav:
Stop all the [speculation on] last days! Everything depends upon repentance and good deeds."[19]

At the time of the Hadrianic persecutions, the rabbis speculated on
the fate of the Roman conquerors and their role in the messianic drama.
Rabbi Yose urged his contemporary, Hananiah ben Teradyon, to observe
the Roman edict prohibiting the teaching of Torah. He believed that
Rome was ordained to rule over Israel until the Messiah arrived.[20] He
predicted that the Persians and Medes would first penetrate the area
through the gate of Caesarea Philippi, located at the Banias spring in
northern Israel. After three attempts, Persia would defeat the Romans.
When that occurred, the Messiah would arrive.[21]

The tradition sees messianism as an abrupt end to Jewish suffering.
The only remaining question is whether human moral actions can hasten the arrival of the Messiah. The sense of the sources is that religious
and moral regeneration might help, but the arrival of the Messiah is, in
the end, not predictable.

THE DYING MESSIAH

The rabbis of the Mishnah and Talmud speculated on the nature of the
messianic era, but no systematic theory emerged. Some rabbis predicted
that the messianic era would begin with catastrophic events, while others thought events would unfold in a more rational sequence. It became
increasingly difficult to reconcile the contradictory views on the events
leading up to the arrival of the Messiah. One solution to this problem
was the introduction of the idea that there are really two messianic figures. The first, Messiah son of Joseph (*ben Yosef*), follows the arrival of
Elijah but he himself dies before the messianic era begins. The second,
Messiah son of David, is the figure who concludes the process, restores
the Davidic throne, and ushers in the end of days.

There was a tradition that a descendant of Jacob would defeat Edom,
the offspring of his brother Esau and a euphemism for Israel's enemies,
especially Rome. This defeat of Esau was linked to the idea that Joseph,

Jacob's favorite son, would serve as the agent of revenge.[22] The avenger, called a Messiah of Battle, would be victorious and defeat Rome. Another early source, the Aramaic Targum, suggested that there would be two redeemers—the Messiah son of David and the Messiah son of Ephraim.[23] The identification of the second Messiah with Ephraim is based on the fact that Joseph was the father of Ephraim. Here we have another variation on the notion that the line of Joseph will produce a Messiah. The question is, however, why two Messiahs? The answer lies partly in the fact that there are two traditions about the Messiah. The dominant tradition sees the line of David as producing the redeemer. A second, lesser tradition associates Jacob, Joseph, and Ephraim with the defeat of Esau (Edom or Rome). The latter reflects the particular degree of Jewish animosity toward Rome, which occupied Palestine and suppressed Jewish destiny. After the Hadrianic persecutions in the second century, this tradition gained greater prominence.[24]

THE MESSIANIC ERA

A central question that preoccupied the rabbis was how the messianic age would differ from the present age. One concern was that many Gentiles would convert to Judaism at the last moment just in order to participate in the new age. Some sages concluded, therefore, that "converts are not received in the days of the Messiah," just as they were not welcome in the days of David and Solomon.[25] A dispute arose among the rabbinic sages about the desirability of encouraging Gentiles to convert to Judaism. While most welcomed converts, others raised doubts about their sincerity. Rabbi Helbo, who mistrusted the sincerity of converts, stated that "converts are more difficult for Israel than a sore."[26] Others suspected that converts might not remain loyal during the messianic era. They decided that converts could be accepted, but with difficulty because they were likely to revert to their former ways in the heat of the messianic upheavals.[27]

Foreign nations would not be obliterated in the messianic era. Nations such as Rome would come to the Messiah to pay tribute to him, but their appeals for favor would be rejected.[28]

Some rabbis faced the messanic age with anticipation, others with dread. One viewpoint suggested that knowledge of Torah would continue to decline in the messianic age: "A bad announcement was conveyed to Israel at that moment. In the future, the Torah will be forgotten."[29] Others forecast that in "the future era, the synagogues and academies of Babylonia will be transported to the Land of Israel."[30] Still others held that humans would take on a new appearance: some thought that man would achieve a height of 160 feet, while another suggested he might double that. There is no suggestion that the Messiah himself is a wonder worker, but many sages believed that the messianic age would be a time of wonders. Women would give birth painlessly, hens lay eggs continuously, and food appear in abundance.[31]

There were controversies about the nature of the messianic era. Followers of the sage Samuel maintained that it would be similar to their own era, except that the Jewish people would be returned to Israel and the Davidic monarchy restored. Samuel saw "no difference between this world and the messianic age other than subjugation to dispersions."[32] Others, such as Rabbi Eliezer, believed that the next era would be unprecedented and qualitatively different. This debate represented the two poles of Jewish belief about the messianic era. One view sees it in terms of normal human existence under conditions of Jewish political independence; the other as something wholly new that defies prediction.

During the messianic era, the Messiah will reign victorious and rebuild the Temple. He will restore the priesthood to the Temple, and the traditional sacrifices will be reinstated. The return to the golden age of the Jewish people will be complete. Many popular Jewish prayers express this messianic longing for the rebuilding of the Temple and above all for the return to Zion. Perhaps even more than the coming of the Messiah, traditional Judaism has sought this dream of the return to Zion.

THE RESURRECTION OF THE DEAD AND THE DAY OF JUDGMENT

There is an end to the messianic era, although views differed on how long it might last. Some believed it would be brief, while others thought it would continue for years. At the end of the messianic era, the "day of the Lord" will bring a time of judgment to all humanity. Every person who has ever lived will be resurrected (*techiyyat ha-meitim*) from his grave for a final judgment, which will take place on Mount Zion in

Jerusalem. This is one reason why many traditional Jews prefer to be buried near Mount Zion: on the day of resurrection, they want to be closer to the front. Each individual will be accountable for his or her own actions. Those who are judged worthy will be rewarded with eternal life in the heavenly paradise. Those who are judged as unredeemed sinners will be condemned to Gehinnom, a nether world where the evil suffer eternal torment.

Jews and Gentiles alike have the same opportunity to be judged on the merits of their individual actions. One school of thought maintains that righteous Gentiles have the same likelihood as righteous Jews to be judged favorably.[33] Maimonides said that "the pious of the nations of the world have a place in the world to come."[34] Another approach assumes that all Gentiles will be presumed guilty for not having followed the teachings of the Torah.

THE TIME-TO-COME

Following the end of the messianic era begins the time-to-come, which has no end. The time-to-come (*olam ha-ba*) has two meanings in Judaism. It refers to the world that is constituted after the messianic era as well as to the period of life after death of the individual. This discussion considers only the messianic sense of the term. Once the Messiah arrives, the messianic era endures for between forty and two thousand years.[35] The rabbis have offered various forecasts about the length of this transitional period. Seeing this, other sages prohibited speculation about the end of the messianic era and the beginning of the time-to-come. As one sage raged, "May the bones of those who calculate the End rot!"[36]

The time-to-come, the end of history—when it comes—will be different from previous epochs in human history. According to Rabbi Yohanan, a Palestinian rabbi, the biblical prophecies of a utopian era refer to the messianic age, but the time-to-come is uncharted and unknown. According to Samuel, the postmessianic era, like the messianic one, will be no different from the present, with one exception: the Jewish people will be free from political subjugation by its enemies.[37]

Rav states that, in the time-to-come, life will be entirely spiritual, with none of the challenges of contemporary life. It will be lived as one continuous divine rapture. In the time-to-come there is no eating, drinking, procreation, commerce, jealousy, hate, or competition. There are only the righteous sitting with their crowns upon their heads and enjoying the radiance of the *Shekhinah*. True nourishment in the final era is not physical but spiritual. It consists of the continuous spiritual contemplation of Torah in God's presence.

MAIMONIDES' CODIFICATION OF MESSIANISM

There have been continual attempts to describe the messianic era and the time-to-come. Most of these are based on the biblical ideas of redemption and are developed, as they were in the rabbinic writings, in a highly unsystematic manner. Moses Maimonides tried to consolidate and systematize the various views into a Jewish theory of messianism. No formulation since the Talmud has had as great an impact in defining Jewish messianism as that of Maimonides.

Maimonides' approach to messianism is decidedly restorationist rather than utopian. He believed that the messianic age would be characterized by the restoration of the ideal kingship rather than the arrival of a utopian spiritual paradise. His view of the messianic age is that the King Messiah (*melech ha-mashiach*) will arise and restore the kingdom of David to its original state. He will rebuild the sanctuary and gather the dispersed of Israel. All the ancient laws governing the worship of God in the Temple will be reinstated. Sacrifices will again be offered, and all the laws of the ancient kingdom of Israel will be observed according to the commandments.[38]

This is a political messianism devoid of the supernaturalism that pervades many of the rabbinic statements. Maimonides advised against believing that the King Messiah would perform signs and wonders, bring anything new into being, revive the dead, or do similar things. The Messiah is not expected to perform miracles. As a mortal king, the Messiah will die and be succeeded by his son and descendants in a conventional line of Davidic succession.[39]

Maimonides specified the criteria for determining the authencity of the Messiah. The true Messiah will be a king descended from the house of David, a scholar who is knowledgeable in the Torah, occupies himself with the commandments, and observes the precepts of the Written and the Oral Law. He should be able to prevail upon Israel to walk in the way of the Torah and to lead Israel into battle against the enemies of the Lord. If he fulfills all these conditions, it may be assumed that he is the Messiah. If he further rebuilds the sanctuary on its site and gathers the dispersed of Israel, he is beyond all doubt the Messiah.[40] The messianic era is a natural progression from the present era. Maimonides cautioned against believing that in the days of the Messiah any of the laws of nature would be set aside or any innovation be introduced into creation. The world will follow its normal course.[41]

In Maimonides' scenario, Israel will experience a secure existence among her neighbors, non-Jews will accept Judaism, and "the sole difference between the present and the messianic days [will be] delivery from servitude to foreign powers."[42] Beyond this, he dismissed the various rabbinic theories about the nature of this era as mere speculation. He subscribed to the idea that Israel will be free to devote itself to the study of the Torah and will benefit from peace and human comfort. The king of Israel will reign for the course of a normal lifetime. After his death, he will be succeeded by his son through a natural course of succession.

According to Maimonides, the dead will be resurrected into life at the beginning of the messianic era—but not eternal life. The Messiah will not resurrect the dead himself. At the end of the era, those who were resurrected will again die a natural death, but they will endure, although not as physical bodies. The eternal part of the human soul—the intellect—will endure forever as a pure mind contemplating God.

Maimonides' formulation of resurrection provoked a widespread controversy among his opponents, who saw his views as insincere or distortions of traditional Jewish belief. He subsequently wrote a separate treatise on resurrection to reaffirm his belief in this tenet, but he did so in such a way that it still appeared insincere. Maimonides probably did not believe in the bodily resurrection of the dead. Some of his followers even went so far as to state that the doctrine of the resurrection of the dead was not a Jewish belief.

Maimonides rejected the attempts to portray the future as something new and different. The messianic era will be a progression into the ideal past, where Israel lives free in its land, under its king, and worships God in pure ways. In reality, Maimonides probably thought that this future would always be out of reach. His views represented not so much an expectation of an imminent restoration as a model of perfect human and Jewish life that would remain an unattainable ideal. Like many other Jewish thinkers, for him messianism was a deeply held belief that belonged eternally in the future.

DIFFERENCES BETWEEN JUDAISM AND CHRISTIANITY

What is it, after all, that marks the difference between Christians and Jews? Jews and Christians share a common stake in humanity and participate in the same social arena in most modern societies. Believing Jews and Christians, however, have incompatible views on the world. Jews believe in the eventual fulfillment of an elusive dream of a perfect world. Christians believe that the world has already been saved by the crucifixion and resurrection of the Messiah Jesus. The difference between the belief in future redemption and realized redemption is the chasm that separates Jewish from Christian thinking.

Christianity emerged out of a Jewish environment and against the backdrop of Jewish messianism in the late Second Temple period. The beliefs of early Jewish Christians were based on Jewish teaching of the first century C.E. John the Baptist was among the Jewish figures of the first century who believed in the cataclysmic prophecies about the impending disaster facing Israel if it did not repent. Jesus saw himself as a prophet—perhaps the last prophet—sent by God to gather Israel in a movement of national repentance before the imminent disaster.[43] The Jewish sects of the period differed about messianism. Some anticipated the imminent coming of the Davidic kingship, while others expected a more spiritual end of days which did not rely on the coming of a king. The messianic message was everywhere in first-century Israel.

Jesus was a Jewish preacher who lived at the end of this period, a time when messianic expectation was high. The ideas expressed in the Book of Enoch were widespread throughout the Jewish community. The Jews of Roman Palestine debated whether the messianic era was imminent and thus whether one ought to attack the Romans to hasten the End or wait passively apart from civilization to prepare for the Messiah. Jesus was a product of his times who followed the religious views of such Jewish teachers as Hillel, who emphasized ethics as the expression of devotion to God. Jesus went further than Hillel and his Pharisaic contemporaries in stressing the spiritual status of the poor and the oppressed and the holiness of poverty.

The New Testament explicitly identifies Jesus as the Davidic Messiah. In fact, the word "Christ" is a Greek translation of the Hebrew *mashiach*. The Romans, who tried and executed Jesus, recognized the inherent political danger of the messianic move toward Jewish national independence. They found Jesus guilty of claiming to fulfill the predictions for the restoration of the Davidic throne.

Although Jesus did not naturally fit the prophetic criteria for messianic authenticity, the authors of the gospels of Matthew and Luke composed a biography that attributed such characteristics to him. They created for him a lineage that traced his ancestry to King David. The legend of his birth in Bethlehem was intended to link him with David's ancestral home. Jesus followed some of the ascetic practices of Jewish sects of the time, which preached the need for repentance through immersion in water—a Jewish custom. The Last Supper—a Passover Seder—shows the degree to which Jesus was an observant Jew who followed the practices of Judaism while introducing new spiritual teachings. His teachings were part of the ferment of first-century Judaism under Roman occupation, in which deep differences about Jewish belief and practice were still being worked out.

Jesus did not always see himself as the Messiah. Early on, he accepted the view that the Messiah would soon come to judge Israel in the "end of days." Jesus often spoke about "the son of man," the term used by Jews in this period to describe the Messiah. He did not, however, identify himself with the son of man until the last years of his life. Although he may not have seen himself as the Messiah, many of his followers did. Soon after his martyrdom, he was widely seen by the Jewish Christians as the Messiah of Israel who alone brings the possibility of salvation to all humanity. Jesus was viewed by Jews at the time as one of the many contemporary spiritualists, who deserved no special attention. Insofar as the rabbis took notice, they dismissed him as a rabbinical student who disgraced his teachers by straying from the true path.[44]

Many early Christian ideas were inspired by a new approach to the meaning of the prophetic writings. The prophets often wrote metaphorically about events in their own lifetime, including politics, morality, and religion. They would also write about their hopes for future renewal and restoration in poetic terms. The followers of Jesus read these prophecies not as reflections of the prophets' historical situation and hope for the future but rather as specific predictions which they sought to match with the circumstances of Jesus' life. Many of their interpretations were based on the wide currency of messianic fervor during the first century—coupled with a misreading of the prophetic writings.

What were some examples of creative misreading? Jacob's blessing of his sons, shortly before his death, includes a promise to Judah, his son by Leah: "The scepter shall not depart from Judah, nor the ruler's staff between his feet; so that tribute shall come to him [*shiloh*][45] and the homage of peoples be his" (Genesis 49:10). Many scholars believe this passage to be an insertion from the time of King David, a descendant of the tribe of Judah. The passage reflects the view among David's supporters that the continuous reign of the house of David represents the fulfillment of Jacob's promise to Judah, predicting, as it does, that the line of Judah will produce the future kings of Israel. Jesus' followers, however, believed that *shiloh* referred to Jesus, who was alleged to have descended from King David and thus also Judah, on his paternal side (Matthew 1:2–16).

Later, Isaiah describes his image of the restoration king with the euphemism "God is with us [*immanuel*]" (Isaiah 7:14). This is a contemporary reference to King Hezekiah, the successor to Ahaz. Isaiah (9:5–6) describes Hezekiah as a "child [who] has been born to us," that is, a successor to King David. The reference to Hezekiah was picked up by the followers of Jesus. Early Christians attributed Davidic ancestry to Jesus and read this historical reference as a prophecy alluding to the birth and infancy of Jesus.

The motifs of redemption, which continue throughout Deutero-Isaiah, date from the period of the destruction of Solomon's Temple. In the song of the "servant of the Lord" (Isaiah 42:1–4), Deutero-Isaiah prophesies about the redemption of Israel, "My servant." The "suffering servant" is a metaphor that has two meanings in these passages. Sometimes the servant refers to one of the kings of Israel, in keeping with the notion of Davidic restoration. At others, it becomes an idealization of the people Israel, an image that suggests Israel's future as God's chosen people (Isaiah 51:8, 54:1). In either case, the servant is a symbol for the future restoration of Israel. Although Israel is oppressed by the gentile nations, Deutero-Isaiah holds out the hope that eventually the religious and moral teachings of Israel will spread to the other nations. Israel will serve as an exemplar, "a light of the nations," who will lead the others from darkness to light. Deutero-Isaiah teaches that, in the end of days, all the nations will bow down before God.

Deutero-Isaiah describes the disparity between the condition of the Jewish people and the glorious destiny for which they are intended. This image became known as the "suffering servant" passage. The heart of the passage is a memorial hymn to a wounded or defeated figure (Isaiah 53:1–5):

> Indeed, My servant shall prosper,
> Be exalted and raised to great heights.
> Just as the many were appalled at him—
> So marred was his appearance, unlike that of a man,
> His form, beyond human semblance—
> Just so he shall startle many nations.
> Kings shall be silenced because of him,
> For they shall see what has not been told them,
> Shall behold what they have never heard. (Isaiah 52:13–15)

The "suffering servant" passage was a memorial ode to King Josiah, a Davidic descendant, who was killed in a battle at Megiddo (2 Kings 23:29). In the Christian tradition, however, it was taken to mean that Christ had died for the sins of the people. Not knowing the original intent of the passage, Christians read their prediction into the text after the fact. In medieval times, this passage and its differing interpretation by Jews and Christians became something of a battleground between the two religions.

Why do Jews and Christians read these passages so differently? Jews read them in the historical context in which they were written. The passages refer to the sufferings and hope for restoration of the Jewish kingdom in all its moral and religious glory. Jews understand the metaphors in these passages in the context of Jewish historical events, which refer to real persons and kings. Christians take them out of their historical context and read them as predictions.

The prophet Jeremiah continues Isaiah's warnings about the impending national disaster. He warns frequently: "Behold, days are coming" (Jeremiah 7:32, 9:24) when the kingdom of Judah will pay the price of its infidelities and suffer defeat at the hands of its enemies (34:8–22). This oracle came to pass with the destruction of the Temple, the conquering of the kingdom, and the exile of its leading families by the Babylonian king Nebuchadnezzar in 586 B.C.E. Like Isaiah and Micah, Jeremiah also predicted that after the national catastrophe, the Davidic kingdom would be restored, Israel and Judah would be reunited, the Sinai covenant would be reaffirmed, and the people Israel would assume a new character of devotion to God and moral goodness:

> See, a time is coming—declares the Lord—when I will make a new covenant with the house of Israel and the house of Judah. It will not be like the covenant I made with their fathers, when I took them by the hand to lead them out of the land of Egypt, a covenant which they broke, so that I rejected them—declares the Lord. But such is the covenant I will make with the house of Israel after these days—declares the Lord: I will put my teaching [Torah] into their inmost being and inscribe it upon their hearts. Then I will be their God, and they shall be My people. (Jeremiah 31:30–32)

Christians understood this passage as suggesting that the Torah would someday be replaced by faith in Jesus, although the passage explicitly states that God will reaffirm the Torah as the covenant binding the people to God.

Each of these passages reflects specific prophetic teachings in the context of actual events in the history of Israel. Jesus' followers, however, did not read them as such. Because they were also meant to be predictive, the followers of Jesus were following common Jewish practice when they interpreted them as messianic hints. There was nothing un-Jewish about viewing these passages predictively. The conclusion that they referred to Jesus was not surprising, given the messianic anticipation and eclecticism common among Jewish sects in the first century.

What was surprising was that Jesus, a Jewish sectarian, should be seen as the fulfillment of Jewish messianic hopes after his death. For, within the decades after his death, the obvious fact that he failed to fulfill Jewish messianic expectations should have led to the decrease among his followers. The success of the early Christian movement among the Jews is a testimony to the power that messianism held within the community. The forced interpretations of Scripture by Jesus' followers were used to justify him as the fulfillment of Jewish prophecy. Subsequent events show that Jesus was but one of the many messiahs who have appeared in Jewish history. The main point of contention between Judaism and Christianity on the issue of the Messiah is whether Jesus satisfies the criteria accepted by the rabbinic tradition. From the Christian point of view, Jesus fulfills the predictions about the Messiah in the prophetic writings. From the Jewish point of view, the Christians misread the prophecies, some of which refer to past events while others describe the future in metaphorical terms. The major Jewish objection to Christianity is that Judaism regards the Messiah as a human being, and the Christian deification of a person constitutes idolatry. Moreover, since none of the events predicted for the messianic era have come true, Jews cannot accept the Christian claim that the world has been redeemed or that the Messiah has come. Nevertheless, it is primarily through the spread of Christian teaching, from the early Jewish Christians to the later Gentiles, that Jewish messianism has become a part of world culture.

JEWISH MESSIANIC MOVEMENTS

Real expectation of the coming of the Messiah has been fundamental to postbiblical Judaism. The idea is too deeply rooted and too powerful not to erupt occasionally into messianic movements. There has also been a deep bias against the belief that the Messiah has arrived. Jewish messianism is best understood as an unrealizable promise, a dream unfulfilled. It is ironic that Judaism devotes so much attention to the conditions and circumstances of messianism, but is loathe to declare the arrival of a Messiah. Thus, Jewish messianism is both the theory of messianism and the history of false messiahs and messianic disappointments.

Christianity is the first major messianic movement to have emerged from Jewish messianism. Judaism views Jesus as one of many false messiahs in first-century Jerusalem. The New Testament itself makes reference to several false messiahs of the period (Acts 5:36–37). Josephus, the first-century chronicler of the Jewish revolt against Rome, identifies a certain Menahem as a real historical figure in the war against Rome (66–70 C.E.). Menahem was a leader in the revolt who, early on, recaptured Masada from the Romans. He is said to have then appeared in the Temple courtyard in Jerusalem dressed as the king of Israel. He was murdered there by other Jewish insurgents who saw him as a royal pretender of inferior origins.[46]

The most important Jewish messianic figure in antiquity was Bar Kokhba (died 135 B.C.E.), the leader of the Jewish revolt in Judea against Rome. Rome had destroyed the Second Temple in 70 C.E. and sent many Jews into exile throughout the Roman Empire. By 132, Jewish groups had begun to mount effective resistance to the Roman occupation by stealing weapons and seizing small towns and villages in Judea. Rome responded by pouring in a large army to suppress the insurrection. But soon the conflict expanded into a full-scale revolt which exacted a severe toll on the Roman forces.

The rebels captured Jerusalem for a time, until the Roman forces crushed the revolt and ended the Jewish occupation of the city. The rebel forces made their final stand at Betar in the Judean hills outside Jerusalem, where Bar Kokhba was killed. The revolt had spread to the Galilee, the Golan, the coastal plain, Judea, and the Judean Desert. For a time, the rebels held the upper hand and claimed a short-lived independence from Rome. By 135, the revolt was crushed and its leaders killed. The Midrash of the Ten Martyrs, the martyrology recited in the Yom Kippur service, recalls the Roman persecutions and massacre of the Jewish sages in 135.

The revolt was led by Bar Kokhba, the military and administrative leader of the Jewish community who held the title of *nasi* (chief). Rabbi Akiva, the leading sage of the period, identified Bar Kokhba as King Messiah who would fulfill the messianic aspirations of Israel. Many viewed Bar Kokhba as the Messiah, and the revolt contributed to a greatly heightened sense of messianic expectation. All this abruptly ended with the defeat of the revolt and Bar Kokhba's death. Many Jews throughout Judea were massacred or enslaved. This tragedy extinguished Jewish messianic hopes but contributed many of the fantastical theories about messianism that were included in the Talmud.

Small outbreaks of local messianic hope continued to erupt throughout Jewish history. In eighth-century Persia, Abu Isa of Isfahan claimed to be the precursor of the Messiah. He led a military revolt against the Muslim authorities which lasted several years. It, too, died and left a continuing residue of disappointment within the Jewish community. Later, during a period of Muslim persecution of the Jews, Maimonides himself felt compelled to warn the Jews of Yemen against believing in a man who claimed to be the Messiah.

The period from the First to Second Crusades (1096–1146) was a time of war between Christianity and Islam. Jewish communities in Europe and the Middle East were not spared suffering, death, and dispersion as armed Crusaders made their way to the Holy Land. In Kurdistan and Baghdad, major centers of Muslim and Jewish life, a short-lived messianic movement appeared. David Alroy, who claimed to be the Messiah, urged the Jews to arm themselves and prepare to establish the messianic kingdom. This movement too was crushed and its leader killed. These episodes reflect how Jews have sometimes resorted to messianism in times of persecution. Messianism served as an outlet for the deep and painful experiences and frustrations of Jewish history, but in most cases misplaced political rebellion resulted in greater calamity and suffering.

Other messianic pretenders offered strange and imaginative schemes which had a profound impact upon wide circles of Jews throughout the world. The most important and bizarre case is that of Sabbatai Zvi (1626–76). He was born to a wealthy merchant family in Izmir (Turkey) and was educated in rabbinics and Kabbalah. He gained a following of students and seemed destined for a respectable, if not distinguished, rabbinic career. But he also displayed signs in early adulthood of a manic-depressive disorder. During the manic cycle, he began to commit violations of Jewish law. During the depressive state, he would withdraw from contact with his contemporaries and struggle with what he thought were demons and satanic forces. He developed a reputation as a gifted, charismatic, but disturbed personality. At times he claimed to be the Messiah. He was aware of his own bizarre behavior and sought to exorcise his demons through spiritual practices. He wandered through Greece, Turkey, Egypt, and Israel in search of a cure.

Sabbatai Zvi was a student of the Lurianic system of Kabbalah, which taught that God's holy and pure light is trapped and hidden within the world. God's light is mired in the broken vessels that constitute the reality of everyday life; redemption comes from finding and elevating the divine light trapped in the vessels of this world. Lurianic Kabbalah taught that the divine light could be elevated through performance of the *mitzvot*.

The period itself was one of heightened messianic expectation. The Chmielnicki pogroms of 1648 in the Ukraine devastated many East European Jewish communities. Speculation about messianism grew in proportion to the extent of the tragedy. Although the pogroms occurred in the Ukraine, news of them shook the entire Jewish world. Moreover, the *gematria*—the numerical value—of the Hebrew word for "birthpangs of Messiah" was equivalent to the year 1648 in the Hebrew calendar.

The pogroms seemed to confirm the talmudic predictions that the Messiah would come when Jewish suffering increased. Against this background, Sabbatai Zvi met Nathan of Gaza, a young Kabbalist, in 1665. Nathan persuaded him that he was indeed the Messiah and that his cycles of elation and despair were not psychological but theological states. He convinced Sabbatai Zvi that the agonized soul of the Messiah reflected the conflict between illumination of the divine light and the affliction of the broken vessels. The despair Sabbatai Zvi experienced as a result of his inner conflict was a microcosm of the mystical conflict between good and evil. The cosmic battle between the light and the broken vessels was being played out within the soul of the Messiah. Sabbatai Zvi became convinced that he was the Messiah, and his and Nathan's messianic propaganda gained currency.

The popularity of the kabbalistic teachings contributed to the spread of Sabbatean messianism. Sabbatai Zvi's following grew in Turkey and throughout the Jewish world, including Italy, Yemen, and Poland. Never before had so many Jewish leaders and their communities been swept up into a messianic movement. Rumors began to spread throughout the Diaspora that the Messiah had been crowned king and was about to gather the exiled Jewish communities in Israel. But in the face of growing insurrection among the Jews, the Turkish sultan had Sabbatai Zvi arrested in 1666. He was held in various prisons for eight months, during which time the enthusiasm of his followers increased. The sultan finally presented him with the choice of conversion to Islam or death. On September 15, 1666, Sabbatai Zvi converted to Islam.

The disappointment among his followers was profound. Many turned back to their routines and attempted to conceal the evidence in their communities about their support for the false Messiah. But another group, influenced by Nathan of Gaza's propaganda, was persuaded that his apostasy was a necessary stage of the Messiah's mission. The Messiah, Nathan argued, must descend into the very depths of evil, symbolized by conversion to Islam, in order to redeem the light trapped within the shattered vessels. The theory of the paradoxical Messiah continued to gain currency throughout the next century. Faced with the apparent treachery of Sabbatai Zvi, many Kabbalists found the theory plausible.

Surprisingly, the number of his followers grew rather than diminished through the eighteenth century. Some followed him into Islam, and even today this group exists and is known as the Donmeh sect in Turkey. His Jewish followers constituted two distinct groups. One consisted of secret Sabbateans, who overtly followed traditional Judaism while privately believing in the Sabbatean truth. They were practicing Jews and secret adherents of Sabbateanism. The second group, the radical Sabbateans, practiced a discipline of "redemption through sin," in imitation of their Messiah's apostasy. They violated the Jewish commandments— some publicly, others privately—and practiced Sabbatean rites as the fulfillment of their faith in Sabbatai Zvi. They were Jewish heretics in both practice and belief. Some even converted to Catholicism as the ultimate act of their faith. Jewish communities were torn apart by accusations and witch hunts in search of these Sabbateans. Jewish communities also suffered persecution at the hands of radical Sabbateans, especially those who converted to Christianity.

The Sabbatean crisis eventually dissipated. The result of this episode was to discredit messianism among large segments of European Jewry. In the wake of the Sabbatean heresy, Jewish intellectuals recognized that active messianism was a divisive, destructive force in the life of the Jewish people. They sought to replace the messianic energy and neutralize the messianic element in Judaism with less lethal forms of spiritual teachings. Religious leaders warned against attempts to force the Messiah's arrival. By the end of the eighteenth century, active messianism had faded as a potent force in Jewish life.

At the same time, messianism remained a fundamental Jewish belief that explained to Jews that the sufferings of this world would end someday. It promised that Jews would live in a free, independent Jewish state under ideal religious and political circumstances. Although the messianic dream seemed more remote than ever, its power never diminished.

CONTEMPORARY JEWISH MESSIANISM

The notion of a linear progression of history from creation to messianic redemption is a very potent idea in Judaism. It has appeal to religious and secular Jews alike because it is based on the idea that human beings can perfect the world. Even if we ourselves never reach the goal, the vision of a better world continues to motivate and inspire us. We believe that our efforts contribute to the realization of the vision and that without us the world would be less than it is or can be. This messianic idea empowers us as the agents who move history forward on its course.

The traditional belief in the arrival of a Messiah, accompanied by the events that were predicted by the rabbis of the Talmud and Maimonides, seems unnatural and fantastic today. Yet this vision of the future has inspired Jews throughout history and continues to excite some segments of the Orthodox community. For the modern Jew, the messianic dream has been transformed and lives on in ways that are greatly different from the traditional belief.

For centuries, traditional Jews have found comfort in messianic belief, especially during periods of oppression and insecurity. This hope has been expressed in a brief verse, "*Ani Maamin*" (I believe), based on Maimonides' twelfth principle of belief which has been set to a plaintive melody: "I believe with complete faith in the coming of the Messiah and, even if he should tarry, yet I will wait for him."[47] Messianism has often been the last source of hope and comfort to the Jewish people and an expression of their deepest faith. Jews on their way to certain death in the Nazi gas chambers continued to sing this song of hope even when all hope was lost. The faith in the eventual coming of the Messiah offered more than solace; Maimonides' credo expressed their ardent conviction that God would not allow the destruction of their people and would not let the oppressors go unpunished. It is, at bottom, a plea for divine justice and salvation.

In the decades before the Holocaust, the belief in the Messiah was the subject of considerable debate within the Jewish communities of Eastern Europe. Many young Jews rejected the Orthodoxy of their parents and turned to the great Jewish secular movements of Zionism, socialism, and Bundism. They viewed their parents' faith in the eventual coming of the Messiah as a dangerous passivity in the face of imminent danger to the Jewish people. They took their fate into their own hands and created new forms of secular Jewish messianic activity. Their concern for changing the world by rejecting their religious background shows how deeply they were immersed in the Jewish search for redemption.

Hasidism, the eighteenth-century spiritual movement, also concerned itself with new approaches to redemption. After the Sabbatean debacle of the previous century, Hasidism abandoned active forms of messianism for a system of redemption within the individual. The Baal Shem Tov, the founder of Hasidism, taught that one need not look outside one's own soul for redemption: "All our prayers for redemption are essentially bound to be prayers for the redemption of the individual."[48] He urged that we turn inward and seek redemption through seeking transcendence in all our actions and transactions. As Martin Buber, a leading interpreter of Hasidism said, "There is no definite magic action that is effective for redemption; only the hallowing of all actions without distinction possesses redemptive power. Only out of the redemption of the everyday does the Day of Redemption grow."

Even though it appeared that the idea of a Messiah had run its course, traditional Jewish messianism endures. The Habad-Lubavitch Hasidim, one of the largest of the remaining hasidic sects, believes that the messianic age is imminent. They point to the events of the last several decades—the recapture of Jerusalem in 1967; the ingathering of the immigrants from the Soviet Union, Ethiopia, Syria, and Yemen; the Gulf War; and the collapse of Communism in the former Soviet Union and

Eastern Europe—as signs. They believe that if the great majority of Jews repent and return to observance, the Messiah will arrive immediately. Their task, as they see it, is to stand ready for the arrival of the Messiah. The late Lubavitcher rebbe, Menahem Mendel Schneerson, said that this "generation is the last generation of Exile and the first generation of Redemption."[49] Many of his followers believed that he was the Messiah. They point out that he fit the description of the human redeemer whose good works have brought many Jews back to Judaism. If it turns out that the messianic age is not upon us, they will attribute that not to him but to the lack of readiness of this generation. The Lubavitchers seized on his hints and innuendoes about their rabbi's role as the Messiah, but in the meantime they poured their energy into the observance of the *mitzvot*. They have a very different outlook from the extreme religious messianists in Israel, who are preparing to establish the Third Temple on the Temple Mount in anticipation of the Messiah's imminent arrival. Among the latter are weavers, smiths, and other artisans who have even crafted the vestments, utensils, and paraphernalia necessary to conduct the priestly sacrifices in the rebuilt Temple.

The messianic idea, as opposed to a literal belief in the Messiah, fueled many of the modern Jewish political movements. Zionism, which gained force among the unemancipated Jews of Eastern Europe after 1881, was based on several powerful forces—some modern, some traditional. Zionism sprouted from the modern political judgment that anti-Semitism was endemic to European regimes and could not be solved through attempts at societal reform. It also drew upon the romantic nationalistic idea that every people is a nation and every nation should have a state as a national home. Despite the opposition of traditionalists, the modern political aspirations of Jewish nationalists found their deepest psychological support in the Jewish tradition of the messianic return to Zion. Religious Zionists saw their efforts to rebuild Zion as a partnership with the Messiah. Paradoxically, the popular support for the secular Zionists' return to Zion came from the centuries-old tradition of restorationist Jewish messianism, despite the fact that this "return to Zion" would result in a secular parliamentary democracy, not a theocracy.

Jewish radicalism can also be seen as a form of modern Jewish messianism. Karl Marx, Rosa Luxemburg, Leon Trotsky and other Bolsheviks, and the New Left of the 1960s are often described as secular Jewish messianists in a "search for redemption that is so strong in Jewish history."[50] According to this theory, you can take a Jew out of the tradition, but you cannot take messianism out of a Jew. Irving Howe saw messianism as "the most urgent force in Jewish tradition, the force that could send a quiescent people into moments of transport and even collective frenzy."[51] He saw socialism and Zionism as secular expressions of this force. The essence of Judaism, in his view, is the hope for a Messiah, which these movements have transformed into a commitment to radical political change.

Modern religious denominations have also had to come to terms with the messianic belief. Reform Judaism rejected traditional Jewish messianism. Its liturgical changes included the removal from the prayer book of all references to the Messiah and to an eventual return to the Land of Israel.[52] The idea of the personal Messiah was reinterpreted as the longing for universal brotherhood within the context of ethical monotheism. More recently, the Reform concept of messianism has come to mean the result of human effort on behalf of creating the perfect world. Despite the extremely positive references to the State of Israel in the modern prayer books, there is no preaching of a personal return. This is a messianic age without a Messiah—the fulfillment of the particular destiny of the Jewish people in a modern, universalistic mode.[53]

Conservative Judaism understands the body of rabbinic ideas on messianism as "elaborate metaphors generated by deep-seated human and communal needs."[54] The various images of the messianic age express the longing for a time of universal peace and social justice and for the ingathering of all Jews to Israel. The Conservative movement, however, has replaced the idea of the messianic rebuilding of the Temple by anticipating an age in which the religious and ethical teachings of the Torah will become universal. The Final Judgment is not meant to be taken literally; it is understood as the idea of God's justice. The Conservative credo is agnostic on the question of the Messiah: "We do not know when the Messiah will come, nor whether he will be a charismatic human figure or is a symbol of the redemption of humankind from the evils of the world. Through the doctrine of a messianic figure, Judaism teaches us that every individual human being must live as if he or she, individually, has the responsibility to bring about the messianic age."[55]

Messianism runs deep in the Jewish tradition. The belief in the future restoration of Jewish independence or the utopian anticipation of a better age are fundamental teachings of Judaism. Despite centuries of active messianic hope, Judaism is more comfortable with deferred than attainable messianism. Historically, we have had disastrous experiences with messianic activism. Nevertheless, Judaism requires that Jews work assiduously to bring about the messianic age. Messianism is the perpetually unfulfilled promise of the future. Our sacred myths tell us that the Messiah is always coming and that he might arrive at any moment. Throughout Jewish history, messianism has provided a means for the Jewish people to express their dreams and hopes for a better world in terms both of their particular destiny and of the redemption of all humanity. Jews recognize that the messianic task can never be complete until the world is a better place for all. The broadest definition of Jewish messianism is hope for a better future for humanity. The figure of the Messiah embodies our belief that this is God's hope as well.

The messianic task is not meant to divert us from our responsibilities in the world. It is meant to focus our awareness on the ideal toward which we should be exerting every effort in the world. Jews believe that the work of creating a perfect world is more important than the Messiah. Rabbi Yohanan ben Zakkai said that if you are planting a tree and someone tells you to stop your work because the Messiah has arrived, you should ignore him and continue your planting. When you are done, you can go out to greet the Messiah.[56]

9

Why Be Jewish?
A Letter to My Children

Dear Judah, Micah, and Aviva,

There is a custom in our tradition for parents to write a *tzavaah*, an ethical will, to our children in which we convey our hopes and concerns for you. This tradition goes back to Isaac, who blessed his sons Jacob and Esau. Jacob in turn called his sons together and said, "Come together, that I may tell you what is to befall you in the days to come" (Genesis 49:1). I would not presume to predict the future, but I wish to speak to you about our future as Jews. Although I have taken this unusual step of publishing your *tzavaah*, I hope you will permit my public display of intimacy.

Although it might now appear unlikely, someday each of you will ask yourself, "Why be Jewish?" This is an unusual question, since you probably will never ask, "Why be American?" or "Why be a man or a woman?" I wish matters were such that you could always take your Jewishness for granted. On the other hand, I would not want you to leave your Jewishness unexamined any more than I would want you not to reflect on who you are in other regards. I think, though, that examining your Jewishness will involve more than reflection. You will find that being and remaining Jewish will require an active effort, a determined decision, on your part.

No parent can take for granted that his or her children will remain Jewish. You might find that you have no room in your heart for the particular concerns of the Jewish people. You might find another spiritual teaching more compelling for you. You might find that being a good person is satisfaction enough. I hope not, but I realize that I cannot take your Jewish self for granted. Your parents hope to create a home and a community in which the choice to be Jewish will be inevitable. We realize, however, that you make your own decisions despite us.

Why be Jewish? There are many ways I could answer this question. I could tell you that since you are Jewish, and were raised Jewish, you can never be anything other than that. I know that you can make many choices, including one as profound as attempting to throw off one identity for another. But even if you should deny your Jewish self, others will remind you of who you are. You should be prepared to assert the positive value of who you are, because others will be less kind. There is a deep Jewish spark within you which cannot be denied. If you think you can discard it, you will be disappointed. This reminds me of what Freud said to a Jewish colleague who was thinking of raising his children outside of the Jewish tradition: "If you do not let your son grow up as a Jew, you will deprive him of those sources of energy which cannot be replaced by anything else. He will have to struggle as a Jew, and you ought to help him develop all the energy he will need for that struggle. Do not deprive him of that advantage." What are those sources of energy that cannot be replaced by anything else? I hope they are the Jewish drive for transcendence, for perfection, for seeing the world as it can be, not just as it is.

I might also appeal to you on the grounds of simple loyalty. Do not abandon the religion that is yours by birth, the faith of your parents and ancestors. Judaism is your inheritance. The God of Judaism is my God and its people are my people. I am often drawn to what I read about other cultures and find deep inspiration there. "Who is wise?" our sages ask. "One who learns from all." I do not believe that Judaism has the monopoly on truth, but I do find that I feel closer to the sacred myths of my own people. I find myself wondering who my ancestors were, what they read, and what they believed. The likelihood that they thought about the same things I do, that we have stepped into the same river at the same point, offers me a sense of continuity and belonging I could not find anywhere else. I know that this in itself is not sufficient to persuade you to remain Jewish. There are many other elements of your birthright and ancestry that you are free to keep or abandon. I could not expect you to choose to live where I live, share my political opinions, or follow in the footsteps of my career. So why should I expect you to be Jewish simply because it is your inheritance?

The world needs you to be Jewish. Our society faces new and seemingly unprecedented challenges, including creating opportunities for better lives for millions of people and finding ways to realize the opportunities of new technologies. Even the newest challenges reflect perennial human concerns and will require moral and critical judgments. Judaism represents a serious and sustained effort over centuries to address human concerns in light of a value system that is open to change and growth.

From a purely intellectual point of view, Judaism is the longest continuous culture within Western civilization. It is an invaluable key to understanding that civilization. Jewish culture played a critical role in the transmission of the classical civilization of ancient Greece and Rome to the West during the Renaissance. Jewish literature often served as the vehicle for the preservation and dissemination of the classical tradition from one part of the world to another. Jewish culture is the connective tissue between the humanistic traditions of antiquity and modernity.

It would be an irrevocable loss to world culture if Judaism were to disappear. The Jewish role in modern culture—the arts, sciences, and literature—has shaped American culture. The growing phenomenon of assimilation threatens to destroy the ties of American Jews to their own culture which has contributed so much. It seems to me that the disintegration of Jewish culture would constitute something more serious than the loss of an immigrant culture. It would represent the loss of one of the great world traditions, a loss of one of the constituent cultures of Western civilization, and a further homogenization of the American polity into an indistinguishable blend of popular cultures. Further, in an age when some political forces seek to impose particular religious values upon a diverse American society, Jewish culture serves as a reminder of the pluralistic character of our society and its tolerant traditions.

There are dimensions of American cultural literacy that emerge from the Jewish tradition and are important to all people. These include the Hebrew Bible—monotheism, the Ten Commandments, the Prophets—and the work of great Jewish philosophers and thinkers. We must help transmit this legacy to all children.

I recognize that the rationale for Jewish survival is, ultimately, personal and beyond rational explanation. A Jew knows instinctively the importance of Jewish continuity, although it might require a lifetime of exploration to explain it even to himself. The search may in fact lead you to take a class, join a congregation, take a trip to Israel, or read more books, all of which fall within the range of traditional Jewish activities. The most persuasive reason for being Jewish is the satisfaction you can find in taking part in the all-encompassing life of the Jewish people.

The sacred myths of Judaism offer answers to the fundamental questions concerning the individual's place in the world different from those of other cultures or religions. Our culture cannot be preserved unless its elements are so compelling that they provide more than any other system that competes for our attention. The Jewish way must seem to us a better way.

The fact that Judaism places the quest for finding a transcendent purpose within life at the center of the Jewish enterprise seems to me the element that most distinguishes Judaism. Although every religion has its own set of answers, the sacred myths of Judaism are constantly challenging the accepted answers and posing new approaches. Judaism is the always self-correcting spiritual process of finding transcendent meaning and purpose. This process is perpetual and commits us in advance to intellectual honesty. Ours will not be the last generation to struggle with the issue of Jewish destiny.

So far, I have given you my reasons why this enterprise we call Judaism and the survival of the Jewish people deserve your support and involvement. If Jews do not care about Judaism, who will? And if Jews cease to be Jews, who will represent this vision of a higher purpose of life to the world? But the real answer to the question "Why be Jewish?" has to do with you. If you choose to disregard your Jewish heritage, you will lose something that cannot be replaced by anything else. We lead our lives within this world somewhat precariously. Judaism helps us to navigate the world, to fill it with magnificence, and to reach occasional glimpses of eternity. It provides us with a spiritual orientation that does not deny the importance of the everyday but rather shows us how to elevate the mundane. I am concerned about how you will live your lives. In passing along the faith of our ancestors to you, I do it with the hope that you will use your God-given potential to make life extraordinary.

My own answer is that Judaism is the right system of belief and action to guide you through the world. Ultimately, Judaism is a teaching about how we can experience the transcendent dimensions of life and strengthen the image of God within ourselves. We can envision it as God reaching out to us and drawing us to a higher level of existence or we can describe it as realizing God in the everyday. Perhaps the clearest expression of these goals is found in a letter written by a Jewish mother to her child living in the Warsaw Ghetto in 1940, shortly before they were murdered by the Nazis:

> Judaism, my child, is the struggle to bring down God upon earth, a struggle for the sanctification of the human heart. This struggle your people wages not with physical force but with spirit and by constant striving for truth and justice. So, do you understand, my child, how we are distinct from others and wherein lies the secret of our existence on earth?

The most compelling of all our beliefs is the dual belief in divine transcendence and human empowerment. The destiny of the Jewish people is to create a kingdom of priests and a holy nation. The Jewish belief in human destiny sets a standard for me that no other culture does. Judaism challenges me to be consistent in my words, deeds, and thoughts. I know of no other system of meaning that expects so much of me but promises so much in return.

To be Jewish is to be a seeker of the unlimited ways in which God can be realized within our lives. A hasidic saying urges us to hold on to two thoughts: that "the world was created for my sake" and that "I am but dust and ashes." When we feel small and insignificant, we must re-

member that we are created in God's image and that the world was created for our sake. When we are feeling powerful, we must recall our
mortality. Our lives have purpose and ultimate significance as the manifestation of God in the world.

Every generation of Jews sees the same goal, but in its own way, and
expresses it in the language of its own day. What one generation calls
"seeking God," another might call "seeking transdendence." What one
generation calls "covenant," another might call "responsibility." What
one generation refers to as "the divine image," another might call
"human destiny."

The great sacred myth of the destiny of the Jewish people explains
that the search for higher meaning animates every aspect of Jewish life.
It means that we constantly strive to recognize that all people are created in the divine image. As individuals, our spirituality is expressed in
strengthening the divine image within ourself. The search for transcendence takes us into the garden of Torah to fathom God's message to us
and along the path of Jewish spirituality which teaches us to express our
deepest beliefs in actions. Just as God reaches out to us, we respond
with the service of our heart.

We believe that God is the hidden ideal to which we always aspire
through our daily routines, our religious practices, our learning, and our
prayers. The higher world is the world to which we aspire, but it is also
one that we can realize only within ourself, in our relationships, and in
our community. Touching the transcendent reality greater than ourself
is the spiritual goal of Judaism. The realization of our aspiration can
only be achieved within the world we know.

And, so, my children, this is your *tzavaah*. Remember, your life is like
a book. Write in it what you want to be known of you.

With love,
Your Abba

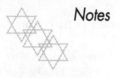

Notes

References to the Hebrew Bible are based on the English translation of *Tanakh: A New Translation of the Holy Scriptures According to the Traditional Hebrew Text* (Philadelphia, 1985). Talmudic references are to the standard pagination of the tractates of the Babylonian Talmud.

Introduction

1. Mary Douglas, *Purity and Danger* (London, 1966), p. 39; quoted in Lawrence Hoffman, *Beyond the Text* (Bloomington, Ind., 1987), p. 38.
2. Matthew Fox, "A Mystical Cosmology: Towards a Postmodern Spirituality," in *Sacred Interconnections,* ed. David Ray Griffin (Albany, N.Y., 1990), p. 16; quoted in Wade Clark Roof, *A Generation of Seekers* (San Francisco, 1993), p. 64.
3. Gershom Scholem, "Reflections on Jewish Theology," in Scholem, *On Jews and Judaism in Crisis* (New York, 1976), p. 265.

Chapter 1: God

1. David R. Griffin, *God and Religion in the Postmodern World* (Albany, N.Y., 1989), p. 52; quoted in Roof, *Generation of Seekers,* p. 74.

2. James Pritchard, *Ancient Near Eastern Texts* (Princeton, N.J., 1955), tablet 1, II. 1–30.
3. Avot 3:2.
4. Sota 14a.
5. Hullin 60a; Hayim Nahman Bialik and Yehoshua Hana Ravnitzky, *The Book of Legends / Sefer Ha-Aggadah* (New York, 1992), p. 505.
6. *Pirkei de-Rabbi Eliezer* (Warsaw, 1852) 12:24; quoted in Barry Holtz, *Finding Our Way* (New York, 1990), p. 103.
7. *Sifre: A Tannaitic Commentary on the Book of Deuteronomy*, ed. Reuven Hammer (New Haven, 1986), *Ekev* 49; quoted in Holtz, *Finding Our Way*, p. 65.
8. *Pesikta de-Rav Kahana*, ed. Bernard Mandelbaum (New York, 1962); quoted in George F. Moore, *Judaism in the First Centuries of the Christian Era* (New York, 1971), vol. 2, p. 203.
9. Bava Metzia 59b.
10. *Pesikta de-Rav Kahana* 3.
11. Lamentations Rabbah, ed. Solomon Buber (Vilna, 1899), proem 29.
12. *Mahzor for Rosh Hashanah and Yom Kippur*, ed. Jules Harlow (New York, 1972), pp. 153f.
13. Plato, *The Dialogues of Plato*, trans. B. Jowett (New York, 1937), vol. 2, *Timaeus* 29.
14. Midrash Rabbah, ed. Moshe Mirkin (Tel Aviv, 1968), *Shemot* 23:13; Bialik and Ravnitzky, *Book of Legends*, p. 503.
15. David S. Ariel, *The Mystic Quest* (Northvale, N.J., 1988), pp. 54–68.
16. Harry A. Wolfson, *The Philosophy of Spinoza* (New York, 1969), vol. 2, p. 10.
17. Ibid., vol. 1, p. 223.
18. Ariel, *Mystic Quest*, pp. 175–77.
19. Eugene B. Borowitz, *Renewing the Covenant* (Philadelphia, 1991), p. 81.
20. Ibid.
21. Ibid., p. 114.
22. Ibid., p. 266.
23. *Emet ve-Emunah: Statement of Principles of Conservative Judaism* (New York, 1988), p. 17.
24. Ibid., p. 8.
25. Ibid., p. 18.
26. Paul Mendes-Flohr, "Martin Buber's Conception of God," in Mendes-Flohr, *Divided Passions: Jewish Intellectuals and the Experience of Modernity* (Detroit, 1991), pp. 237–82.

27. Martin Buber, *Hasidism and Modern Man* (New York, 1958), p. 42.
28. Ibid., p. 237.
29. Abraham Joshua Heschel, *The Earth Is the Lord's* (New York, 1966), p. 76.

Chapter 2: Human Destiny

1. Bereshit Rabbah, ed. J. Theodor and C. Albeck (Jerusalem, 1965), 8:3–4.
2. Sanhedrin 4:5; Bialik and Ravnitzky, *Book of Legends*, p. 14.
3. Bereshit Rabbah 8:1; Bialik and Ravnitzky, *Book of Legends*, p. 15.
4. Ecclesiastes Rabbah 7:13; Bialik and Ravnitzky, *Book of Legends*, pp. 14–15.
5. *Sifre: A Tannaitic Commentary*, p. 306.
6. Bialik and Ravnitzky, *Book of Legends*, pp. 206, 593.
7. Berakhot 10a; Bialik and Ravnitzky, *Book of Legends*, p. 585.
8. *Zohar Hadash*, Bereshit 27b–28a; quoted in Tishby, *Mishnat ha-Zohar* 2:96–98.
9. Ariel, *Mystic Quest*, p. 126.
10. Ibid., p. 127.
11. Ibid.
12. Michael Walzer, *Exodus and Revolution* (New York, 1985), p. 53.
13. Abraham Joshua Heschel, *The Prophets* (New York, 1962), p. 4.
14. Ibid., p. 205.
15. Ibid., p. 217.
16. Ibid., p. 219.
17. Makkot 24a.
18. Moses Maimonides, *Shemoneh Perakim* 4.
19. Moses Maimonides, *Mishneh Torah, Hilkhot Deot* 2:2.
20. Solomon Schimmel, *The Seven Deadly Sins* (New York, 1992), p. 24.
21. Yevamot 47a.
22. Maimonides, *Mishneh Torah, Hilkhot Matanot le-Evyonim* 10:1.
23. Avot 4:1.
24. Avot 2:7.
25. Moshe Alshekh, *Torat Moshe* (Warsaw, 1879), on Leviticus 19:9.
26. Immanuel Etkes, "Rabbi Israel Salanter and His Psychology of Mussar," in *Jewish Spirituality: From the Sixteenth Century Revival to the Present*, ed. Arthur Green (New York, 1987), p. 214.
27. Ibid., pp. 232ff.

28. It is interetsing to note that Etkes cites Rabbi Menahem Mendel Lefin as the literary source for Salanter's theory of tricking oneself into behavioral change. Lefin, in turn, learned this technique from Benjamin Franklin's autobiography.
29. Etkes, "Rabbi Israel Salanter," pp. 238ff.
30. Irving Howe, *World of Our Fathers* (New York, 1976), p. 645.
31. Moshe Waldoks, "Mentsh," in *Contemporary Jewish Religious Thought*, ed. Arthur A. Cohen and Paul Mendes-Flohr (New York, 1987), p. 587.
32. Ibid., p. 588.
33. Avot 5:21; Bialik and Ravnitzky, *Book of Legends*, p. 578.
34. Yevamot 62b; Bialik and Ravnitzky, *Book of Legends*, p. 614.
35. Yevamot 63b.
36. Kiddushin 29b; Bialik and Ravnitzky, *Book of Legends*, p. 615.
37. Sota 44a; Bialik and Ravnitzky, *Book of Legends*, p. 614.
38. Bereshit Rabbah 68:3; Bialik and Ravnitzky, *Book of Legends*, p. 616.
39. Sota 2a; Bialik and Ravnitzky, *Book of Legends*, p. 616.
40. Sota 17a; Bialik and Ravnitzky, *Book of Legends*, p. 620.
41. Bava Batra 110a; Bialik and Ravnitzky, *Book of Legends*, p. 617.
42. Gerald Blidstein, *Honor Thy Father and Mother: Filial Responsibility in Jewish Law and Ethics* (New York, 1975), pp. 4ff.
43. Maimonides, *Mishneh Torah, Shoftim, Hilkhot Mamrim*, 6:3.
44. Midrash Tanhuma, ed. S. Buber (Vilna, 1885), *Ekev* 2.
45. Kiddushin 29a.
46. Pesahim 112a; Bialik and Ravnitzky, *Book of Legends*, p. 628.
47. Gittin 4:5.
48. Yoma 69b.
49. Berakhot 58b.
50. Tosefta Berakhot 6:4; Bialik and Ravnitzky, *Book of Legends*, p. 586.
51. Berakhot 43b.
52. Niddah 30b; Bialik and Ravnitzky, *Book of Legends*, p. 576.
53. Ibid.
54. Sanhedrin 91b.
55. Yevamot 69b.
56. Bereshit Rabbah 8:9; Bialik and Ravnitzky, *Book of Legends*, p. 614.
57. Yevamot 6:6.
58. See Genesis 37:35; Isaiah 14:9–11; Psalms 88:4–7.
59. Bereshit Rabbah 16:6.
60. Bereshit Rabbah 30:8.
61. Sanhedrin 10:1.

62. Avot 4:16.
63. Avot 4:17.
64. Ecclesiastes Rabbah 1:15.
65. Avot 1:14.
66. Avot 1:3.
67. Berakhot 28b.
68. Berakhot 17a.
69. Shabbat 152b.
70. Immanuel of Rome, *Tophet and Eden,* trans. Hermann Gollancz (Longon, 1921), pp. 35ff; quoted in Rifat Sonsino and Daniel Syme, *What Happens after I Die?* (New York, 1990), pp. 27f.
71. Maimonides, *Mishneh Torah, Hilkhot Teshuvah* 8:1, 5.
72. Zohar I:224b; quoted in Gershom Scholem, *Zohar: The Book of Splendor* (New York, 1963), pp. 72–73.
73. Zohar I:201a; quoted in Tishby, *Mishnat ha-Zohar* 2:154.
74. Zohar III: 126a–b; quoted in Tishby, *Mishnat ha-Zohar* 2:162–63.
75. Shabbat 152b.
76. Martin Buber, *Tales of the Hasidim: The Early Masters* (New York, 1947), pp. 69–70.
77. Ibid., p. 251.
78. Ibid., p. 124.

Chapter 3: Good and Evil

1. Sanhedrin 91b; Bialik and Ravnitzky, *Book of Legends,* p. 538.
2. *Avot de-Rabbi Nathan,* ed. Solomon Schecter (Vienna, 1887), 16; Bialik and Ravnitzky, *Book of Legends,* p. 538.
3. *Avot de-Rabbi Nathan,* 16; Bialik and Ravnitzky, *Book of Legends,* p. 539.
4. Bereshit Rabbah 9:7; Bialik and Ravnitzky, *Book of Legends,* p. 543.
5. Sukkah 52a: Bialik and Ravnitzky, *Book of Legends,* p. 541.
6. Avot 4:1.
7. Bahya ibn Pakuda, *The Book of Direction to the Duties of the Heart,* trans. Menachem Mansoor (London, 1973), p. 277.
8. Maimonides, *Shemoneh Perakim* 6.
9. Gershom Scholem, *Major Trends in Jewish Myticism* (New York, 1941), p. 92.
10. Ibid.

11. Martin Buber, *Ten Rungs: Hasidic Sayings* (New York, 1947), p. 95.
12. Rivka Schatz Uffenheimer, *Hasidism as Mysticism* (Princeton, N.J., 1993), pp. 58f.
13. Yoma 86b; Bialik and Ravnitzky, *Book of Legends*, p. 545.
14. Avot 4:2.
15. *Sifre: A Tannaitic Commentary* 186–87; Bialik and Ravnitzky, *Book of Legends*, p. 545.
16. *Avot de-Rabbi Nathan* 33; Bialik and Ravnitzky, *Book of Legends*, p. 545.
17. Kiddushin 40b; Bialik and Ravnitzky, *Book of Legends*, p. 544.
18. Avot 3:9; Avot de-Rabbi Nathan 22; Bialik and Ravnitzky, *Book of Legends*, p. 544.
19. Shabbat 153a; quoted in Bialik and Ravnitzky, *Book of Legends*, p. 556.
20. Kiddushin 40b; Bialik and Ravnitzky, *Book of Legends*, p. 548.
21. Shemot Rabbah 19:4, Bialik and Ravnitzky, *Book of Legends*, p. 558.
22. Yoma 38b; Bialik and Ravnitzky, *Book of Legends*, p. 558.
23. *Pesikta Rabbati,* ed. Meir Friedmann (Vienna, 1880), 44, p. 185a; Bialik and Ravnitzky, *Book of Legends*, p. 558.
24. Berakhot 34b; Bialik and Ravnitzky, *Book of Legends*, p. 560.
25. Yoma 86b; Bialik and Ravnitzky, *Book of Legends*, p. 559.
26. Yoma 8:9; Bialik and Ravnitzky, *Book of Legends*, p. 560.
27. Sanhedrin 107b; Bialik and Ravnitzky, *Book of Legends*, p. 561.
28. Saadya Gaon, *Sefer Emunot ve-Deot,* ed. Joseph Kapah (Jerusalem, 1970) 5:5.
29. Scholem, *Major Trends*, p. 105.
30. Ibid., p. 106.
31. Niddah 16b; Bialik and Ravnitzky, *Book of Legends*, p. 547.
32. Avot 3:15.
33. Maimonides, *Mishneh Torah, Hilkhot Teshuvah* 5.
34. Ibid.
35. Robert Alter, *The Art of Biblical Narrative* (New York, 1981), p. 45.
36. Bereshit Rabbah 33:1; Bialik and Ravnitzky, *Book of Legends*, p. 566.
37. Berakhot 7a; Bialik and Ravnitzky, *Book of Legends*, p. 566.
38. Bereshit Rabbah 32:3; Bialik and Ravnitzky, *Book of Legends*, p. 567.
39. Avot 4:15.
40. Pesach Schindler, *Hasidic Responses to the Holocaust in the Light of Hasidic Thought* (New York, 1990), p. 20.
41. Emil Fackenheim, "To Mend the World," in *Fackenheim: German Idealism and Jewish Thought,* eds. L. Greenspan and G. Nicholson (Toronto, 1992), pp. 247ff.

Chapter 4: The Chosen People

1. The references to *yehudim* in Jeremiah and Esther mean Judeans, not Jews.

2. *Sifre: A Tannaitic Commentary* 343; Bialik and Ravnitzky, *Book of Legends,* pp. 78–79.

3. Shabbat 88a; Bialik and Ravnitzky, *Book of Legends,* p. 79.

4. Ariel, *Mystic Quest,* p. 132.

5. Saadya Gaon, *Sefer Emunot ve-Deot,* ed. Joseph Kapah (Jerusalem, 1970) 3:7.

6. Maimonides, *Commentary to Mishnah Sanhedrin,* ed. Joseph Kapah (Jerusalem, 1964–67), 10:3.

7. Maimonides, *Mishneh Torah, Hilkhot Avodah Zarah* 2:5.

8. Maimonides, *Mishneh Torah, Hilkhot Evel* 1:10; Menahem Kellner, *Maimonides on Judaism and the Jewish People* (Albany, N.Y., 1991), p. 87.

9. Maimonides, *The Guide of the Perplexed,* trans. Shlomo Pines (Chicago, 1963), 3:32.

10. Sigmund Freud, "Address to the Society of B'nai Brith," in *The Standard Edition of the Complete Psychological Works of Sigmund Freud,* ed. James Strachey (London, 1959), vol. 20, p. 274. See also Yosef Hayim Yerushalmi, *Freud's Moses* (New Haven, 1991), p. 12.

11. Ernst Simon, "Sigmund Freud, the Jew," *Leo Baeck Institute Yearbook* 2 (1957), pp. 270–305.

12. Martin Buber, "Renewal of Judaism," in Buber, *On Judaism* (New York, 1967), p. 40.

13. Ibid., p. 42.

14. Ibid., p. 54.

15. Abraham Joshua Heschel, *The Insecurity of Freedom: Essays on Human Existence* (New York, 1972), p. 215.

16. Shemot Rabbah 2:5.

17. Felix Levy, "How Judaism Might Be Advanced," in *His Own Torah: Felix A. Levy Memorial Volume,* ed. Sefton Temkin; quoted in Arnold Eisen, *The Chosen People in America* (Bloomington, Ind., 1983), p. 54.

18. Martin Buber, *Ten Rungs: Hasidic Sayings* (New York, 1947), p. 15.

19. Megillah 13a.

20. Maimonides, *Mishneh Torah,* Introduction.

21. Salo W. Baron, *A Social and Religious History of the Jews* (New York, 1952), vol. 1, p. 283.

22. Yevamot 24b; Maimonides, *Mishneh Torah, Hilkhot Issurei Biah* 13:17.

23. *Mekilta de-Rabbi Ishmael,* ed. Jacob Z. Lauterbach (Philadelphia, 1933–35), Pischa 15.
24. Ibid., Nezikin 18.
25. Pesahim 87b.
26. Va-yikra Rabbah 2:9.
27. Moses Maimonides, *Responsa of Maimonides,* ed. Freimann (Jerusalem, 1934), pp. 40ff.
28. Moses Maimonides, "Letter to Obadiah the Proselyte," in Maimonides, *Crisis and Leadership: Epistles of Maimonides.*
29. Ibid.
30. *Mekilta de-Rabbi Ishmael,* Amalek 2.
31. Ecclesiastes Rabbah 1:8.
32. Josephus, *Contra Apion,* trans. Henry St. John Thackeray, Ralph Marcus, and Louis Feldman (Cambridge, Mass., 1926–65) 2:123.
33. Midrash Ruth Zuta, ed. Solomon Buber (Vilna, 1925), 1:12.
34. Yevamot 47b.
35. Yevamot 47a.
36. Sota 47a.

Chapter 5: The Meaning of Torah

1. *Sefer ha-Zohar,* ed. Reuven Margoliot (Jerusalem, 1970), 3:73a; Isaiah Tishby, *Mishnat ha-Zohar* (Jerusalem, 1961), 2:372.
2. Hayim Halevy Donin, *To Be a Jew* (New York, 1972), p. 35.
3. Sanhedrin 10:1.
4. Sanhedrin 99a.
5. *Sifre: A Tannaitic Commentary, Shelakh* 112.
6. Sota 37b.
7. Bava Batra 14b.
8. Bava Batra 15a.
9. Avot 5:25.
10. Avot 1:1.
11. Menahot 29b.
12. Moses Maimonides, *Commentary to the Mishnah Sanhedrin* 10.
13. Yevamot 71a.
14. Moses Nahmanides, *Perush ha-Ramban al ha-Torah,* ed. C. D. Chavel (Jerusalem, 1959), Introduction.
15. *Sefer ha-Zohar* 3:152a; *Zohar: The Book of Enlightenment,* trans. Daniel C. Matt (New York, 1983), pp. 43–45.

16. Gershom Scholem, "Reflections on Jewish Theology," in Scholem, *On Jews and Judaism in Crisis* (New York, 1976), p. 270.
17. Ibid., pp. 270f.
18. Michael Fishbane, *The Garments of Torah* (Bloomington, Ind., 1989), pp. 84ff.
19. Neil Gillman, *Sacred Fragments: Recovering Theology for the Modern Jew* (Philadelphia, 1990), p. 18.
20. Scholem, "Reflections on Jewish Theology," p. 269.
21. See Yehezkel Kaufmann, *The Religion of Israel* (Chicago, 1960), p. 153.
22. Abraham Rabinowitch in *The Jerusalem Post*, March 10, 1990.
23. Nahum Sarna, *Understanding Genesis* (New York, 1970), p. xxi.
24. Alter, *Art of the Biblical Narrative* p. 11.
25. Ibid.
26. Ibid., p. 12.
27. Ibid..
28. Ibid., p. 26.
29. Donin, *To Be a Jew*, p. 25.
30. Moshe Davis, *The Emergence of Conservative Judaism* (Philadelphia, 1963), p. 296.
31. Mordecai Waxman, *Tradition and Change* (New York, 1958), pp. 377ff.
32. *Emet ve-Emunah*, pp. 19f.

Chapter 6: The *Mitzvot*

1. See also Leviticus 26:3 and Exodus 16:4; Ephraim E. Urbach, *The Halakhah: Its Sources and Development* (Jerusalem, 1986), p. 2.
2. Urbach, *Halakhah,* p. 3.
3. Makkot 23b.
4. Pesakhim 10a.
5. Kiddushin 1:7.
6. Jacob Neusner, *First Century Judaism in Crisis* (New York, 1975), p. 36.
7. Sanhedrin 88b.
8. Makkot 3:16.
9. Holtz, *Finding Our Way*, p. 43. Holtz translates "trying" as "purified," thus offering a modernist and spiritual interpretation of the purpose of *mitzvot*.
10. Bereshit Rabbah 44:1.
11. Bereshit Rabbah 34:8.
12. Maimonides, *Guide of the Perplexed* 3:51.

13. *Emet ve-Emunah,* p. 56.
14. Ibid., p. 57.
15. Ibid., pp. 21–23.
16. Mordecai Kaplan, *The Religion of Ethical Nationhood: Judaism's Contribution to World Peace* (New York, 1970), p. 16.
17. Yoma 67b.
18. *Letter of Aristeas,* ed. Henry St. John Thackeray (London, 1918), 142–47.
19. *Sifra,* ed. Israel Meir Cohen (Jerusalem, 1970), Kedoshim 9:12.
20. Maimonides, *Guide of the Perplexed* 3:48.
21. Ibid.
22. Isaac Arama, *Akedat Yitzhak* 8:60.
23. Samson Raphael Hirsch, *Horeb: A Philosophy of Jewish Laws and Observances,* trans. I. Grunfeld (London, 1962), p. 328.
24. *The Changing World of Reform Judaism: The Pittsburgh Platform in Retrospect,* ed. Walter Jacob (Pittsburgh, 1985), pp. 107–9.
25. Samuel Dresner, *The Jewish Dietary Laws* (New York, 1966), p. 54.
26. Joseph Soloveitchik, *Halakhic Man,* trans. Lawrence Kaplan (Philadelphia, 1983), p. 94.
27. Hayyim of Volozhin, *Sefer Nefesh ha-Hayyim* (Vilna, 1824), 4:25.
28. Eugene Borowitz, *Liberal Judaism* (New York, 1984), p. 331.
29. Ibid.
30. Abraham Joshua Heschel, *The Sabbath: Its Meaning for Modern Man* (New York, 1951), pp. 30f.

Chapter 7: Prayer

1. Berakhot 26b.
2. Midrash Tehillim, ed. Solomon Buber (Vilna, 1891; Jerusalem, 1965), 18:4.
3. Megillah 17b–18a.
4. Joseph Heinemann, *Prayer in the Talmud* (New York, 1977), p. 10.
5. Ibid., pp. 14–15.
6. Gavriel Cohen, *Ha-Tefillah ha-Yehudit: Hemshekh ve-Hiddush* (Jerusalem, 1978), p. 7.
7. Midrash Tanhuma, ed. Solomon Buber (Vilna, 1885), *Vezot Haberachah* 7.
8. Bialik and Ravnitzky, *Book of Legends,* p. 524.
9. Midrash Tehillim 4:3.

10. Sota 5a; Bialik and Ravnitzky, *Book of Legends,* p. 526.
11. Berakhot 28b.
12. Berakhot 5:1.
13. Bahya ibn Pakuda, *Duties of the Heart,* p. 365.
14. Zohar III:294a–b.
15. Zohar III:126a; quoted in Tishby, *Mishnat ha-Zohar* 2:308–9.
16. *Sifre: A Tannaitic Commentary, Devarim* 41.
17. Zohar II:59b; quoted in Tishby, *Mishnat ha-Zohar* 2:30 7–8.
18. Quoted in *Your Word Is Fire,* ed. and trans. Arthur Green and Barry Holtz (New York, 1977), p. 25.
19. Rivka Schatz, "Contemplative Prayer in Hasidism," in *Studies in Mysticism and Religion Presented to Gershom Scholem,* ed. Ephraim Urbach (Jerusalem, 1968), p. 209.
20. Buber, *Tales of the Hasidim,* p. 103.
21. Berakhot 24a.
22. Susan Grossman and Rivka Haut, *Daughters of the King: Women and the Synagogue* (Philadelphia, 1992), p. 4.
23. Berakhot 3:3.
24. Grossman and Haut, *Daughters of the King,* pp. 73ff. See also Chava Weissler, "The Traditional Piety of Ashkenazic Women," in *Jewish Spirituality,* ed. Arthur Green, vol. 2, pp. 245–75; and Ellen Umansky and Diane Ashton, *Four Centuries of Jewish Women's Spirituality* (Boston, 1992).
25. *The Sabbath and Festival Prayer Book* (New York, 1946), p. 35.
26. *Siddur Sim Shalom* (New York, 1985), p. 742.
27. *The Union Prayer Book* (Cincinnati, 1945), p. 192.
28. *Gates of Prayer* (New York, 1975), p. 721.
29. *Kol Haneshamah* (Wyncote, Pa., 1989), p. 80.
30. Heschel, *The Earth Is the Lord's,* p. 76.
31. Heschel, *The Insecurity of Freedom,* p. 215.
32. Hullin 78a; Bialik and Ravnitzky, *Book of Legends,* p. 525.
33. Hayim Halevy Donin, *To Pray as a Jew* (New York, 1980), p. 250.
34. Holtz, *Finding Our Way,* p. 126.

Chapter 8: The Messiah

1. See also Joel 1:15; 2:1; 3:4; 4:14; Obadiah 1:15; Zephaniah 1:17–18; Malachi 3:23.
2. See Isaiah 10:21–22; 11:11, 16; 28:5; 37:32.

3. Most of these works were written in Hebrew or Aramaic. None is included in the Hebrew Bible. Some appear in the Christian Apocrypha and the Pseudepigrapha.
4. Joseph Klausner, *The Messianic Idea in Israel* (Philadelphia, 1955), pp. 289ff.
5. While this is an apparent reference to Isaiah 49:6 *(le-or goyyim)*, it is not used in the later sense of a missionary. It is probably used in the same sense as Isaiah, i.e., an agent of good fortune.
6. Berakhot 28b.
7. Sanhedrin 94a.
8. Sanhedrin 99a.
9. *Tanna de-Vei Eliyahu,* ed. M. Friedmann (Vienna, 1904), pp. 27ff.
10. Sanhedrin 10:3.
11. Pesahim 13a.
12. Jerusalem Talmud (New York, 1948), *Pesahim* 3:6.
13. *Mekilta de-Rabbi Ishmael,* Pischa 14.
14. Sota 9:15.
15. Sanhedrin 97a.
16. Shabbat 118b.
17. Yevamot 62a; Avodah Zarah 5a; Niddah 13b; Va-yikra Rabbah 15: Rashi on Avodah Zarah 5a.
18. Sanhedrin 97b.
19. Ibid.
20. Avodah Zarah 18a.
21. Sanhedrin 98a–b.
22. Bereshit Rabbah 3:99.
23. Targum on Song of Songs 5:4.
24. Sukkah 52a.
25. Yevamot 24b.
26. Niddah 13b.
27. Avodah Zarah 3b.
28. Pesahim 118b.
29. *Mekilta de-Rabbi Ishmael,* Pischa 12.
30. Megillah 29a.
31. Shabbat 30b.
32. Shabbat 63a.
33. Tosefta Sanhedrin 13:2.
34. Maimonides, *Mishneh Torah, Hilkhot Teshuvah* 3:5.
35. Sanhedrin 99a.

36. Sanhedrin 97b.
37. Sanhedrin 99a.
38. Maimonides, *Mishneh Torah, Sefer Shoftim, Hilkhot Melakhim* 11:1.
39. Ibid., 11:3.
40. Ibid., 11:4.
41. Ibid., 12:1.
42. Ibid., 12:2, quoting Sanhedrin 91b.
43. John P. Meier, "Reflections on Jesus-of-History Research Today," in *Jesus' Jewishness,* ed. James H. Charlesworth (New York, 1991), pp. 90f.
44. Berakhot 17b.
45. Targum Onkelos and Rashi read *shiloh* as *shelo,* rendering the passage as "until he to whom obedience is due arrives." Klausner *(The Messianic Idea in Israel)* and others read it as a form of *Shelomo* (Solomon), suggesting that this passage was an insertion from the time of Solomon.
46. Josephus, *Jewish War* 2., 444–48.
47. Based on Maimonides, *Commentary on the Mishnah,* introduction to *Perek Helek.*
48. Gershom Scholem, *The Messianic Idea in Judaism* (New York, 1971), p. 194.
49. *Me-Golah le-Geulah,* ed. Eliahu Friedman (New York, 1991), p. 101.
50. Nora Levin, *While the Messiah Tarried: Jewish Socialist Movements, 1871–1917* (New York, 1977), foreword.
51. Howe, *World of Our Fathers,* p. 223.
52. Paul Mendes-Flohr and Jehuda Reinharz, eds. *The Jew in the Modern World: A Documentary History* (New York, 1980), p. 163.
53. Borowitz, *Renewing the Covenant,* p. 18.
54. *Emet ve-Emunah,* p. 29.
55. Ibid., pp. 31f.
56. *Avot de-Rabbi Nathan* 31; quoted in Bialik and Ravnitzky, *Book of Legends,* p. 361.

 *Glossary*

ASHKENAZIM—Jews of central and eastern Europe; many migrated from Germany to Poland and Russia during the twelfth to sixteenth centuries.

B.C.E.—Abbreviation for Before the Common Era, the Jewish term used instead of B.C. (Before Christ).

BIBLE—The writings that constitute the Bible or *Tanakh*. Christians call this canon the Old Testament because they believe it has been superseded by the New Testament. The biblical writings are the earliest sources of Judaism and cover the period prior to 167 B.C.E., the time of the Maccabean revolt.

C.E.—Abbreviation for Common Era, the Jewish term used instead of A.D. (Anno Domini, "In the Year of Our Lord").

EMANCIPATION—The Jewish movement for political and civil rights in late eighteenth and nineteenth century Europe.

HALAKHAH—Jewish law.

HASIDISM—A Jewish spiritual movement that was founded in Poland and Ukraine in the eighteenth century and continues today as a fundamentalist movement within Orthodox Judaism.

KABBALAH—A medieval Jewish mystical tradition that originated in Spain after 1200. The word Kabbalah means "tradition."

KETUVIM—The Hebrew word for Writings, the third section of the Hebrew Bible, which includes the books of Psalms, Proverbs, Job, Song of Songs, and others.

MEDIEVAL PERIOD (Middle Ages)—Generally, the period between the completion of the Talmud and the French Revolution in 1789, the date that marks the beginning of the modern Jewish Emancipation. Its major communities were Ashkenazic, Sephardic, and Mediterranean Jewry. The predominant movements among the medieval Jewish communities were Jewish philosophy, Jewish mysticism (Kabbalah), East European Hasidism, and traditional Judaism (which had not yet called itself Orthodoxy).

MIDRASH—A genre of Hebrew literature comprising biblical commentaries, law, and legends from the first centuries until the late Middle Ages that were directed at the popular Jewish audiences of the time.

MISHNAH—The earliest postbiblical code of Jewish law, compiled around 200 C.E.

MITZVAH (pl. *mitzvot*)—A commandment or religiously required action according to Jewish law.

MODERN PERIOD—A designation referring to the developments in Judaism since 1789, particularly in Europe, North Ameria, and Israel. The period includes the development of the four modern religious denominations—Orthodox, Conservative, Reconstructionist, and Reform Judaism.

NEVIIM—Prophets, the second section of the Hebrew Bible, which includes historical works such as Joshua, Judges, Samuel, and Kings, and the prophetic books of Isaiah, Jeremiah, Ezekiel, Hosea, Amos, Jonah, Micah, and others.

RABBINIC PERIOD—The postbiblical era after the turn of the first millennium, when Judaism was defined by rabbis rather than by kings, priests, or prophets. For the purposes of this book, the period covers the first six centuries of the Common Era. The word *rabbis* as employed in this book refers to the scholars and sages whose teachings shaped Judaism in this period, not to the rabbis who serve as the contemporary religious authorities of Judaism. Their views are quoted in the literature of the period, including the Mishnah, Talmud, and Midrash.

SEPHARDIM— Jews who lived in Spain, before the Expulsion of 1492; afterward they migrated to North Africa, other parts of Europe, and the Ottoman Empire.

TALMUD—The expansion and elaboration of the Mishnah (just as U.S. Supreme Court decisions expand and elaborate constitutional law).

TANAKH—An acronym for the Hebrew Bible which includes the Torah, Neviim, and Ketuvim.

TORAH—The Five Books of Moses: Genesis, Exodus, Leviticus, Numbers, and Deuteronomy.

Bibliography

Albeck, H., and H. Yalon, eds. *Shishah Sidrei Mishnah*. 6 vols. Jerusalem, 1952–56.

Alshekh, Moshe. *Torat Moshe*. Warsaw, 1879.

Alter, Robert. *The Art of Biblical Narrative*. New York, 1981.

Arama, Isaac. *Akedat Yitzhak*. Pressburg, 1849.

Arrel, David S. *The Mystic Quest*. Northvale, N.J., 1988.

Avot de-Rabbi Nathan. Edited by Solomon Schechter. Vienna, 1887.

Babylonian Talmud. Vilna, 1886.

Bahya ibn Pakuda. *The Book of Direction to the Duties of the Heart*. Translated by Menachem Mansoor. London, 1973.

Baron, Salo W. *A Social and Religious History of the Jews*. 17 vols. New York, 1952.

Bereshit Rabbah. *See* Midrash Bereshit Rabbah.

Berkovits, Eliezer. *Not in Heaven: The Nature and Function of Halakha*. New York, 1983.

Blidstein, Gerald. *Honor Thy Father and Mother: Filial Responsibility in Jewish Law and Ethics.* New York, 1975.

Borowitz, Eugene. *Liberal Judaism.* New York, 1984.

————. *Renewing the Covenant.* Philadelphia, 1991.

Bialik, Hayim Nahman, and Yehoshua Hana Ravnitzky. *The Book of Legends / Sefer Ha-Aggadah.* New York, 1992.

Buber, Martin. *The Eclipse of God.* New York, 1957.

————. *Hasidism and Modern Man.* New York, 1958.

————. *Moses: The Revelation and the Covenant.* New York, 1958.

————. *On Judaism.* New York, 1967.

————. *The Origin and Meaning of Hasidism.* New York, 1960.

————. *Tales of the Hasidim: The Early Masters.* New York, 1947.

————. *Ten Rungs: Hasidic Sayings.* New York, 1947.

Charlesworth, James H., ed. *Jesus' Jewishness.* New York, 1991.

Cohen, Arthur A., and Paul Mendes-Flohr, eds. *Contemporary Jewish Religious Thought.* New York, 1987.

Cohen, Gavriel. *Ha-Tefillah ha-Yehudit: Hemshekh ve-Hiddush.* Jerusalem, 1978.

Davis, Moshe. *The Emergence of Conservative Judaism.* Philadelphia, 1963.

Donin, Hayim Halevy. *To Be a Jew.* New York, 1972.

————. *To Pray as a Jew.* New York, 1980.

Douglas, Mary. *Purity and Danger.* London, 1966.

Dresner, Samuel. *The Jewish Dietary Laws.* New York, 1966.

Ecclesiastes Rabbah. Vilna, 1887.

Eisen, Arnold. *The Chosen People in America.* Bloomington, Ind., 1983.

Emet ve-Emunah: Statement of Principles of Conservative Judaism. New York, 1988.

Epstein, Lawrence J. *The Theory and Practice of Welcoming Converts to Judaism.* Lewiston, N.Y., 1992.

Etkes, Immanuel. "Rabbi Israel Salanter and His Psychology of *Mussar.*" In *Jewish Spirituality: From the Sixteenth Century Revival to the Present,* edited by Arthur Green. New York, 1987.

Fackenheim, Emil. "To Mend the World." In *Fackenheim: German Idealism and Jewish Thought,* edited by L. Greenspan and G. Nicholson. Toronto, 1992.

Fishbane, Michael. *The Garments of Torah.* Bloomington, Ind., 1989.

Fox, Marvin. *Interpreting Maimonides.* Chicago, 1990.

Fox, Matthew. "A Mystical Cosmology: Towards a Postmodern Spirituality." In *Sacred Interconnections,* edited by David Ray Griffin. Albany, N.Y., 1990.

Freud, Sigmund. "Address to the Society of B'nai Brith." In *The Standard Edition of the Complete Psychological Works of Sigmund Freud,* edited by James Strachey, vol. 20. London, 1959.

Gates of Prayer. New York, 1975.

Gillman, Neil. *Conservative Judaism.* New York, 1993.

—————. *Sacred Fragments: Recovering Theology for the Modern Jew.* Philadelphia, 1990.

Glatzer, Nahum. *Language of Faith: A Selection from the Most Expressive Jewish Prayers.* New York, 1975.

Goldsmith, Emanuel, Mel Scult, and Robert Seltzer. *The American Judaism of Mordecai M. Kaplan.* New York, 1990.

Green, Arthur, ed. *Jewish Spirituality: From the Sixteenth Century Revival to the Present.* 2 vols. New York, 1987.

—————, and Barry Holtz, ed. and trans. *Your Word Is Fire.* New York, 1977.

Griffin, David R. *God and Religion in the Postmodern World.* Albany, N.Y., 1989.

Grossman, Susan, and Rivka Haut. *Daughters of the King: Women and the Synagogue.* Philadelphia, 1992.

Halevi, Judah. *Sefer ha-Kuzari.* Edited by Yehudah ibn Shmuel. Tel Aviv, 1972.

Hammer, Reuven. *Entering Jewish Prayer: A Guide to Personal Devotion and the Worship Service.* New York, 1994.

Hartman, David. *Conflicting Visions.* New York, 1990.

———. *A Living Covenant: The Innovative Spirit in Traditional Judaism.* New York, 1985.

Hayyim of Volozhin. *Sefer Nefesh ha-Hayyim.* Vilna, 1824.

Heinemann, Joseph. *Prayer in the Talmud.* New York, 1977.

Heschel, Abraham Joshua. *The Earth Is the Lord's.* New York, 1966.

———. *God in Search of Man: A Philosophy of Judaism.* New York, 1955.

———. *The Insecurity of Freedom: Essays on Human Existence.* New York, 1972.

———. *Man's Quest for God: Studies in Prayer and Symbolism.* New York, 1954.

———. *The Prophets.* New York, 1962.

———. *The Sabbath: Its Meaning for Modern Man.* New York, 1951.

Hirsch, Samson Raphael. *Horeb: A Philosophy of Jewish Laws and Observances.* Translated by I. Grunfeld. London, 1962.

Hoffman, Lawrence. *Beyond the Text.* Bloomington, Ind., 1987.

Holtz, Barry. *Finding Our Way.* New York, 1990.

Howe, Irving. *World of Our Fathers.* New York, 1976.

Immanuel of Rome. *Tophet and Eden.* Translated by Hermann Gollancz. London, 1921.

Jacob, Walter, ed. *The Changing World of Reform Judaism: The Pittsburgh Platform in Retrospect.* Pittsburgh, 1985.

Jerusalem Talmud. New York, 1948.

Josephus. *Contra Apion.* Translated by Henry St. John Thackeray, Ralph Marcus, Louis Feldman. 9 vols. Cambridge, Mass., 1926–65.

———. *The Jewish War.* Translated by G. A. Williamson. Baltimore, 1970.

Kadushin, Max. *The Rabbinic Mind.* New York, 1971.

Kaplan, Mordecai M. *Judaism as a Civilization.* New York, 1967.

————. *The Religion of Ethical Nationhood: Judaism's Contribution to World Peace.* New York, 1970.

Kaufmann, Yehezkel. *The Religion of Israel.* Chicago, 1960.

Kellner, Menahem. *Maimonides on Judaism and the Jewish People.* Albany, N.Y., 1991.

Klausner, Joseph. *The Messianic Idea in Israel.* Philadelphia, 1955.

Kol Haneshamah. Wyncote, Pa., 1989.

Lamentations Rabbah. Edited by Solomon Buber. Vilna, 1899.

Letter of Aristeas. Edited by Henry St. John Thackeray. London, 1918.

Levin, Nora. *While the Messiah Tarried: Jewish Socialist Movements, 1871–1917.* New York, 1977.

Levy Felix. "How Judaism Might Be Advanced." In *His Own Torah: Felix A. Levy Memorial Volume,* edited by Sefton Temkin.

Mahzor for Rosh Hashanah and Yom Kippur. Edited by Jules Harlow. New York, 1972.

Maimonides, Moses. *Commentary to the Mishnah.* Edited by Joseph Kapah. 2 vols. Jerusalem, 1964–67.

————. *Crisis and Leadership: Epistles of Maimonides.* Translated by A. Halkin and D. Hartman. Philadelphia, 1985.

————. *The Guide of the Perplexed.* Translated by Shlomo Pines. Chicago, 1963.

————. *Mishneh Torah.* Jerusalem, 1964.

————. *Responsa of Maimonides.* Edited by Freimann. Jerusalem, 1934.

————. *Shemoneh Perakim.* Tel Aviv, 1944.

————. *Treatise on Resurrection.* Translated by Fred Rosner. New York, 1982.

Matt, Daniel C., trans. *Zohar: The Book of Enlightenment.* New York, 1983.

Me-Golah le-Geulah. Edited by Eliahu Friedman. New York, 1991.

Meier, John P. "Reflections on Jesus-of-History Research Today." In *Jesus' Jewishness,* edited by James H. Charlesworth. New York, 1991.

Mekilta de-Rabbi Ishmael. Edited by Jacob Z. Lauterbach. 3 vols. Philadelphia, 1933–35.

Mendes-Flohr, Paul. *Divided Passions: Jewish Intellectuals and the Experience of Modernity.* Detroit, 1991.

———, and Jehuda Reinharz, eds. *The Jew in the Modern World: A Documentary History.* New York, 1980.

Midrash Bereshit Rabbah. Edited by J. Theodor and C. Albeck. Reprint. Jerusalem, 1965.

Midrash Rabbah. Edited by Moshe Mirkin. 11 vols. Tel Aviv, 1968.

Midrash Ruth Zuta. Edited by Solomon Buber. Vilna, 1925.

Midrash Tanhuma. Edited by Solomon Buber. Vilna, 1885.

Midrash Tehillim. Edited by Solomon Buber. Vilna, 1891; Jerusalem, 1965.

Mikraot Gedolot. New York, 1951.

Moore, George F. *Judaism in the First Centuries of the Christian Era.* 3 vols. Reprint. New York, 1971.

Nahmanides, Moses. *Perush ha-Ramban al ha-Torah.* Edited by C. D. Chavel. Jerusalem, 1959.

Neusner, Jacob. *First Century Judaism in Crisis.* New York, 1975.

Pesikta de-Rav Kahana. Edited by Bernard Mandelbaum. 2 vols. New York, 1962.

Pesikta Rabbati. Edited by Meir Friedmann. Vienna, 1880.

Pirkei de-Rabbi Eliezer. Warsaw, 1852.

Plato. *The Dialogues of Plato.* Translated by B. Jowett. 2 vols. New York, 1937.

Pritchard, James. *Ancient Near Eastern Texts.* Princeton, N.J., 1955.

Roof, Wade Clark. *A Generation of Seekers.* San Francisco, 1993.

Saadya Gaon. *Sefer Emunot ve-Deot.* Edited by Joseph Kapah. Jerusalem, 1970.

The Sabbath and Festival Prayer Book. New York, 1946.

Sarna, Nahum. *Understanding Genesis.* New York, 1970.

Schatz, Rivka. "Contemplative Prayer in Hasidism." In *Studies in Mysticism and Religion Presented to Gershom Scholem,* edited by Ephraim Urbach. Jerusalem, 1968.

Schatz Uffenheimer, Rivka. *Hasidism as Mysticism.* Princeton, N.J., 1993.

Schimmel, Solomon. *The Seven Deadly Sins.* New York, 1992.

Schindler, Pesach. *Hasidic Responses to the Holocaust in the Light of Hasidic Thought.* New York, 1990.

Scholem, Gershom. *Major Trends in Jewish Mysticism.* New York, 1941.

————. *The Messianic Idea in Judaism.* New York, 1971.

————. *On Jews and Judaism in Crisis.* New York, 1976.

————. *Zohar: The Book of Splendor.* New York, 1963.

Sefer ha-Zohar. Edited by Reuven Margoliot. Jerusalem, 1970.

Siddur Sim Shalom. New York, 1985.

Sifra. Edited by Israel Meir Cohen. Jerusalem, 1970.

Sifre: A Tannaitic Commentary on the Book of Deuteronomy. Edited by Reuven Hammer. New Haven, 1986.

Simon, Ernst. "Sigmund Freud, the Jew." *Leo Baeck Institute Yearbook* 2 (1957).

Soloveitchik, Joseph. *Halakhic Man.* Translated by Lawrence Kaplan. Philadelphia, 1983.

Sonsino, Rifat, and Daniel Syme. *What Happens after I Die?* New York, 1990.

Tanakh: A New Translation of the Holy Scriptures According to the Traditional Hebrew Text. Philadelphia, 1985.

Tanna de-Vei Eliyahu. Edited by M. Friedmann. Vienna, 1904.

Tishby, Isaiah. *Mishnat ha-Zohar.* 2 vols. Jerusalem, 1961.

Tosefta. Edited by Saul Lieberman. 3 vols. New York, 1955.

Umansky, Ellen, and Diane Ashton. *Four Centuries of Jewish Women's Spirituality.* Boston, 1992.

The Union Prayer Book. Cincinnati, 1945.

Urbach, Ephraim E. *The Halakhah: Its Sources and Development.* Jerusalem, 1986.

————. *The Sages: Their Concepts and Beliefs.* 2 vols. Jerusalem, 1975.

Walzer, Michael. *Exodus and Revolution.* New York, 1985.

Waxman, Mordecai. *Tradition and Change.* New York, 1958.

Wolfson, Harry A. *The Philosophy of Spinoza.* 2 vols. New York, 1969.

Yerushalmi, Yosef Hayim. *Freud's Moses.* New Haven, 1991.

Zohar Hadash. Venice, 1658.

Index

Aaron, 141, 142
Abbaye, 87
abortion, 71
Abraham, 16–17, 19, 33, 110, 111–12, 149, 157, 192, 204, 205
Abu Isa of Isfahan, 239
Adam, 51–54, 83, 100, 127
    sin of, 73, 74, 78, 79, 85, 89, 100, 101
afterlife, 73–81, 91, 101–2, 218
agnosticism, 14, 42
Ahad Haam, 121–22
Akiva, Rabbi, 76, 97, 101–2, 129, 138–39, 143, 166, 224, 238
Aleinu, 109, 114
Alroy, David, 239
Alter, Robert, 154
Amidah, 114, 130, 192, 205, 224
Amos, 59, 60, 213, 214

angels, 54–55, 71, 147
animals, 21, 54–55, 59, 81, 128
    dietary laws and, 176–77
Antiochus IV Epiphanes, 218
apocalyptic literature, 218
Aristotle, 31, 32, 34, 35, 40, 41, 61
asceticism, 62, 89
Ashkenazim, 89, 96, 172, 267, 268
astral body, 78
atheism, 12

Baal Shem Tov (Israel ben Eliezer; Besht), 42, 43, 81–82, 90, 201, 202, 243
Babylonia, 17, 19, 20, 28, 31, 33–34, 116, 161, 162, 164, 165, 166, 191, 192, 193, 228, 236
Baeck, Leo, 119
Bahya ben Joseph ibn Pakuda, 88, 196

Balaam, 140
Bar Kokhba, 238–39
B.C.E., 267
Ben-Gurion, David, 213
Besht, *see* Baal Shem Tov
Bialik, Hayim Nahman, 121
Bible, 134, 162, 166, 194, 217, 267,
    268
    see also Torah
Birnbaum, Philip, 194
birth, 70–72, 85, 205
blessings, 160, 195, 209
Borowitz, Eugene, 44–45
Buber, Martin, 46–47, 48, 49, 50,
    90, 123, 127, 150–51, 183, 184,
    243

Caesar, Julius, 23
Canaan, 111
Catholicism, 115, 241
C.E. (Common Era), 267, 268
children, 69
    birth of, 70–72, 85, 205
    death of, 103
    evil impulse and, 85–86
    suffering of, 102, 103
Chmielnicki pogroms, 240
chosen people, chosenness, 108–33,
    160, 235
    converts and, 128–32
    and distinctiveness of Jewish iden-
        tity, 109–10, 117–18, 120,
        121–28, 132, 133, 205, 206
    egalitarianism and, 109, 110, 120
    and Israel as "light of nations,"
        116–21, 126
    mission-people concept and,
        119–20, 207
    prayer reform and, 206, 207–8

Reform Judaism and, 118–20,
    206–7
sacred myth of, 108, 111–16,
    118–21, 125, 132
    see also Israel
Christians, Christianity, 159, 162, 164,
    182, 195, 213, 218, 220, 221,
    237–38, 239
    chosenness and, 114, 117
    converts and, 131
    Holocaust and, 106
    Jewish messianism vs., 211, 212,
        232–37
    penitence in, 96
    sin as seen in, 84–85, 89, 100, 101
circumcision, 112, 184, 205
Cohen, Hermann, 65
commandments, *see mitzvot;* Ten
    Commandments
Common Era (C.E.), 267, 268
conception, 71, 72, 85
Conservative Judaism, 44, 45–46, 48,
    120, 172–74, 204, 268
    dietary laws and, 179–80
    Messiah and, 245–46
    prayer book reform in, 194, 205,
        206
    Torah and, 155–56
Crusades, 239
Cultural Zionism, 121–23

Daniel, Book of, 218, 220
David, King, 60, 129, 212–13, 215,
    217, 220, 222, 226, 227, 228,
    230, 232, 233, 234, 236
death:
    life after, 73–81, 91, 101–2, 218
    repentance and, 94
    resurrection after, 218, 228–29, 231

derash, see midrash
destiny, *see* human destiny
Deuteronomy, Book of, 134, 139–40, 161, 269
Diaspora, 122, 123, 129, 130, 164, 165, 191–92, 216, 224
dietary laws *(kashrut),* 163, 171, 172, 173, 176–80, 185
divorce, 70

Edom, 115, 226, 227
Eli, 190
Elijah, 216, 223, 224, 226
Emancipation, 171, 267
Emet ve-Emunah, 45
Enoch, Book of, 219, 220–21, 232
Ephraim, 161, 227
Epicureans, 137, 138
Esau, 101, 112, 115, 226, 227, 247
eschatology, 218, 219, 226
Essenes, 221
ethics, *see* morality and ethics
Eve, 52, 73, 78, 127
evil, *see* good and evil
Exodus from Egypt, 7, 59, 136, 158, 160
Eyn Sof, 38, 39, 58, 202
Ezekiel, 216, 220
Ezra, 153

family, 69, 87
   see also marriage
Flood, 32, 176
freedom, 59, 84, 97, 156, 160
free will, 96–98
Freud, Sigmund, 11, 12, 63, 121

Garden of Eden, heavenly, 75, 76–77, 78

Gehinnom (hell), 75, 76, 77, 79, 81, 229
Gemara, 162, 166
gematria, 150
Ginzburg, Asher, 121–22
glossary, 267–69
Gnostics, Jewish, 99–100
God, 11–49
   agnosticism and, 14, 42
   anthropomorphic descriptions of, 22, 23, 34, 35–37, 39, 197
   anthropopathic descriptions of, 22, 34, 35–37, 39, 197
   Aristotle's concept of, 31, 32, 34
   belief in, belief in science compared with, 17
   Buber on, 46–47, 48, 49
   Conservative Judaism and, 44, 45–46, 48
   as creator of universe, 12, 15, 16, 17, 18, 19–20, 32, 33, 160, 188
   as dead, 106
   diversity in Jewish beliefs about, 13–14
   feminine aspect of, 40, 199
   Hasidism on, 42–44, 46 47, 48
   Heschel on, 48, 49
   as hidden and unknowable, 13, 14–15, 17–18, 20, 21, 22, 23 24, 35, 38, 39, 41, 42, 65, 103–5
   Holocaust and, 105–6, 107
   humans created in image of, 15, 18, 20, 50, 51–53, 56, 189
   idolatry and, 15, 18, 36, 37, 127–28, 160
   images of, 12–13, 18, 24, 31
   immanence of, 14, 15, 16, 21, 22, 24, 29, 34, 38, 48, 49

God *cont.*
  Israel's relationship with, 108–9,
    113–14, 214
  Kabbalists on, 37–40, 42
  as king and judge, 30–31, 33, 34
  knowable aspects of *(Sefirot),*
    38–40, 43, 58, 71–72, 198–99
  Maimonides on, 34–37
  masculine, fatherly images of, 13,
    14, 25–29, 30–31, 34, 40
  modern Jewish beliefs about,
    44–49
  moral nature of, 12, 13, 17, 18–21,
    23, 32, 33, 34, 60
  nature as, 41
  one, belief in, 13, 17, 19, 20
  oneness of, 13, 16–18, 24
  Orthodox Judaism and, 44, 46
  as parent, 13, 25–29, 30–31
  Plato's concept of, 31–32, 34
  presence of, in daily life, 13, 20,
    21–24, 29
  punishment by, *see* punishment
  Reconstructionism and, 44, 46
  Reform Judaism and, 44–45
  sacred myths of, 14, 15–16
  simplistic conceptions of, 12, 13
  as sole reality, 42–44
  Spinoza on, 40–41
  suffering and, 12, 13, 29, 84, 101–7
  as transcendent, 13, 14, 15, 16, 21,
    22, 23–24, 28, 29, 33, 34, 35, 36,
    38, 40, 45, 48, 49, 120
  withdrawal of, 27–29, 105
good and evil, 15, 16, 41, 49, 60,
    84–107
  free will and, 96–98
  God as source of, 98–100
  Hasidism on, 89–91

impulses for, 85–91
Kabbalists on, 98–101
and reason and judgment, 88
repentance and change, 93–96
repetition of behaviors and, 92
sexual temptation and, 87–88,
    90–91
suffering and, 101–7
superstition and, 98–101
see also mitzvot; morality and ethics
Greek civilization, 31–32
Griffin, David R., 13
Guide of the Perplexed (Maimonides),
    35, 197

Habad-Lubavitch Hasidism, 43–44,
    243–44
Habakkuk, 61
Hadrianic persecutions, 226, 227
Haggadah, 7
Halakhah, 129, 161–70
  dietary laws, 163, 171, 172, 173,
    176–80, 185
  modern life and, 170–76
  prayer and, 186, 193, 195, 196, 200,
    201, 204; *see also* prayer
  spiritual dimension of, 180–85
  see also mitzvot; Torah
Halevi, Judah, 131
Hannah, 190
Hanukkah, 163, 164, 218
Haredim, 175
Hasidim, Hasidism, 62, 105, 158, 175,
    194, 243, 267, 268
  Ashkenazic, 89, 96
  God as seen in, 42–44, 46, 47, 48
  on good and evil, 89–91
  Habad-Lubavitch, 43–44, 243–44
  on human destiny, 81–82

Messiah and, 243–44
Polish-Ukrainian, 89
prayer and, 201–3
Hasmoneans, 219
heaven, 75, 76–77, 78, 79
Hebrew, 122, 123, 173, 187
prayer reform and, 205–6, 207
hell, *see* Gehinnom
hermeneutics, 149
Herzl, Theodor, 213
Heschel, Abraham Joshua, 48, 49, 124, 184, 208
Hezekiah, 222, 234
Hillel, 74, 165, 233
Hillel son of Gameliel, 222
Hillel the Elder, 55
Hirsch, Samson Raphael, 172, 178–79
holiness *(kedushah),* 22, 50, 51, 126–27, 184, 190
Holocaust, 12, 105–7, 243
Hosea, 59, 60, 214
Howe, Irving, 66–67
hukkim, 88–89, 110, 163, 177
human destiny, 20, 50–83, 84, 91, 92–93
afterlife in, 73–81, 91, 101–2, 218
changing course of, 93–94
ethics and, *see* morality and ethics
Hasidism on, 81–82
image of God in, 50, 51–53, 56
Kabbalists on, 71–72
and quest for spirituality, 81–83
soul and, 53–58
and stages of life, 67–73
suffering and, *see* suffering

I and Thou (Buber), 47
idolatry, 15, 18, 36, 37, 127–28, 160, 163, 178, 237

Immanuel of Rome, 76
Isaac, 111, 112, 157, 192, 204, 205, 247
Isaiah, 33, 59, 60–61, 116, 214–16, 222, 234–35, 236
Ishmael, 112, 115
Ishmael, Rabbi, 138, 139, 145
Islam, Muslims, 35, 117, 162, 195, 239, 241
Israel, 7, 15, 16, 17, 48, 49, 59, 122–23, 134–35, 136, 164, 165, 171, 175, 190, 192, 193
dietary laws and, 177–78
gathering of exiles into, 216–17, 223–24, 230, 231
God's relationship with, 108–9, 113–14, 214
as "heart of humanity," 117
idolatry and, 128
as "light of nations," 116–21, 126, 189, 235
Messianism and, 213, 214, 215–17, 218–19, 223–24 225, 226, 228, 230, 231, 234, 235, 236, 245
prayer and, 189
in sacred myth of chosen people, 108, 109, 111, 112, 113, 114–16; *see also* chosen people, chosenness
see also Zionism
Israel ben Eliezer, *see* Baal Shem Tov
Israelite sectarians, 118

Jacob, 101, 110, 112, 157, 192, 204, 205, 226–27, 234, 247
Jeremiah, 59–60, 236
Jesus, 213, 232–33, 234, 235, 236–37, 238
Jew, use of term, 110, 111

Jewish identity, 109–10, 117–18, 120,
    121–28, 132, 133
  author's letter to his children on,
    247–52
  synagogue and, 187, 209
  see also chosen people, chosenness;
    Judaism
Job, 103–5
Joel, 216
John the Baptist, 232
Joseph, 157, 161, 226–27
Josephus, 129, 131, 238
Joshua, 113, 141, 142
Judah, 110, 111, 214, 216, 234, 236
Judah Halevi, 117
Judah Ha-Nasi, 162, 165
Judaism:
  author's letter to his children on,
    247–52
  Christian messianism vs., 211, 212,
    232–37
  Conservative, *see* Conservative Ju-
    daism
  converts to, 128–32, 227
  education in, 6, 156
  ethics as essence of, 65–67, 171,
    172
  evolving beliefs in, 4, 6–8, 13, 188,
    195, 205–8
  Orthodox, *see* Orthodox Judaism
  persistence of, 110
  Reconstructionist, *see* Reconstruc-
    tionist Judaism
  Reform, *see* Reform Judaism
  Rosenzweig on, 151–52
  sacred myths of, 5–8, 14, 48–49,
    133, 159–60, 184, 186–87
  spirituality in, 5–6, 44, 124–25,
    126–27, 167, 180–85

  use of term, 110, 111
  see also Jewish identity
Judea, 111, 238–39
judgment, 30, 99
judgment day, 216, 217, 218, 228–29,
    245
justice, 13, 20, 60, 160
  suffering and, 101, 104, 105
  see also punishment

Kabbalists, Kabbalah, 16, 55, 58, 126,
    268
  on afterlife, 78
  on death of children, 103
  on evil, 98–101
  on God, 37–40, 42
  on human destiny, 71–72
  Lurianic, 240, 241
  prayer and, 194–95, 196, 198–200
  on Torah, 145–50
  Zohar, 57, 73, 77, 79–80, 117
Kant, Immanuel, 64–65, 66, 170–71
Kaplan, Mordecai, 46, 120, 152,
    174–75
Karaite sect, 161–62
kashrut, see dietary laws
kavanah (intention), 90, 196, 200
kedushah, see holiness
Ketuvim, 268, 269
Kokhba, Bar, 238–39
Kook, Abraham Isaac, 12
korban (sacrifice), 190–92, 193, 197,
    200
kosher foods, 177
  see also dietary laws
Kuzari (Halevi), 117

land, 21
law(s), 110, 161, 163, 170–76

dietary, 163, 171, 172, 173, 176–80, 185

see also Halakhah; *mitzvot*

Leah, 204, 205, 234

Letter of Aristeas, 177

Lilith, 100

love, 44, 45, 72–73, 87

Maccabean revolt, 218, 219

Maggid of Mezritch, 48, 82, 202, 203

Maimonides, *see* Moses ben Maimon

Malachi, 216

marriage, 67, 68–69, 70

 mixed or forbidden, 129, 132, 171, 223

Platonic love and, 72–73

Marx, Karl, 11, 12, 245

mashiach, 212, 217–218, 219–21

materialism, 127

medieval period, 16, 34, 41, 55, 56, 95, 135, 144–45, 268

see also Kabbalists, Kabbalah

Messiah, 171, 211–46

arrival of, 223, 224–26

death of, 223, 226–27

Elijah as precursor of, 223, 224, 226

ingathering of exiles by, 216–17, 223–24, 230, 231

Jesus as, 213, 232–33, 234, 235, 236–37, 238

as personal redeemer, 212, 217–18, 219–21

Third Temple and, 244

two traditions about, 226–27

messianic era, 218, 223, 227–28

resurrection and day of judgment following, 228–29

time-to-come following, 223, 229–30

messianism, 211–46

contemporary Jewish, 242–46

false messiahs and, 237–42

Jewish vs. Christian, 211, 212, 232–37

Maimonides on, 229, 230–32, 239, 242

origins of, 212–23

Micah, 59, 60, 61, 214, 236

midrash *(derash),* 148, 149, 154, 156, 166, 194, 268

Midrash of the Ten Martyrs, 194, 238

minyan (prayer quorum), 193, 199, 204, 209

miracles, 25, 26–27, 208

Mishnah, 137, 138, 140, 162, 165–66, 194, 268, 269

Mishneh Torah (Maimonides), 34–35, 162, 167, 169, 197

mishpatim, 89, 110, 163

mitzvot (commandments), 60–61, 62, 64, 82, 85, 86, 88–89, 91–93, 106, 110, 142, 159–85, 187, 206, 207, 240, 244, 268

afterlife and, 74, 75

categories of, 163

dietary laws, 163, 171, 172, 173, 176–80, 185

as folkways, 174

Maimonides on, 167–70

marriage and, 69

modern life and, 170–76

prayer and, 186, 187; *see also* prayer

rational vs. irrational, 88–89, 159, 163, 177

Reform movement and, 119

Rosenzweig on, 151, 152

mitzvot (commandments) *cont.*
    Sabbateanism and, 241
    seven universal, 128
    613 individual, 162–67
    spiritual dimension of, 180–85
    teshuvah and, 93–96
    transmigration and, 80
    violations of, 85, 86, 88–89, 91–93
    women and, 204
    see also Halakhah
modern period, 268
monotheism, 13, 17, 19, 20
morality and ethics, 58–67, 160, 161,
        170–71, 181, 189, 193
    as essence of Judaism, 65–67, 171,
        172
    golden mean in, 61
    idolatry and, 127–28
    and Jews as chosen pepole, 117,
        119–20
    Kant on, 64–65, 66
    Maimonides on, 61–62
    mentshlichkeyt and, 66–67
    messianism and, 226
    mitzvot and, 60–61
    and moral nature of God, 12, 13,
        17, 18–21, 23, 32, 33, 34, 60
    Musar movement and, 63–64
    see also good and evil; law; *mitzvot;*
        sin
moral truths, 65
Moses, 17–18, 82, 102, 112, 113, 126,
        134–46, 151, 152, 153, 154, 157,
        161, 166–67, 193
    Five Books of, 134, 136–37, 155;
        see also Torah
Moses ben Maimon (Maimonides;
        Rambam), 34–37, 40, 41, 52
    on adherence to Torah, 118

    on afterlife, 76, 77, 81
    on converts, 130
    on dietary laws, 178
    on divine omniscience, 97–98
    on evil impulse, 88–89
    on free will, 97, 98
    Guide of the Perplexed, 35, 197
    Kabbalists on, 38
    on law and spirituality, 167–70
    on messianism, 229, 230–32, 239,
        242
    Mishneh Torah, 34–35, 162, 167,
        169, 197
    on morality, 61–62
    on origin of Torah, 144, 145
    on parent-child relationship, 69
    prayer and, 194, 196–98
Mount Sinai, 134, 136, 137, 145, 146,
        151, 152, 158, 166
Mount Zion, 228–29
Musar movement, 63–64
Muslims, Islam, 35, 117, 162, 195,
        239, 241
mysticism, *see* Kabbalists, Kabbalah
myths, *see* sacred myths

Nachman of Bratslav, 202–3
Nahmanides, 145, 146, 148
Nathan, 217
Nathan of Gaza, 240, 241
nature, 15, 16, 23, 33, 41, 48, 49, 112
nefesh, 53–54, 55, 56, 57, 58, 72, 80,
        117
neshamah, 54, 55, 56, 57, 58, 77, 80,
        117
Neviim, 268, 269
Noah, 32, 128, 167, 176
Numbers, Book of, 134, 139, 140,
        269

original sin, 73, 74, 78, 79, 85, 89,
    100, 101
Orthodox Judaism, 44, 46, 66, 81,
    120, 124, 135, 155, 172–73,
    175–76, 181, 182, 193–94,
    203–4, 209, 242, 243, 268
  dietary laws and, 177, 178–79
  Messiah and, 212
  see also Hasidim, Hasidism

Palestine, 110–11, 218, 220, 227,
    232
PaRDeS, 148
parent-child relationship, 69
Passover, 7, 114, 158, 160, 164, 191,
    224, 233
Paul, 84–85
peshat, 148–49, 156
Petuchowski, Jacob, 209
Pharisees, 74, 221
Philistines, 110, 213
Plato, 31–32, 34, 35, 72–73
pleasure, 63, 70, 96
polytheism, 17, 19, 20
prayer(s), 22, 38, 39, 82, 161,
    186–210, 228
  community and, 209–10
  consciousness transformed by, 187
  efficacy of, 187–88
  experience of, 208–10
  Hasidic, 201–3
  Kabbalists and, 194–95, 196,
      198–200
  libidinous thoughts during, 91
  Maimonides on, 196–98
  purposes of, 195–96
  types of, 188, 195–96
  women and, 203–5
prayer books, 193–95, 205

reform of, 205–8, 245
  Siddur, 186, 188, 190–95, 205–8
prayer quorum *(minyan),* 193, 199,
    204, 209
procreation, 68, 70–71, 81
prophets, 213–17, 218, 234, 268
punishment, 30, 63, 74, 75, 76, 92, 96,
    216, 217
  God's withdrawal as, 105
  Holocaust as, 105–7
  inherited, 102, 103
  suffering as, 101–7
  transmigration as, 80–81
purgatory, 76, 81
Purim, 164

rabbinic period, 268
Rachel, 101, 204, 205
Rebecca, 204, 205
Reconstructionist Judaism, 44, 46,
    120, 174–75, 268
  prayer book reform in, 194, 205,
      206, 207–8
Reform Judaism, 44–45, 66, 118–20,
    122, 124, 172–73, 181–82, 204,
    268
  chosen-people concept and,
      118–20
  dietary laws and, 179
  messianism and, 245
  prayer and, 194, 205, 206–7, 245
  ritual and, 172
  traditionalist shift in, 120
remez, 148, 149–50, 156
repentance, 93–96
resurrection, 218, 228–29, 231
righteousness, 62, 132–33
ritual(s), 16, 57, 114, 119, 123, 163,
    170, 171, 172, 191, 192–93, 198

ritual(s) *cont.*
    consciousness transformed by, 187
    evil countered by, 100–101
    Reform Judaism and, 172
    see also law; prayer
Roman Empire, 23, 28, 110, 111, 129,
    164, 165, 212, 219, 220, 226,
    227, 232, 233, 238
Rosenzweig, Franz, 123–24, 151–52,
    173, 182–83, 185
Rosh Hashanah, 114, 160, 192, 194
ruah, 54, 55, 57–58, 80
Rubenstein, Richard, 106
Ruth, 129

Sabbatai Zvi, 239–41, 243
Sabbath, 15, 16, 20–21, 48–49, 59,
    135, 150, 158, 160, 161, 163,
    164, 173, 174, 184, 185, 190,
    195, 204–5, 224
sacred myths, 4–5
    of Judaism, 5–8, 14, 48–49, 133,
    159–60, 184, 186–87
sacrifice *(korban),* 190–92, 193, 197,
    200
Sadducees, 74, 138, 141, 142
Salanter, Israel, 63–64
Samael, 100
Samaritans, 161
Samuel, 190, 228, 229
Sanhedrin, 161
Sarah, 111, 204, 205
Sarna, Nahum, 154
Satan, 99, 103
Saul, 217
Schneerson, Menahem Mendel,
    244
Scholem, Gershom, 8, 152
Seder, 7, 193, 233

Sefirot, 38–40, 43, 58, 71–72, 198–
    99
    good and evil and, 99, 100
    prayer and, 199, 200
    Torah and, 146, 147, 150
Senesh, Hannah, 49
Sephardim, 172, 268, 269
sexuality, 70, 87–88, 90–91
Shavuot, 114, 160, 191
Shekhinah, 22, 23, 29, 40, 199, 200,
    230
Shneur Zalman, 43–44
Siddur, 186, 188, 190–95, 205–8
sin(s), 60, 62, 63, 80, 91, 93, 189
    Christian vs. Jewish views of,
    84–85, 89
    God's withdrawal caused by, 28–29,
    105
    original, 73, 74, 78, 79, 85, 89, 100,
    101
    repetition of, 91–92
    Sabbateanism and, 241
    teshuvah and, 95
    transmigration and, 80
    see also good and evil; morality and
    ethics
slavery, 59, 160
sod, 148, 150, 156
Sodom and Gomorrah, 33
Solomon, King, 213
Soloveitchik, Joseph, 180–81, 209
soul(s), 53–58, 71–73, 91, 231
    in afterlife, 73–81, 91
    birth and, 71–72
    body and, 39, 53–55, 71, 72
    masculine and feminine compo-
    nents of, 72
    nefesh, 53–54, 55, 56, 57, 58, 72, 80,
    117

neshamah, 54, 55, 56, 57, 58, 79, 80, 117

Platonic love and, 72–73

ruah, 54, 55, 57–58, 80

transmigration of, 80–81

Spinoza, Baruch (Benedict), 40–41, 153

spirituality, 5–6, 13, 44, 81–83, 124–25, 126–27, 167, 180–85

suffering, 13, 29, 84, 92, 98, 101–7, 189

in the Holocaust, 12, 105–7

messianism and, 226

as test of faith, 102–3

Sukkot, 114, 160, 163, 164, 191

superstition, 98–101

Symposium (Plato), 73

synagogues, 187, 192, 193, 200, 204, 209

Talmud, 63, 140, 161, 162, 166, 170, 181, 194, 196, 218, 239, 268, 269

Gemara 162, 166

Mishnah, 137, 138, 140, 162, 165–66, 194, 268, 269

Tanakh, 267, 269

see also Bible

techines, 204–5

tefillah, 188

Ten Commandments, 14–15, 17, 112, 117, 134, 136–37, 138, 139, 140, 142

teshuvah, 93–96

Tillich, Paul, 45

Tofet ve-Eden, 76

Torah, 7, 17, 34, 36, 110, 127, 134–58, 159, 160, 165, 167, 170, 189, 190, 194, 227–28, 229, 269

birth and, 70–71

commandments in, 142; *see also mitzvot*

divine origin of, 134–40, 143–44, 145, 146, 151, 153, 155–56, 157, 158

idea of freedom in, 59

Jewish identity and, 117, 118

Kabbalists and, 38, 145–50

as living document, 141

medieval beliefs about, 144–45

modern ideas on, 150–56

multiple authors of, 153–54

Oral, 137, 139, 140–44, 145, 155, 161

preexistent archetype of, 146

public reading of, 191, 192

rabbinic innovations and, 142–44, 163

and sacred myth of chosen people, 113, 114, 115–16

study and interpretation of, 22, 24, 55, 68, 82, 135, 141, 142, 146–47, 148–50, 156–58, 163, 164, 181, 185, 191, 192–93, 204

value of, in modern life, 157–58

Written (Five Books of Moses), 134, 136–37, 155

see also Halakhah; *mitzvot*

transcendence, 50, 51, 55, 126–27, 133, 148, 159, 186, 187, 208, 243

transmigration of souls, 80–81

Trial of God, The (Wiesel), 106

tzavaah (ethical will), 247–52

wealth, 63

Wellhausen, Julius, 153

Wiesel, Elie, 106
Wise, Isaac Mayer, 119
women, 9, 160, 174
    mitzvot and, 163–64
    prayer and, 203–5

yetzer ha-ra, 85, 88, 89
yetzer ha-tov, 85, 99
Yiddish culture, 66–67, 204–5
yiddishe neshomeh, 117–18
Yohanan, Rabbi, 229

Yohanan ben Zakkai, 75, 164–65,
    221–22, 223, 225, 246
Yom Kippur, 114, 160, 194, 238

Zechariah, 216
Zerubavel, 216
Zionism, 12, 106, 122, 124, 207, 213,
    243, 244, 245
    Cultural, 121–23
Zohar, 57, 73, 77, 79–80, 117, 147,
    148, 200

About the author

DAVID S. ARIEL earned his doctorate in Jewish philosophy at Brandeis University. He is president of the Cleveland College of Jewish Studies and is the author of *The Mystic Quest: An Introduction to Jewish Mysticism*. He lives in Shaker Heights, Ohio, with his wife and three children.